THE WORLD OF GENDER JUSTICE

THE WORLD OF GENDER JUSTICE

For
Dear Mike
with warm affection,
Murlidhar Bhandare
Grand-father of Ananya,
Teesta.

Edited by

MURLIDHAR C. BHANDARE

HAR-ANAND
PUBLICATIONS PVT LTD

HAR-ANAND PUBLICATIONS PVT LTD
E-49/3, Okhla Industrial Area, Phase-II, New Delhi-110020
Tel.: 41603490 Fax: 011-41708607
E-mail: haranand@rediffmail.com
Website: www.haranandpublications.com

Reprint, 2014

Published by Ashok Gosain and Ashish Gosain for
Har-Anand Publications Pvt Ltd

Printed in India by Everest Press

This book is dedicated to Sunanda, to women everywhere—and those who fight their cause.

WOMAN

is the companion of man,
gifted with equal
mental capacities.
She has the right
to participate
in the minutest details
in the activities of man,
and she has an equal right
of freedom
and liberty with him.

Mahatma Gandhi - 1917

Acknowledgment

Federico Mayor, the Director General of UNESCO is highly regarded as a visionary for a culture of peace. It is his belief, as is the Justice Sunanda Bhandare Foundation's, that there can be no culture of peace without gender justice. To him goes my deep gratitude for his unflinching support to this book right from the day when I first discussed it with him. Contributors have been equally supportive. All of them have a life long commitment and contribution to human rights particularly women's rights. Each one of them is an expert in his or her field and despite very busy schedules, have devoted valuable time not only to write but also encourage this project at every step. I do not have words enough to thank them.

I will be remiss if I fail to mention the energetic and ever enthusiastic Narendra Kumar and his sons Ashok and Ashish of Har-Anand Publications, who did not hesitate for a second when I first broached this project with them.

My dear friend and former neighbour Adrian Cawasjee designed the logo for the Foundation when it was set up in 1994. Little did we realise then that it would become the cover for the Foundation's first publication. Many thanks to Poonam Shahi who suggested we use the logo and then designed the cover.

Prof. Lakshmi Jambholkar assisted me in editing. Vineet Bakshi prepared the rear index in record time. Shalini Bhalla, a young and energetic trainee, helped with the research. My able Secretary H.N. Gandhi burnt the midnight oil and put in long hours to see this book to fruition. Mr. Kanwarpal co-ordinated all the preparation.

Finally, my sister-in-law Namita Gokhale provided sage advice and with her customary cheerfulness saw this book through and my daughter-in-law Namita Bhandare gave all help and assistance in getting the book ready on time.

To all these and many, many more silent supporters, I am for ever indebted for ably seeing through production of this work.

Murlidhar C. Bhandare

Foreword

"The World of Gender Justice" is a most welcome contribution to the commemoration of the 50th anniversary of the Universal Declaration of Human Rights, reaching as it does to the heart of the question: how do we ensure human rights become a reality for all, in particular for women and other vulnerable groups?

Women are the voice of half of the world and that voice is too often silenced, marginalised or circumscribed. Women account for less than 12 per cent of the world's parliamentarians and only 7.1 per cent of National Assembly Presidents. We at UNESCO believe that education is the key to changing this situation. When countries like India invest in education, they show how significantly this puts women and girls in charge of their own lives and influences the size of their families. As Justice Sunanda Bhandare showed in her life and work, the link between gender, the law and human rights is also crucial.

In many countries today girls are increasingly choosing to study law and this is a very encouraging trend. But it is not enough to see parity being achieved at undergraduate level in law faculties. Women must also be fully represented where the laws are made: in parliaments and governments. They must be fully represented where the law is implemented: in courts of law, as judges and magistrates from high courts to rural tribunals. They must be fully represented across the whole spectrum of the legal professions, on law councils and in public prosecutors' offices.

Women must also enjoy their full rights as users of the law and this raises questions of access to legal aid, of the level of literacy required to understand legal documents and procedures, of access to information on laws and conventions. Only by overcoming all these barriers can we ensure that women around the world are able to make full use of justice systems which are truly just from a gender perspective. It is my firm belief that this will not only restore the voice and dignity of all humankind, it will open the way to endogenous, sustainable development within a framework of justice, equality and freedom.

These are goals to which UNESCO attaches great importance and to which the co-authors of this book make an important contribution. There is still a long way to go to a world of true gender justice, but let us make sure that already, no one can say:

Woman,
you brought
with you
a new song.
But we did not let you
speak out
although yours
is the voice
of half
the earth.

Federico Mayor

Contributors

Mr. Federico Mayor,
Director General, UNESCO

Ms. Mary Robinson
High Commissioner for Human Rights, U.N.
Former President of Ireland

Justice M.N. Venkatachaliah
Chairman, National Human Rights Commission, India;
Former Chief Justice of India

Justice Sunanda Bhandare

Justice Sujata V. Manohar,
Judge, Supreme Court of India

Justice Silvia Cartwright DBE
Judge, New Zealand High Court;
Member of U.N. Committee of Experts, CEDAW
(Convention on the Elimination of All Forms
of Discrimination against Women)

Justice V.R. Krishna Iyer
Former Judge, Supreme Court of India

Prof. Savitri Goonesekere
Professor of Law, University of Colombo, Sri Lanka
Member of U.N. Committee of Experts, CEDAW
(Convention on the Elimination of All Forms
of Discrimination against Women)

Justice Leila Seth
Member, Law Commission of India;
Former Chief Justice of Himachal Pradesh
High Court

Dr. V. Mohini Giri,
Chairperson, Guild of Services, India.

Ms. Halima Embarek Warzazi
Member, U.N. Sub-Commission for Prevention of Discrimination and Protection of Minorities

Mr. Nitin Desai
U.N. Under Secretary-General

Dr. Vina Mazumdar
Chairperson, Centre for Women's Development Studies, New Delhi and the Indian Association for Women's Studies

Dr. Sarla Gopalan, IAS (Retd.)
Former Secretary to Government of India, Ministry of Human Resource Development

Dr. Vandana Shiva
Director, Research Foundation for Science, Technology & Ecology

Ms. Ingeborg Breines
Director, UNESCO Culture of Peace Project, UNESCO

Prof. Sushila Kaushik
Director, Women's Studies & Development Centre, Delhi University

Ms. Chandni Joshi
Regional Programme Advisor, UNIFEM (United Nations Development Fund for Women, South Asia Regional Office, New Delhi)

Dr. Mira Shiva
Head, Public Policy Division
Voluntary Health Association of India

Ms. Kusum
Associate Research Professor
Indian Law Institute, New Delhi

Contents

Introduction

Universal awareness of the equality of sexes and gender justice was ushered in with the formation of the United Nations after the second World War. The United Nations has been built on the edifice of equality. The first major and decisive step to "re-affirm faith in fundamental human rights, in the dignity and worth of the human person, in the equal rights of men and women" expressed in the U.N. Charter was the adoption by the U.N. General Assembly on 10th December, 1948 at Paris of the Universal Declaration of Human Rights, elaborated by the Commission of Human Rights under the able chairpersonship of Eleanor Roosevelt. Article 1 of the Universal Declaration of Human Rights underlines the basic concept of freedom and equality by asserting "all human beings are born free and equal in dignity and rights. They are endowed with reason and conscience and should act in a spirit of brotherhood". It is a reflection at once of the humanity's urge for peace and human rights. Human rights, be they civil, political, economic, social and cultural, are all inter-dependent, inalienable and inviolable. They are, thus, universal.

Justice Sunanda Bhandare was a child of the Independence movement in India and had a strong commitment to human dignity, which could be preserved and enriched only through freedom and equality. Her motto in life which she practised more than she preached, the *freedom to choose and the right to excel,* is now also the motto of the Foundation. The Justice Sunanda Bhandare Foundation endeavours to commemorate today the Golden Jubilee of the adoption of the Universal Declaration of Human Rights with this publication.

The Justice Sunanda Bhandare Foundation was established in 1994 to perpetuate the memory of Justice Sunanda Bhandare, a sitting judge of the Delhi High Court. In a brief career, Justice Bhandare worked ceaselessly to establish an egalitarian society where women and the weaker sections of society had the right to live with dignity. It is to fulfil this task that the Foundation has been instituted. Its chief endeavour is to ensure gender justice through various activities.

Equality of sexes and gender justice have indeed made very slow progress. The subordination of women to men has subsisted through the millennia in all societies and countries without exception. It is only now at the fag end of the 20th century that these twin factors are being increasingly recognised and rectified.

The American Declaration of Independence on 4th July, 1776 mentions only men as being created free and equal. Liberty and justice are the main attributes of equality. Justice has been depicted as a goddess, holding a pair of scales in her hand. U.S.A.'s Statue of Liberty depicts a woman holding a torch in her raised right hand proclaiming a new life of freedom. At her feet lie the broken shackles of slavery. In real life, women are still not free from most of these shackles. In U.S.A. it took from 1840 to 1920 — 80 years — for women to get the right to vote. France, the land of liberty, equality and fraternity conferred to its women citizens the right to vote only in 1944. In Switzerland it was secured as recently as 1971. Even the right to practice law was denied to women. In the U.S. the claim of Myra Bradwell to practice law was rejected on the facile and ridiculous ground that the "paramount destiny and mission of women is to fulfil the noble and benign offices of wife and mother. This is the law of the creator". Even in India, Sudhanshu Bala Hazara a young woman in Calcutta was refused the right to practice law on the ground that women were not fit for the "hurly burly of the legal profession".

The U.N. has been at the forefront for advancing gender justice. In fact as early as in 1946 it constituted the Commission on Status of Women. 1975 was observed as International Women's Year when the First World Conference on Women was organised in Mexico City. It was followed in 1979 by the General Assembly adopting the Convention on the Elimination of All Forms of Discrimination against Women (CEDAW), which is a *magna carta* for women. The second and the third world conferences on women were held respectively in Copenhagen in 1980 and in Nairobi in 1985. In Nairobi forward-looking strategies for the advancement of women to the year 2000 gave an excellent plan at the national, regional and international level to promote the empowerment and advancement of women.

More significant events followed with the Vienna Conference on Human Rights in 1993. This gave a decisive momentum to women's rights at the global level. The Vienna declaration and programme of action underlines the importance of the integration and participation of women as both agents and beneficiaries in the development process. It assured the integration of the equal status of women and their human rights into the mainstream of United Nations systemwise activity.

The World Conference on Human Rights stressed the importance of working towards the elimination of violence against women in public and private life, the elimination of all forms of sexual harassment, exploitation and trafficking in women, the elimination of gender bias in the administration of justice and the eradication of any conflicts which may arise between the rights of women and the harmful effects of traditional and customary practices, cultural prejudices and religious extremism. It called for elimination of all kinds of violence including murder, systematic rape, sexual slavery, and forced pregnancy, as also eradication of all forms of discrimination against women both hidden and overt.

This was followed by the Beijing Conference on Women in 1995, which brought in its wake the famous Beijing Declaration. The Beijing Declaration includes women's empowerment and their full participation on the basis of equality in all spheres of human rights. It acknowledges women's rights as human rights. In sheer terms of representation no other U.N. conference matches the Beijing Conference. All these very salutary and heart-warming events have provided momentum to the movement of gender justice.

Women are vulnerable because of a vicious circle of gender stereotypes. To remove these, laws can play a vital, or even pivotal role. Laws provide for an equality that does not exist in actual life. It tries to protect the weak, vulnerable and discriminated sections of society. The courts have a positive role to play in setting right such inequalities, remove discrimination and abolish derogatory practices against women. An awareness of the law results in the assertion of rights and the assertion of rights results in change of attitudes in society. The law works as a catalyst to change not only adverse conditions but also the attitudes of the people. In India, the courts, particularly the Supreme Court, have demonstrated sensitivity in every branch of law affecting the rights and protection of women including matters of marriage, guardianship, maintenance, residence and inheritance in civil matters. They have also played a role in abolishing unfair treatment to women in criminal trials involving offences against women including rape. But the law alone cannot do much. An attitudinal change in society is as important as legal reform. All sections of society have to work for this transformation and this is where N.G.Os, the media and the people's representatives have to play a major role.

The discrimination against women is spread widely in areas of education, employment and health. Education is the key to human advancement, which is not handed down to a majority of women. Most of the women's work, inside the house goes unnoticed and unremunerated. Even outside the family they remain underpaid. Equal pay for equal work remains a guarantee on paper.

Neglect of women, particularly girls, is a black mark on our society. As the Regional Health Report of WHO for 1998 points out, 74 million women in South Asia are simply missing. Equally, this is the only region in the world where men outnumber women in the total population. According to Nobel laureate and economist Amartya Sen a detailed comparison of mortality rates, morbidity rates, hospital care and nutritional attention made in India confirm a fairly decisive picture of the systematical deprivation of women in large parts of the country especially rural India. If four boys from a village need hospitalisation, at least three, if not all four, will get it. But if four girls need hospitalisation, even one may not reach the hospital. Better food is reserved for boys and men. In most families they eat first—served by the women who prepare the food and reserve the choicest portions for them. Women get to eat the left-overs. Malnutrition of women is almost the order of the day.

Violence against women is a grave area needing immediate attention. Violence is not limited to domestic violence. Women at all times are exposed to abuse, mental and sexual harassment and even rape. Apart from individual violence, women and children continue to be the natural targets and worst sufferers both in the man-made and natural calamities. Thus famines, cyclones and earthquakes as well as communal riots, workers' struggles, poverty and indebtedness, fundamentalism, extremism, casteism and regional fanaticism, attack the women first. Women continue to live in an endangered environment.

There is complete international consensus that human rights, international peace and development are inter-dependent. When human rights are disregarded, both international peace and development are threatened. Equally, development is crucial to both human rights and international peace. Development is a third generation human right. Its importance is heightened by the gross and growing poverty in the majority of the nations in the world. Political colonisation is being increasingly substituted by economic colonisation. Twenty per cent of the world's population lives on eighty per cent of its resources. The equal world is only growing grossly unequal. Breaking down trade barriers often has the deleterious effect of breaking the financial backbones of weaker nations. The Brettonwood institutions like the World Bank and I.M.F. are realising that their cures are not working. The concept of market democracy must now yield to human democracy. In human democracy, development must not compromise alleviation of poverty, equity and social justice. Poverty bears the stamp of woman. Seventyfive per cent of the world's poor are women. Underdevelopment thus endangers gender justice.

Gender justice is genuine equality among human beings where neither man is superior nor woman inferior. Gender justice envisages the equality of sexes in each and every sphere. However, it does not claim any preferential treatment for women over men. Gender justice is not based on biological differences. Its object is to eradicate man-made differences in areas economic, social, cultural, political and civil.

In earlier days, the superiority of man over woman was due to his superior physical power, which alone could help in subsistence. However, with the growth of science and technology, physical power has been almost completely overtaken by intellectual power. The mind is growing and the body is shrinking as far as the effort for existence and subsistence and advancement in life is concerned. In fact one can, in modern times, with the tip of a finger produce hundred times more than one produces with the use of both the hands. Biological differences matter less because human beings are singularly endowed with reason and conscience as emphasised by the Universal Declaration of Human Rights. With reason and conscience playing a dominant role, wc have a world of equal dignity.

Discriminatory and derogatory practices take their own time to leave society. Sex equality and gender justice have made very slow progress. With apartheid and racial discrimination abolished and slavery slaughtered, the time is ripe to eliminate sex discrimination and sex inequality and to ensure gender justice in our society.

We are coming to the close of the 20th century which will be remembered as the bloodiest century in the history of humankind. Its first half was ridden with two of the worst world wars entailing incalculable loss of human life and property. The second World War saw the detonation of the atom bomb, a weapon invented by man sufficient to wipe human beings off from the face of the planet. We have also witnessed an unprecedented building up of nuclear and other deadly arsenals even in the second half of the century. The relative peace that has prevailed throughout this period is out of fear of war and not for love of peace. We languish in the culture of violence instead of basking in the sunshine of a culture of peace. But the second half of the century has been heart-warming with the promise of an upsurge for human rights. Every nation today is free. The membership of the U.N. which was 51 in 1945 has gone upto 185. This upsurge for human rights and development must be enhanced. Let us, therefore, march into the 21st century and the next millennium with the full awareness that the key to peace, human rights and development is gender justice.

The time has come, therefore, to remove all the conflicts between the rights of women and the harmful effects of certain traditional and customary practices, cultural prejudices and religious fundamentalism. As has been stated in the UNESCO Statement on Women's Contribution to a Culture of Peace, "there can be no lasting peace without development and ushering of full equality between man and woman. Only together, women and men in parity and partnership, can we overcome obstacles, inertia, silence and frustration and ensure the insight, political will, creative thinking and concrete actions needed for a global transition from the culture of violence to a culture of peace."

To commemorate the Golden Jubilee of Universal Declaration of Human Rights, let us pledge to usher in an era of gender justice. This is the most appropriate moment for us to rededicate ourselves to the cause of women's empowerment and related values which Justice Sunanda Bhandare throughout her life cherished. Let us acknowledge an obligation to provide women of this planet *"Freedom to Choose and Right to Excel"*.

1

The Principle of Equality

Mary Robinson

The best hope for realising the human rights of women lies in the efforts of women themselves. On 10 December 1998, the international community will commemorate the 50th Anniversary of the Universal Declaration of Human Rights. Article I of the Universal Declaration states that:

> *"All human beings are born free and equal in dignity and rights. They are endowed with reason and conscience and should act towards one another in a spirit of brotherhood."*

This anniversary should be an occasion for the international community to ensure the realization of equality among all human beings; men and women as reflected in all international instruments. Equality should be a basis for the realization of human rights.

The principle of equality is inherent to the notion of human rights. The Convention on the Elimination of all Forms of Discrimination against Women demands in its article 1 that not only women should be accorded rights equal to those of men, but that they should be able to enjoy all their rights. In some words, there should be no *de jure* discrimination:

> *"For the purpose of the present Convention, the term discrimination against women shall mean any distinction, exclusion or restriction made on the basis of sex which has the effect or purpose of impairing or nullifying the recognition, enjoyment or exercise by women, irrespective of their marital status, on a basis of equality of men and women, of human rights and fundamental freedoms in the political, economic, social, cultural, civil or any other field."*

This requires that other-than-legal obstacles be identified and eliminated. Eliminating *de facto* discrimination is much more complex and difficult than enacting laws which recognize equal rights for all.

Equality is the cornerstone of every democratic society which aspires to social justice and human rights. In most societies and spheres of activity women are subject to all kinds of inequalities *de jure* and *de facto*. This situation is both caused and exacerbated by the existence of discrimination in the family, in the community and in the workplace. While causes and consequences may vary from country to country, discrimination against women is widespread. It is perpetuated by the survival of stereotypes and of traditional cultures, religious practices and beliefs detrimental to women.

The Vienna Conference on Human Rights in 1993 was one of the main turning points in women's rights emerging as a major concern at the international level. Women's groups were determined to make women's rights human rights. Their lobbying effort succeeded. Article 18 of the Vienna Declaration and Programme of Action states:

> *"The human rights of women and of the girl-child are an inalienable, integral and indivisible part of universal human rights. The full and equal participation of women in political, civil, economic, social and cultural life, at the national, regional and international levels, and the eradication of all forms of discrimination on grounds of sex are priority objectives of the international community.... The human rights of women should form an integral part of the United Nations human rights activities, including the promotion of all human rights instruments relating to women".*

Women are entitled to the enjoyment of all human rights, including those relating to economic development and resources, as part of their equal entitlement to all human rights. Lack of equal access represents a denial of rights, which creates obstacles to equality between men and women and thus women's enjoyment of human rights and results in the perpetuation of women's poverty. Women's equal access to resources and opportunities and equal treatment in economic and social life are cornerstones for the full realization of these rights.

Special Rapporteur on human rights and extreme poverty of the Sub-Commission on Prevention of Discrimination and Protection of Minorities, in his final report, reiterated the Platform for Action's finding that while poverty affected households as a whole, because of the gender division of labour and responsibilities, women bore a disproportionate burden and had to manage household consumption and production under conditions of increasing scarcity.

Criteria for a juridical definition of extreme poverty was elaborated by the Special Rapporteur. He noted that extreme poverty involved the denial, not of a single right or a given category of rights, but of human rights as a whole. According to the Special Rapporteur, the issue at stake was not the "recognition" of human rights, but the real and effective "exercise" of all human rights and fundamental freedoms by the extremely poor. The indivisibility and interdependence of human rights showed that denial or deprivation of one right could have repercussions on the exercise of other rights.*

Denial of equal rights to women in the access to economic resources is reflected in their overall unequal economic and social situation. Ensuring women's full enjoyment of their human rights is a crucial strategy for women's empowerment and for overcoming the disadvantages women continue to face in economic, political and social terms.

Alarming statistics on the economic and social gaps between women and men have been produced by the United Nations. The document reflects the real situation of women in the world. Women are most of the world's poor and the number of women living in rural poverty has increased by 50 per cent since 1975. Women are the majority of worlds' illiterate; the number rose from 543 million to 597 million between 1970 and 1985. Women in Asia and Africa work 13 hours a week more than men and are mostly unpaid. Worldwide, women earn 30 to 40 per cent less than men for doing equal work. Women hold between 10 to 20 per cent of managerial and administrative jobs worldwide and less than 20 per cent of jobs in manufacturing. Women make up less than 5 per cent of the world's heads of State. Women's unpaid housework and family labour, if counted as productive output in national accounts, would increase measures of global output by 25 to 30 per cent.

The concept of equality means much more than treating all persons in the same way. Equality should not be confused with sameness. Each sex has distinct attributes which, when combined allow a relationship to flourish. The gender-based division of labour, with women being primarily responsible for reproductive work and work related to the family, and men for productive work, also contributes to the perpetuation of gender-based inequalities. Equality means that the contributions made in the family or in society, though they may be different, are of equal value. Equal treatment of persons in unequal situations will operate to perpetuate rather than eradicate injustice. True equality can only emerge from efforts directed towards addressing and correcting these situational imbalances. In addition to demanding that women be accorded equal rights with men, the Convention on the Elimination of all Forms of Discrimination against Women goes further by prescribing the measures to be taken to ensure that women every where are able to enjoy the rights to which they are entitled.

What is discrimination? Prohibition implies that differentiation should be on the basis of objective and reasonable criteria, not on the ground of sex, race, ethnic origin, or color.

The Human Rights Committee laid down the distinction between differentiation and discrimination as follows: "Not every differentiation of treatment will

---

*E/CN.4/1998/22-E/CN.6/1998/11, Report of the Secretary-General FOLLOW-UP TO THE FOURTH WORLD CONFERENCE ON WOMEN: REVIEW OF MAINSTREAMING IN ORGANIZATIONS OF THE UNITED NATIONS SYSTEM.

Women's real enjoyment of their human rights, in particular those relating to the elimination of poverty, economic development and economic resources.

constitute discrimination, if the criteria for such differentiation are reasonable and objective and if the aim is to achieve a purpose which is legitimate under the Covenant."

Changes in the relations between sexes as everything else between people can be solved only by mutual efforts of the whole society, first on the global level and then by very organized and synchronized efforts and activities including the small level of society and all spheres of social life. That is why so called "female question" is the least female one i.e. it is not female at all. It is a male and female question, the mutual one, social, global and humane. The absolute equality between the sexes should be realized in all spheres: work, education, politics and decision making.

The obstacles to such equality are great and numerous. The biggest one lies in social inertia. It is so implanted in the consciousness of majority, unfortunately women's too, that it blocks all the efforts that can make them equal members of society in all spheres.

Under the influence of the social inertia present in society, the idea prevails in theory and practice that women should do the traditional female jobs like bringing up children, teaching them at the lower educational levels, service trades, nursing, less complex organizational activities etc. As far as educational levels are concerned, they do not take up schooling that much as men and if they do, few of them go for higher education. Speaking of politics, their presence is almost negligible, specially when world politics is concerned. In decision-making their role is minimized, especially when speaking about institutionalized direct decision-making. The most important stronghold of the social inertia in the family. It is a responsibility which is still and exclusively borne by women. No society treats its women as well as its men, and inequality of the sexes is strongly associated with poverty, it was concluded in the Human Development Report 1997.

Activities should be directed in establishing the equality between sexes and in overcoming the social inertia which is a dominating and characterizing factor. Gender equality means an equal visibility, empowerment and participation of both sexes in all spheres of public and private life.

Our world needs a new vision of equality between men and women—one that rejects the old extreme of one-sex dominance and lockstep gender roles, and also rejects the contemporary extreme of gender-based hostility and separate standards for women and men. Equality of opportunity for all people is essential to the construction of just and democratic societies for the twenty first century. Individuals of both sexes fundamentally believe in genuine equality and understanding between men and women—all that is needed is for that belief to be actively supported in the public arena.

As High Commissioner for Human Rights I encourage and support men and women who work together for the full realization of human rights in all societies. The achievement of equality will only be realized when all human beings will be involved and committed to "reaffirm faith in the equal rights of men and women" as stated in the United Nations Charter.

I would like to salute men and women all around the world who fought for the full realization and full enjoyment of human rights like Justice Sunanda Bhandare, their memory should remind us the purposes of the United Nations which is; "promoting and encouraging respect for human rights and for fundamental freedoms for all without distinction as to race, sex, language or religion."

2

Women & Development—The Indian Perspective

Justice M.N. Venkatachaliah

Justice Sunanda Bhandare was a person of rare sensitivity and promise. She was snatched away by cruel fate ere her time and in the prime of her life. It is impossible to assess the magnitude of this loss which shattered the family and agonised a wide circle of friends. Murli Bhandare has endeavoured to render a touching tribute to her memory. The "Sunanda Bhandare Foundation" for the advancement of women's causes is the sensitive and touching tribute of a devoted husband to the cherished memory of his wife. There could not have been a better one.

I join in this tribute and take the opportunity to refer to some crucial areas in the human development discourse in India. No country can look back with a clear conscience on its treatment of its women. In Britain, till almost 75 years ago, women were subject to scandalous disabilities and immunities. It was said, in lighter vein, that in English Law, 'the husband and wife constituted one person and the husband was that person' and that 'a woman can never be outlawed, for a woman is never in law'. In the United States of America, things were no better. There were queer laws. For instance it was illegal for a woman to weave her daughter's hair without state license. Law held that a husband owned his wife's clothes, and 'if she left his home, he had the right to follow her on the street and remove every stitch of the clothing.'

Indeed, in the famous case of '*Bradwell v. Illinois* (1873)', the American Supreme Court held that women were virtually outside the Fourteenth Amendment. Myra Bradwell was fully qualified to practice law and had herself established a legal journal called 'Chicago Legal News' and 'had ample qualifications to enter the Bar'. She was denied entry into the legal profession because she was a woman. The Supreme Court exhorted that 'the great inequality of man and woman was eternally based in human nature and that law as well as nature herself, has always recognized a wide difference in the respective spheres and destinies of man and woman'. A man, the Court observed 'should be a woman's protector and defender'. Justice Bradley contrasted "those energies and responsibilities, and that decision and firmness which—predominate the sterner sex" with the peculiar characteristics and 'the paramount destiny and mission of woman to fulfil the noble and benign offices of wife and mother'. This, the Judge said, was the law of the creator! But fortunately this stereotype of distinction between the sexes did not survive long, for, Myra Bradwell herself succeeded a decade later in securing a State Law granting the women the right to practice any profession. In 1879, the US Congress passed a law qualifying women to practice before the Supreme Court.

In India, historically women's disabilities have been well-known social checks and retarding factors on the progress of society. In the current Indian debate on economic development and social change the importance of women's education has increasingly come to be realized. The nation can ill-afford to neglect virtually half of its human resource. It is now empirically established that women's education is a single cure for a thousand societal ills. The inverse ratio between female literacy on the one hand, and population-growth, infant mortality, maternal mortality, mal-nutritional, and lower productivity on the other has come to be accepted. Women's education has demonstrated the efficacy of the literacy-route to population-control. Education of the girl child has rightly been perceived as an indispensable and important component of social empowerment which alone would enable the civil society to exact due performance from the political society. Indeed, in a well researched and far-reaching study on India's economic development and social change, the role of female literacy in promoting basic capabilities has been forcefully presented indicating that liberated participation of women in the economy is an essential component of success. This element, according to Jean Dreze and Amartya Sen, has made the State of Kerala a significant study in contrast with the State of Uttar Pradesh. There is striking inter-dependence between the role of the agency of women and expansion of literacy. The expansion of literacy in Kerala itself owes a great deal to that agency, 'reflected in the fact that almost two-thirds of primary-school teachers in Kerala are women (compared with 18 per cent in Uttar Pradesh)'. The table set-out in the work of Jean Dreze and Amartya Sen (See next page).

The education of the child particularly of the girl-child is, indeed, the lynchpin in social change; but the education of the child depends on its ability to absorb education and benefit by it. It presupposes the requisite mental faculties of the child. Here there is a serious problem. 88 per cent of pregnant mothers are anaemic; 40 per cent of the country's infant mortality is because of this maternal anaemia. But what is more alarming is the condition of the children that survive. Maternal anaemia and low-birth-weight-related neurological complications of the child stunt its intellectual growth and to a substantial degree permanently denies to the child the excitement of participation in intellectual life. This congenital condition cannot be compensated after birth. This vicious circle is the most crucial issue in developing social infrastructure. It, therefore, becomes the nodal issue in the programme for development.

India, Uttar Pradesh and Kerala:
Contrasts in Access to Public Services

	India	Uttar Pradesh	Kerala
Percentage of rural children aged 12-14 who have never been enrolled in a School, 1986-87			
Female	51	68	1.8
Male	26	27	0.4
Proportion of children aged 1-13 months who have not received any vaccination, 1992-93(%)	30	43	11
Percentage of recent births preceded by an Ante-natal check-up, 1992-93	49	30	97
Proportion of births taking place in medical institutions, 1991 (%)	24	4	92
No. of hospital beds per million persons, 1991	732	340	2,418
Proportion of villages with medical facilities	14	10	96
Proportion of the population receiving subsidized cereals from the public distribution system (1986-87) (%)	29	3	87

India has 2.9 per cent of share of the earth's surface and 17 per cent of the earth's population. But has only ½ per cent of share in the world trade. It is said that India's share in world's manufacturing output in 1750 was 24.5 per cent; 19.7 per cent in 1800; 17.6 per cent in 1830 and 1.7 per cent in 1900. This was India's diminishment under the colonial rule. This was clearly the result of social inability to respond to and handle the forces of change unleashed by the industrial revolution and the Human Development Report, 1998 gives an idea of the global economic inequalities:

– that three richest people have assets that exceed the combined GDP of the 48 least developed countries.

– The 15 richest have assets that exceed the total GDP of Sub-Saharan Africa.

– The wealth of the 32 richest people exceeds the total GDP of South Asia.

– The assets of the 84 richest exceed the GDP of China, the most populous country, with 1.2 billion inhabitants.

– It is further estimated that the additional cost of achieving and maintaining universal access to basic education for all, basic health care for all, reproductive health care for all women, adequate food for all and safe water and sanitation for all is roughly $40 billion a year. This is less than 4 per cent of the assets of 225 richest persons.

In such a bewildering state of inequality in the international economic order, India's greatest and most urgent need is economic development. But its success is inextricably intertwined with social change. It is an illusion to believe that enduring and stable development can be achieved without social justice and gender equality. This, in turn, depends on education of the girl child which again, in turn, depends for its success on maternal and child health care.

Today, there is alarming phenomenon of 'Missing women', a disturbing demographic denudation in the Male-Female ratio. Women continue to suffer great discrimination. It is said that out of 5003 IAS officers only 528 are women. Out of 540 or so members of the Lok Sabha only 44 are women. In the Rajya Sabha there are only 19 women.

A brochure brought out by the Justice Sunanda Bhandare Foundation says that Sunanda as lawyer had once fought for the inclusion of women into the Armed Forces. But though she did not win this case, she lived to see the first batch of women officers being commissioned to the Indian Air Force. Had she lived, she would have also witnessed the success of her argument in the Supreme Court of the United States. In *United States Vs. State of Virginia* (1996) 1 Butterworths Human Rights Cases 265, the 'all-male-policy' of the single-sex Virginia Military Institute was assailed on grounds of gender discrimination. The Supreme Court of the United States upheld the challenge and struck down the 'all-male' policy. It is appropriate to recall the words of the Court:

> "Today sceptical scrutiny of official action denying rights or opportunities based on sex responds to volumes of history. As a plurality of this Court acknowledged a generation ago, 'our Nation has had a long and unfortunate history of sex discrimination' (see *Frontiero v Richardson* (1973) 411 US 677 at 684). Through a century plus three decades and more of that history, women did not count among voters composing 'We the People'; not until 1920 did women gain a constitutional right to the franchise."

> "Since *Reed*, the Court has repeatedly recognised that neither federal nor state government acts compatibly with the equal protection principle when a law or official policy denies to women, simply because they are women, full citizenship stature-equal opportunity to aspire, achieve, participate in and contribute to society based on their individual talents and capacities."

> 'Inherent differences' between men and women, we have come to appreciate, remain cause for celebration, but not for denigration of the members of either sex or for artificial constraints on an individual's opportunity'. .... 'Measuring the record in this case against the review standard just described, we conclude that Virginia has shown no 'exceedingly persuasive justification' for excluding all women from the citizen-soldier training afforded by VMI."

These great changes in the world and in the outlook of society are a tribute to the tireless tribe all over the world to which Justice Sunanda belonged.

3

Society, Law and Gender Justice

Justice Sunanda Bhandare

Indian mythology places women on a very high pedestal. The goddess of learning in India is Saraswathi, the goddess of power is Parvathi and the goddess of wealth is Laxmi. Gargi and Maitri[1] were both great women philosophers and authorities on the Rigveda and Yajurveda of the days of Yagnavalkya. Women were known by their first name and only the second name appeared of men viz. Sita Ram, Radhey Shyam. Manu,[2] a great Hindu sage, author of 'Manu Samhita' wrote"

यत्र नार्यस्तु पूज्यन्ते रमन्ते तत्र देवत:

(which means where women are honoured, Gods feel delighted).

But the 'Manu Smriti'[3] not only shows contempt for women but goes on to degrade them as slaves. Women were considered to be devoid of intellect and consciously denied any learning. They were denied right to property and were forbidden from performing sacrifices. Manu said "if a man does not pay his father's debt, in his next life he is born as a dog, a slave or a woman." Law conferred second class status to women. The religion also contributed in a substantial measure to aggravate these inequalities. The reasons were many - may be the physical weakness of women because of which they had to depend on man in early days when physical exertion was the main activity to meet daily needs; or the tendency to keep the property within the family and the feeling that a woman is "paraya dhan" (someone else's wealth).

A Hindu woman was given a right to stridhan properties but not to the joint family property in which she had only the right to maintenance. In the law of adoption, her position was an inferior one. A widow could not adopt without the authority of her husband given during his life time and after his death without the authority of his agnates. Her rights to maintenance and property were extremely curtailed. A married woman (*Patni*) was entitled to maintenance only as long as she kept the bed of her lord (husband) unsullied and her status

---

[1]Gargi and Maitri were both great women philosophers and authorities on Rigveda and Yajurveda.

[2]Manu, a great Hindu sage, author of "Manu Samhita."

[3]Manu Smriti is a record of what Manu said.

was determined according to the nature of relationship she had with a man. She was a "Sarvainini" as a wanton woman, "Veshya" as a prostitute, "Kishkashini" as a woman discarded by her paramour or a "Dasi" as a woman kept exclusively by the man.

It was only later during the time of Vijanesvera[4] that the archaic Smriti law was freed from religious fetters and changed for the benefit of women.

Thereafter social reformers like Raja Ram Manohar Roy, Lokmanya Tilak, Mahatma Phule, Agarkar and Mahatma Gandhi took up the cause of women in the promotion of female education, re-marriage of widows', elimination of child marriage and other derogatory practices against women. The concept of widow's estate was developed in respect of property inherited by her from her husband in 1937.

Independence brought in its wake a great consciousness in our society for human dignity and it was realised that gender equality is necessary to ensure such dignity. It ushered in a new era of economic, social and political equality for women. By the time our Constitution came to be framed and adopted, a sea change had taken place though not in adequate proportion.

To fulfil the pledge for an egalitarian society, equality had to be ensured and discrimination and derogatory practices against women eliminated. Thus Articles 14, 15(3), 16, 39(e) and 51 which guarantee equality and special protection for women were enshrined in the Constitution.[5]

Art. 14. The State shall not deny to any person equality before the law or the equal protection of the laws within the territory of India.

Art. 15. (1) The State shall not discriminate against any citizen on grounds only of religion, race caste, sex, place of birth or any of them.

(2) No citizen shall, on grounds only of religion, race, caste, sex, place of birth or any of them be subject to any disability, liability, restriction or condition with regard to-

(a) access to shops, public restaurants, hotels and places of public entertainment; or

(b) the use of wells, tanks, bathing ghats, roads and places of public resort maintained wholly or partly out of State funds or dedicated to the use of the general public.

(3) Nothing in this article shall prevent the State from making any special provision for women and children.

Art. 16. (1) There shall be equality of opportunity for all citizens in matters relating to employment or appointment to any office under the State.

(2) No citizen shall, on grounds only of religion, race, caste, sex, descent, place of birth, residence or any of them, be ineligible for, or discriminated against in respect of, any employment or office under the State.

---

[4]Vijnanesvera author of Mitakshara, the most celebrated and authoritative commentary on the Yajnavalkya Smriti (11th century).

[5]The Constitution of India, adopted on 26 January 1950.

Art. 39 The State shall, in particular, direct its policy towards securing

(a) that the citizen, men and women equally, have the right to an adequate means of livelihood....

(d) that there is equal pay for equal work for both men and women.

(e) that the health and strength of workers, men and women, and the tender age of children are not abused and that citizens are not forced by economic necessity to enter avocations unsuited to their age or strength.

Art. 51A It shall be the duty of every citizen of India ...

(e) to promote harmony and the spirit of common brotherhood amongst all the people of India transcending religious, linguistic and regional or sectional diversities; to renounce practices derogatory to the dignity of women; ...

Similarly the Universal Declaration of Human Rights recognising the equality of men and women in its preamble proclaims:

> Peoples of the United Nations have in the Charter re-affirmed their faith in fundamental human rights, in the dignity and worth of the human person and in the equal rights of men and women and have determined to promote social progress and better standards of life in larger freedom."

Article 1 of the Universal Declaration of Human Rights, adopted on 10th December 1948, provides that all human beings are born free and equal in dignity and rights. Article 2 of the Declaration provides for equality of the sexes by stating that everyone is entitled to all the rights and freedoms without distinction of sex.

Likewise the International Covenant on Civil and Political Rights 1966 urges every Covenant State to respect and to ensure to all individuals within its territory the rights recognised by that Covenant without distinction of sex. Article 3 provides that Covenant States should undertake to ensure equal rights of men and women. Even Articles 2 and 3 of the International Covenant on Economic, Social and Cultural Rights 1966 urge all the Covenant States to ensure equal rights of men and women to the enjoyment of all economic, social and cultural rights.

One had to wait till 1979, thirty one years after the Universal Declaration of Human Rights for the Convention on the Elimination of All Forms of Discrimination Against Women to be adopted by the U.N. General Assembly. This Convention reiterates that discrimination against women violates the principles of equality of rights and respect for women's dignity and is an obstacle to the participation of women on equal terms with men in the political, social, economic and cultural life of their countries, hampers the growth of prosperity of society and the family and makes more difficult the full development of the potentialities of women in the service of their countries and of humanity and urges that change in the traditional role of women as well as role of women in society and in the family is needed to achieve full equality between men and women.

In spite of the enshrinement of these provisions, equality between men and women continues to be an elusive goal not only in our country but all over the world. A wide gap exists between the ideal and the practical in our country partly due to historical reasons. However, the main reason why such discrimination continues in our country is the attitude of inferiority — nay bondage — towards women and an atmosphere in which women are deprived of all basic freedoms, starting with that of education, and are thereby exposed to easy exploitation.

Before we can address ourselves to legal enactments for the prevention of oppression and protection of rights of women, we have to set right these attitudes and atmosphere of prejudice against and neglect towards women. Indian society suffers from the virus of 'son preference'. I remember while attending a family planning programme, one of the speakers observed that if family planning were to be made as simple as to utter a mantra to avoid conception, couples in India would not utter it till a male child was born. Even in matters of health the preference for looking after male children is markedly more than that for female children. This bias results in considerable neglect of female children in matters of nutrition, medical care and education depriving them of the right to equality which remains today only a hollow shell.

Disparity between man and woman stares us in the face and thus several of the following questions still do not have an adequate and satisfactory answer.

(a) How is it that in public life — professions, business and services — women are not adequately represented?

(b) How is it that women put in longer hours of work compared to men and yet do not enjoy equal status or opportunities?

(c) Why is it that property owned by women constitutes a very small fraction of the property owned by men?

(d) Why is it that maternity is not recognised as an essential social function?

(e) Why is the rate of suicide so high among women?

(f) Why is it that fairness vanishes when it comes to giving a fair deal to the 'fair' sex.

Organised religion is one of the main obstacles in the way of liberation of women. Leaders of faith have stood firm against reform which would improve the status of women in social, cultural, economic or political fields. To that extent religion has been more selfish than sublime. Even in the early fifties when reforms of Hindu law were under consideration there was tremendous opposition from the orthodox Hindu community. But Parliament led by Jawaharlal Nehru as the Prime Minister and Dr. B.R. Ambedkar as the Law Minister pushed through the legislation and the Hindu Succession Act which codifies the law relating to inheritance and succession among Hindus came on the Statute book.

The urgent necessity, therefore, is for bringing about a radical change in the attitude of society towards women and to provide a suitable surrounding and atmosphere for accelerating the process of equality between men and women and removing oppression of women in general.

As stated above, good nutrition, proper health care and education are all the more necessary to ensure the dignity and status of women in our country. It is heartening in this connection to note that the Government has announced a policy of free education upto the higher secondary level for girls, but that itself is not enough unless steps are taken to see that they first enroll in the school and then do not drop out until they complete their education. It is only when this is achieved that the laws for eradication of discrimination against women will be effectively implemented, otherwise they are likely to remain a dead letter.

Ultimately, the fundamental question is not one of explaining out the differences between man and woman but of treating both man and woman as human beings, gifted with the same faculties, subject to the same feelings and entitled to equality of opportunity and status to ensure full development of the family and society. One wonders whether the expression 'man' defined to include woman should not be substituted by an expression of a human being, which would include both man and woman. The two expressions 'man' and 'woman' should be used only when relevant to the subject or purpose of legislation. I am, therefore, against suggesting the other extreme that the expression woman includes a man. I think the basic concept of law which talks of man and woman should now be substituted by the concept of a human being. The natural and inalienable rights of human beings are the same whether they are men or women and the right of equality is the primordial right among the basic human rights and fundamental freedoms.

Salutary changes have been made in the Dowry Prohibition Act, 1962, particularly by the Dowry Prohibition (Amendment) Act, 1984. What is, however, necessary is to change the attitude towards the women as a 'paraya dhan'. The feeling that a daughter gets a share only once when she leaves her parents' home is itself contrary to all notions of equity, fair play and justice between the sexes in the matter of property. What is necessary is that daughters should be treated on equal footing with sons in the matter of inheritance of property. Despite the provisions of law providing for equal shares, it is not unknown that married women give up their right to the property of their parents in favour of their brothers. It is this attitude which has resulted in a greater and greater claim for dowry and any woman rightfully claiming her share in her parent's property is considered as a villain. All these things must change. In fact what is most important is to provide an equal share for a woman with that of her husband even when she is not working and contributing to the earnings of the family. The law in the West has undergone considerable change in this regard.

In England as early as in 1823, Lord Stowell in his opinion in the case of *Jane and Matilda*[6] held that women's sex was no bar to her claim for mariner's wages. I may quote from it:

> "The character of woman furnishes a theme at once the most romantic and thrilling in legend and poem, in story and romance. Many of the impressive and dramatic chapters in the world's history take life and colour from memories of the great disadvantages with which she has had to struggle, and the insurmountable barriers which for centuries have hindered the growth and development of her influence; notwithstanding the fact that until but recently the law has been construed and perverted to rob her of individuality by merging her very existence in that of her husband, and despite all the years of injustice and wrong that woman has suffered, she has left the impress of her genius upon the ages, and while poetry is written, the bard will sing the glory of her proud renown—
>
> She walks in beauty, like the night of cloudless climes and starry skies and all that's best of dark and bright meet in her aspect and her eyes."

In England, under Section 5(1)(f) of the Matrimonial Proceedings and Property Act, 1970, a provision has been made that in considering whether to make a transfer of property, the court is to have regard, amongst other things, to:

> "the contributions made by each of the parties to the welfare of the family including any contribution made looking after the home or caring for the family."

In interpreting these provisions, Lord Denning, in *Wachtel Vs. Wachtel* - (1973) All England Reporter 829 (C.A.), observed as follows:

> "In the light thus thrown on the reason for S.5(1)(f), we may take it that Parliament recognised that the wife who looks after the home and family contributes as much to the family assets as the wife who goes out to work. The one contributes in kind. The other in money or money's worth. If the Court comes to the conclusion that the home has been acquired and maintained by the joint efforts of both, then, when the marriage breaks down, it should be regarded as the joint property of both of them no matter in whose name it stands. Just as the wife who makes substantial money contribution usually gets a share, so should the wife who looks after the home and cares for the family for 20 years or more."

[6] 1 HAGG 187.

In India itself, in Goa, under the Portuguese Civil Law, which is still applicable to the residents of Goa, there is a concept of communion of properties and after the marriage, both the spouses share each other's property equally. I think this is a salutary provision and it is worthwhile considering whether a similar provision should not be made for the rest of the country.

Today no civilised society denies the equality of sexes and has also made affirmative provisions against gender discrimination generally. Social science affirms that a woman's place in society marks the level of civilisation.

Violence Against Women

Woman has always been an object of fury and severe violence at the hands of men. The biological weakness of a woman makes her an easy prey particularly to physical domination. She is often a victim of physical violence not only outside her home but inside her home also. In India we have in recent years made far reaching changes in the law to prevent violence against women.

It is the strong agitation by the women and women's organisations that has brought about the Criminal Law Amendment Act, 1983, a substantial qualitative change in the law of sexual offences against women. Not only has the law been changed to punish the men guilty of the offence of rape more deterrently but it has also been moulded to see that the humiliation and shame of the victim is not compounded during or after the trial. The law has particularly been modified to provide the absence of true and genuine consent as the essential ingredient of the law of rape. Thus, the old law which very often permitted the accused to escape on the ground of apparent consent no longer holds the field. The minimum punishment for rape is seven year's imprisonment for ordinary cases but it is ten years' imprisonment for certain aggravated situations. There are seven such established aggravated situations set out in the new law. They refer to the custodial rape by (a) a police officer on a woman in his custody; (b) a public servant on a woman in his custody and subordinate to him by taking advantage of his official position; (c) the member of the staff of a jail, remand home or other place of detention, or a women's or children's institution on an inmate; (d) the manager of a hospital taking advantage of his official position on "a woman in that hospital". (e) a man committing a rape on a woman knowing her to be pregnant; (f) rape on a girl under twelve years of age; and (g) 'gang rape'.

In all the above cases, Section 114(A) of the Evidence Act now provides for a conclusive presumption about absence of consent where sexual intercourse by the accused is proved and the victim states in her evidence before the Court that she did not consent.

The provision for holding the trial in camera and also preventing publication of its proceedings including the name of the victim except in Law Reports, is a salutary provision to protect the victim from further shame and humiliation. Though there are provisions against eve teasing and molestation, the law remains inadequate to meet the purposes and the offences continue to grow.

Over the years judges have made a conscious effort to get out of the rigid mould and break new grounds. Judges have been adopting law to new social ideas and developments of human activity. They thus serve the needs of society. They have in the process loosened considerably the fetters around them. The Supreme Court of India has not felt bound to follow its earlier decisions and in several cases has revised its earlier opinions. There is thus a conscious effort on the part of the judges to carry the law forward through their decisions. It is now recognised by judges that the courts cannot be out of step with society. 'To give just one illustration, on a letter received by the Supreme Court of India, complaining of custodial violence meted out to prisoners in police lock-ups,' the Supreme Court[7] laid down guidelines as to how women in police lock-ups should be treated. The main safeguards provided are —

(i) Separate places of detention should be provided for female suspects.

(ii) Female suspects should be interrogated only in the presence of female police officers.

(iii) Every person who is arrested should be informed of the ground of arrest and of the right to apply for bail. A pamphlet listing these rights should be affixed in every police station.

(iv) The police should intimate the fact of arrest to the nearest legal aid committee and the legal aid committee should take immediate steps to offer to the arrested person the needed legal assistance.

(v) Sessions judges should make surprise visits to police lock-ups periodically.

(vi) On arrest, the police should inform a relative or friend of the arrested person.

(vii) The magistrate before whom an arrested person is produced must inquire whether the arrested person has any complaint of torture or maltreatment in police custody and inform her that under Section 54 of the Code of Criminal Procedure, 1973 she has the right to be medically examined.

Now a word for women lawyers: law has always been regarded as a noble and learned profession. The three attributes of a lawyer are independence, integrity and industry. A woman is naturally gifted both with integrity and industry, more than a man. She has been suppressed over the years and not allowed to be independent. But when on her own, she displays a spirit of independence which is fiercer than that of any man because of her better strength of character. To these she adds the quality of compassion and justice. The picture of a woman as a lawyer has been romanticised by Shakespeare in the Merchant of Venice in his character of Portia who saves the life of her lover Antonio by arguing before the judge for only a pound of flesh without a drop of blood. But like any other occupation, vocation or profession, women have been suppressed even in the profession of law. It was not without difficulty that women started getting a place of their own in the field of law. Nineteenth century British Law prohibited women from entering the Bar both in England

[7]*Sheela Barse v/s State of Maharashtra* (1983) 2SCC 96.

and in India. The solitary Indian woman to earn a law degree in the 19th century was Cornelia Sorabji, a Parsi Christian, who obtained the Degree of Bachelor of Civil Law from Oxford in 1892. She did not practise law but was appointed as a Legal Advisor to the Women's Court of Wards in Calcutta by the Governor of Bengal. In 1921 Sudhanshubala Hazara had to fight right upto the Privy Council to get herself enrolled as a pleader because the High Court of Patna under the Legal Practitioners Act did not permit a lady to be enrolled in the High Court. The Government of India passed the Legal Practitioners (Women) Act in 1923 removing the ban on women practising law. Though women did obtain law degrees, few practised as it was not generally considered respectable among high status families for women to be engaged in the profession. The first known Indian woman who practised law was Mithan Lam, a Parsi, the daughter of women's right activist, Herabai Tata. Mithan Lam was called to the Bar from Lincoln's Inn in 1923 and practised in the Bombay High Court.

The profession of law has opened new vistas for women. It is up to you to work hard and reach the top of the profession. A woman is inferior to no man though she has to be twice as good to go half as far. As in other walks of life you are likely to be exploited even in this profession. You must resist the temptation of becoming only an adjournment counsel or a show-piece in an office of a senior male advocate. You have to make your presence felt by your legal acumen and hard work so that more and more clients come to rely on your professional ability. This is one profession where all lawyers work in open courts under public gaze. It is unlike the profession of medicine where each member works separately in a clinic or hospital. It is, therefore, necessary for women to prove equal, and even superior, to men. Even in matters of fees, the general gender bias continues against women. There is hesitation, in the first instance to brief a woman lawyer and then there is hesitation to pay her fees equal to a male lawyer for the same case. Equally dismal is the picture on the appointment of women to judicial posts. But time has proved that it is possible to practice effectively while looking after home and the children.

It is, therefore, all the more necessary to persevere in practice till you succeed. I have all hope and confidence that in years to come the highest positions both at the bar and on the Bench will be filled by a "galaxy" from amongst you.

Let me end by quoting a poem which captures the spirit of independence of women.

I decided long ago never to walk
in any one's shadow.
If I fail, If I succeed.
At least I will live as I believe
and no matter what they, take from me
They can't take away my dignity
So I learn to depend on me.

4

Judiciary and Gender Justice

Justice Sujata V. Manohar

Today is the birth anniversary of Justice Sunanda Bhandare — a day, which I am sure, holds happy memories for her family and many of us present here. It is appropriate that the first Justice Sunanda Bhandare Memorial Lecture is organised for today. I have known Sunanda and Murli Bhandare for many years when they were in Bombay and then in Delhi. I remember Sunanda as a young lawyer taking an active interest in women's issues. We were together at the biennial Conferences of the Indian Federation of Women Lawyers at Madras and at Hyderabad, and I was impressed by her concern for women's issues and her sound common-sense. She excelled herself as a judge. Her sterling independence, integrity and legal acumen made her a notable judge of the Delhi High Court. Her husband gave her total support and did not allow his own vocation to intrude into her work.

Little did I expect that my first task on coming to Delhi would be to pay a condolence visit to her husband. Destiny plays some strange tricks. Looking to Sunanda's abiding concern for gender justice, it is appropriate that the first lecture in her memory should be on the Judiciary and Gender Justice–two subjects dear to her heart, separately or together.

Background

Gender justice is a wide term which takes in its sweep every facet of life. For centuries, in fact, ever since known history, we have lived in a patriarchal (with some notable exceptions) and feudal society which has assigned to women a subordinate role. Women may be respected and loved, but have been confined to the home and home-making, looking after children, the sick and the elderly in the family. Most of the unpaid work in the world is done by women. Their socio-economic dependence led to their exploitation. The new awareness of this exploitation and the need to restructure society on a more just basis has led to serious attempts to reform and transform our social, moral, economic and political structure including legal and constitutional framework.

How this is to be achieved has elicited varied responses.

Need for Structural Transformation

At the Fourth World Conference on Women, more than 170 Non-Governmental Organisations from all over the world called for a pledge to gender justice. While there is a fair unanimity on the concept of gender justice, the question, how gender justice is to be achieved, has elicited varied, and at times, conflicting responses.

Women now demand not structural adjustment but structural transformation–making it possible for women to participate and contribute, while also fulfilling their responsibilities towards their children, elders and family. Women have also voiced their concern about lack of effective protection against domestic violence, against crimes like rape or molestation and sexual harassment at work, apart from sex based discrimination, making it difficult for women to function effectively in all spheres of significant human activity. There is also a growing fear that we are moving towards feminisation of poverty. The fear is backed by impressive statistics. One out of five of the world's 5.6 billion people lives in absolute poverty–defined as lack of adequate food, safe drinking water, or lack of health care, high infant mortality and lack of education. And 70 per cent of the world's poor are women. Most of world's single parent families are headed by women. And these families form a significant part of the world's poor.

An inherent gender bias pervades world civilizations cutting across countries and cultures. How is it to be overcome?

Rosemarie Tong in her book *Feminist Thought** has summarised differing perceptions of the subject. "Gender justice, insist liberal feminists, requires us, first, to make the rules of the game fair and second, to make certain that none of the runners in the race for society's goods and services is systematically disadvantaged"— this is the socio-legal approach. "Marxist feminists think it is impossible for anyone, especially women to obtain genuine equal opportunity in a class society where the wealth produced by the powerless may end up in the hands of the powerful few." So that economic and political restructuring is advocated. "Radical feminists argue that it is the patriarchal system that oppresses women .... Psychoanalytic feminists find the roots of a woman's oppression embedded deep in her psyche ...."

Law, Judiciary and Structural Transformation

I would like to focus on making and keeping the Rules of the game fair—if necessary by structural transformation, because that is where judiciary can play an effective role. The Constitution has laid the foundation for this transformation in our society. Article 14 enjoins equality and equal protection of the laws. Article 15(1) prohibits the State from discriminating against any citizen on grounds only of religion, race, caste, sex or place of birth. Article 15(3) by providing for special provisions for women and children has opened up the possibility of structural transformation. It is legitimate for the judiciary to enforce constitutional mandates. Vision, empathy and balance in interpreting and applying this mandate and laws flowing from it, are necessary for this transformation of our society and its diverse cultures.

---

*Tong, R., *Feminist Thought: A Comprehensive Introduction*. (London: Unwin Hyan, 1989).

Fortunately, we have a basic constitutional mandate to bring about equality and justice. We have also signed the United Nations Convention on the Elimination of all forms of Discrimination against Women, which came into force on 3rd of September, 1981—though with reservations. Article 2 of the Convention provides: "All appropriate measures shall be taken to abolish existing laws, customs, regulations and practises which are discriminatory against women and to establish adequate legal protection for equal rights of men and women, in particular, (a) the principle of equality of rights shall be embodied in the Constitution or otherwise guaranteed by law ...." Articles 14 and 15 of the Constitution cover some of these constitutional requirements. But the full legal guarantees are still lacking.

Of course, it is not easy to eradicate deep seated cultural values or to alter traditions that perpetuate discrimination. It is fashionable to denigrate the role of law reform in bringing about social change. Obviously law, by itself, may not be enough. Law is only an instrument. It must be effectively used. And this effective use depends as much on a supportive judiciary as on the social will to change. An active social reform movement, if accompanied by legal reform, properly enforced, can transform society. And an effective social reform movement does need the help of law and a sympathetic judiciary to achieve its objectives. An obvious example is the Sati eradication movement. Raja Ram Mohan Roy's campaign for eradication of Sati when backed by Lord Bentinck's Sati Regulation of 1829 brought the practice to an end. The extent of the practice can be gauged by the fact that prior to the Regulation, in Bengal Presidency alone there were 600 satis every year! An attempt to revive and glorify the practice in 1987, — The Roopkunwar episode was fortunately nipped in the bud with the commission of Sati Prevention Act, 1987. In contrast, in the absence of a strong social reform movement, Dowry Prohibition Act, 1961 has not checked the practice of dowry and its accompanying evils.

It is interesting to note that Australia, after it signed the Convention on the Elimination of all forms of Discrimination against Women, in 1993 referred to its Law Reform Commission, the question whether any changes should be made in any of its laws in order to give effect to the principle of equality before the law and Australia's obligations under international law including CEDAW. The Australian Law Reforms Commission was headed by Justice Elizabeth Evatt who had chaired the U.N. Committee which drafted CEDAW. Some of the findings of the Australian Law Reforms Commission are relevant to us also as they reflect on the manner in which the legal system functions.

Crimes Against Women

One of its important findings is to the effect that the legal system fails to deal effectively with violence perpetrated by men on women. Often violence against women is hidden but influential, directing a woman's actions which affect the way the law operates in relation to her. It has recommended, for example, that where the court directs the parties to attend counselling or recommends conciliation, it shall take into account any allegations of violence or reluctance of a party to attend because of violence and the need to ensure the protection of the party against violence. It has recommended training family court personnel in the dynamics of violence. In considering custody and access orders, the Court must take into account the need to protect the child from abuse, ill-treatment or exposure to violence. In criminal law the Commission suggested re-examination of concepts of self-defence and provocation taking a woman's perspective into account. The Commission has also referred to hidden and sometimes unconscious bias in the legal process while dealing with women. For example, gender bias may include lack of credibility given to women as witnesses. The Commission said that women repeatedly claimed that they lacked credibility in the court and their experience ranged from being humiliated or patronised, to simply not being understood. Other examples which it cited were, the belief that a woman's sexual experience is relevant in a rape trial or that when a woman says no, she means yes, or that women provoke domestic violence.

Law Enforcement and Gender Justice

The experience of our women's organisations with our law enforcement machinery has also not been very happy. It is a common complaint that the police are not interested in registering a case of domestic violence — treating it as a domestic personal affair rather than an offence. For example, in 1992 an Additional Commissioner of Police issued a directive to police stations that unless women approach the police stations with bleeding injuries, cases of harassment and cruelty should not be registered. It was only after women's organisations met him and pointed out that Section 498A included mental cruelty also, that he withdrew the directive. Even in cases of dowry deaths and rapes, similar complaints have been voiced. For example, in *Satya Rani Chadha's case,* the Magistrate took five years and a direction from the Supreme Court before he passed a committal order. The setting up of a Crime against Women Cell is a measure to redress this grievance. But such cells will have to be set up on a large scale throughout the country before proper investigation takes place in crimes relating to women. It might be more beneficial to restructure and reorient the police force.

The problem area of investigation of crimes against women is reflected in statistics. There has been a fall in the sex ratio between women and men from 934:1000 in the 1981 census, to 927:1000 in the 1991 census showing lower expectancy of life for women, high infant mortality rate among girls and the consequences which result from oppressive traditions, illiteracy and similar factors. In the years from 1989 to 1993, the incidence of crime against women has increased. For example, rapes have gone up by 22.9 per cent, dowry deaths have increased by 38 per cent, tortures by 19 per cent and eve teasing by 20.9 per cent. These statistics do not take into account domestic violence.

Perhaps some observations of the courts have also reflected sub-conscious gender bias. In one case of sexual molestation, for example, the High Court said, "The accused is married. He is the sole breadwinner and he is in his early twenties. The uncalled for heat of passion is likely to have cooled off by social castigation. So we will restrict the sentence to the period already undergone, — six weeks." Rape victims have also had this kind of experience. In fact, it was the acquittal in the *Mathura Rape* Case that lead to important amendments in the law of custodial rape, shifting the burden of proof on the accused in cases of custodial rape where the woman victim states that she did not consent.

What do these cases indicate?

1. A lot is needed to be done to improve the functioning of the police and its machinery of crime investigation. Women's experiences have brought these inadequacies into sharp focus. If as a result, the entire system improves, women will have done a great service to the country. Some States have set up Women's Cells in some police stations. But a more fundamental process of education and improvement is necessary.

2. Not every judge can be expected to be free from the cultural values and biases of his society. Gender justice education is necessary as a part of the judicial training programme. The experiment of having Mahila Courts is an attempt at overcoming some of the problems faced by women in the legal process. But a basic change in attitudes all round is necessary.

3. As a result of the effective role played by women's organisations and the media in highlighting gender discrimination in crime investigation and prosecutions, the higher judiciary has, to a large extent, been sensitised to this issue. This is increasingly reflected in recent judgements. Unlike some other countries, there is strong positive thinking in our country on the part of the judiciary to support fair laws and fair decisions in cases relating to women.

For example, in the case of *Ashok Kumar v. State of Rajasthan*[1] the Supreme Court upheld the conviction of the brother-in-law of a woman who had been burnt to death. The court expressed its anguish about the evil of dowry and resultant deaths. It said that social reformists and legal jurists should evolve a machinery for debarring the husband of a dowry victim from re-marriage and emphasised the need for social ostracism to curtail the increasing incidence of bride burning. The court upheld the conviction, which is more important. In the case of *Kundla Bala Subramaniam v. State of Andhra Pradesh*[2] the Supreme Court upheld the conviction in the case of a dowry death under Sections 302, 304B and 34 based on circumstantial evidence. Once again the court expressed its distress. It said that the role of courts under the circumstances has assumed greater importance and it is expected that the courts would deal with such cases in a more realistic manner and not allow the criminals to escape on account of

[1]Air 1990 SC 2134.

[2]1993 [2] SCC 684.

procedural technicalities or irrelevant lacunae as otherwise criminals would receive encouragement. The courts are expected to be sensitive in cases involving crime against women. The Supreme Court commented adversely on the verdict of acquittal which was given by the trial court. The High Court had reversed the verdict and the High Court's conviction was upheld by the Supreme Court. These are two illustrative cases of growing sensitivity of the courts to crimes against women.

In *Sudha Goel's case*[3] the Supreme Court observed that the neighbours were reliable and dependable witnesses and that even if there were minor variations between their statements in court and in the statement to the police, there was a ring of truth to them and they could be relied upon.

Incidents of gang rape and rape by people holding fiduciary positions over the victim, such as the police, heads of orphanages or women's institutes, have given rise to some important amendments relating to the law of rape. Here the demand for law reform was occasioned by a judgement in 1979 of the Supreme Court in what has come to be known as the *Mathura Rape Case* (*Tuka Ram v. State of Maharashtra*[4]). The conviction which was recorded by the High Court was set aside by the Supreme Court. Protests from a large number of women's organisations ultimately led to the amendment of the Penal Code and the Evidence Act. Since then, there have been many judgements in this area displaying more sensitivity and understanding of women's plight. For example, in a later case of *State of Maharashtra v. Chander Prakash Kewalchand Jain*[5] which also dealt with the rape of a newly married girl by the police the court headed by our present C.J.I. categorically observed that the prosecutrix cannot be put on a par with an accomplice. She is a victim of the crime. Not only is she a competent witness, but her evidence must carry the same weight as is attached to an injured person who is a victim of violence, unless there are special circumstances which call for caution. The Supreme Court said, "ordinarily, the evidence of the prosecutrix who does not lack understanding must be accepted. To insist on corroboration except in the rarest of rare cases is to equate a woman who is a victim of the lust of another with an accomplice to a crime and thereby insult womanhood." These are very strong observations in support of justice for women in a court of law.

Then in the case of *State of Maharashtra v. Madhukar Narain Mardikar*[6] the Supreme Court held that even a woman of easy virtue is entitled to protect her person. Her evidence cannot be thrown overboard on that count. In the recent case of *Karnal Singh v. State of Madhya Pradesh*[7] the Supreme Court and our C.J.I. once again reiterated, in the case of prosecution for rape, that the evidence

[3]AIR 1986 SC 250.

[4]AIR 1979 SC 185.

[5]1990 [1] SCC 550.

[6]JT 1990(4) SCC 169.

[7]Crl. Appeal No. 877/1995.

of the prosecutrix, the medical evidence of her examination and the evidence of the investigating officer were reliable and there was no risk involved in accepting the version of the prosecutrix. Significantly, the court expressed its unhappiness regarding the manner in which investigation had been carried out and it said that the investigation was casual and defective.

The case illustrates the understanding attitude displayed by the courts in relation to crimes against women and the tardy or casual investigation carried out by the investigating agency in crimes relating to women which enables many guilty people to escape conviction. These are now the two recurring factors which affect prosecutions in courts of law relating to crimes against women. In the case of *State of Punjab v. Iqbal Singh and Ors.*[8] on account of husband persistently making dowry demands from the wife and beating and harassing her, the wife ultimately committed suicide. The court said that the husband by his wilful conduct had created an atmosphere which forced the wife to commit suicide. The conviction of the husband under Section 306 and sentence of seven years rigorous imprisonment recorded by the trial court were upheld. The reversal of conviction by the High Court was set aside. In the case of *State of U.P. v. Ashok Kumar Srivastava*[9] which was prior to the insertion of Section 304-B in the Penal Code, the Supreme Court in the case of a dowry death held that the circumstantial evidence led to the hypothesis of guilt of the accused husband, the father-in-law and the sister-in-law of the deceased. The court observed that while appreciating circumstantial evidence the court must be cautious and should record conviction only when all the links in the chain are completely pointing to the guilt of the accused. But it would not be correct to say that the prosecution must meet each and every hypothesis put forward by the accused. There is thus an effective reversal of the trend from the days of Manju Shree Sarda or Mathura.

Unfortunately, we do not have any separate legal provisions relating to domestic violence. We have to rely upon the Penal Code for the protection of women against domestic violence. This kind of violence, however, has certain special interactable characteristics because it is perpetrated in the privacy of the home. The victim is more vulnerable and the remedy is more difficult. Outsiders, whether it is the police or neighbours or other friends or relatives are reluctant to intervene in what they perceive as a private domestic problem. The abused wife and her children usually depend on their assailant for food, shelter and even for their identity. Abused women often need an emergency temporary shelter. In many countries this is followed by obtaining a protection order from the court asking the husband to desist from violence and where necessary, preventing the husband from entering the matrimonial home. The National Commission of Women has recommended a domestic violence legislation for our country, providing for protection orders and a protection officer. But for women who are faced with chronic abuse, the only viable option is an

[8]1991 (3) SCC 1.

[9]1992 (2) 86.

independent life with decent wages, educational training, jobs, child support, a house, an option which gives them the power to stand up inside the home. Most women do not have this option. And they do not believe that they can change their situation. Providing a counselling service alone merely provide a place where women can express their distress and possibly derive sufficient energy to cope with the abuse, and nothing more.

Sometimes an arrest order can effectively check repeated violence. An experiment in Minneapolis showed that the repeat rate for violence, where an arrest had been effected, was only 13 per cent compared to 26 per cent where no arrest was made. Such an order sends out a message that wife beating will not be tolerated. Its long-term practical efficacy, however, is doubtful.

Property Rights

The second important area of concern for the judiciary relates to property rights of women. The two important laws for Hindu women that ultimately transformed their right to inherit family property are the Hindu Women's Right to Property Act, 1937 and the Hindu Succession Act, 1956. Under the 1937 Act a widow obtained a share on inheritance, in her husband's property equal to that of a son. It was however, only a life estate. After the Hindu Succession Act of 1956 was enacted making this share absolute, there was a spate of litigation relating to Section 14 of that Act. Under Section 14 a Hindu widow's limited estate was abolished and she became the absolute owner of the property. It provided that any property possessed by a female Hindu whether acquired before or after the commencement of the Act shall be held by her as the full owner thereof and not as a limited owner. The question was: what is meant by the expression "possessed by a female Hindu? The Supreme Court in the case of *G.T.M. Kotturuswami v. Setra Verravva*[10] said that the word 'possessed' is used in its widest connotation. It need not be actual physical possession or personal occupation of the property by the female. It can be either actual or constructive. Thus for example the possession of a licensee, lessee or mortgagee from the female owner would be her possession for the purpose of Section 14. In *Mangal Singh v. Rattno*[11] the Supreme Court said that the section would cover all cases of property owned by a female Hindu although she may not be in actual or constructive possession of that property provided she had not parted with her rights and was capable of obtaining possession of the property. In that case, a Hindu widow who was wrongfully dispossessed, filed a suit for possession in March 1956 before the coming into force the Hindu Succession Act. The Court said that on coming into force of the Hindu Succession Act she must be regarded as a female Hindu who possessed the property for the purposes of Section 14 and so she became a full owner of it.

---

[10]1959 Suppl. 1 SCR 968

[11]AIR 1967 SC 1786

The Court has clearly given a very broad interpretation to this section in order to ensure that all rights of limited ownership of female Hindus become their absolute rights. Even the share of a widow declared by a preliminary decree in a partition suit before the commencement of the Succession Act has been considered by the Court as a share possessed by her. Compensation which was awarded in respect of the acquired property of a widow, who did not have an absolute interest in it at the date of acquisition, was considered as her absolute property because the compensation was given to her after the coming into force of the Act. The latest decision in the area of inheritance is the famous *Mary Roy case*[12] where the Supreme Court held that the law applicable to Christian women in Kerala after the integration of States was the Indian Succession Act. A Christian woman in Kerala, therefore, cannot be given a lesser share in inheritance under the old State law.

Employment

In matters of employment Article 15 of the Constitution provides for non-discrimination on the ground of sex in matters of employment under the State. One of the interesting cases which the Court had to consider was that of *Air India v. Nargesh Meerza & Ors.*[13]. The Air Hostesses challenged certain service conditions such as termination of services on first pregnancy, restriction on marriage within the first four years of service, an early retirement at 35 years extendable to 45 years as violative of Article 14 and discriminatory. The Supreme Court said that air hostesses were an entirely separate class governed by a different set of rules and conditions of service. Since they formed a separate category, special conditions attached to the separate category could not be considered as discriminatory. But the conditions, if they are wholly arbitrary and unreasonable, can be struck down under Article 14 as going against the equality clause. The condition relating to termination of service on pregnancy was not only manifestly unreasonable or arbitrary but contained the quality of unfairness, violating Article 14. On the ground of arbitrary discretion being conferred on the Managing Director to extend in a given case the age of retirement upto 45, the Court also struck down the discretion holding that the retirement age would be 45 for all Air Hostesses. The consequences are there for all to see. In the case of *C.B. Muthumma v. Union of India*[14] service conditions of Foreign service personnel requiring female employees to obtain government permission before marriage and denying married women a right to be employed, were struck down as discriminatory.

Occasionally the provisions of Article 15 Clause (3) which provide for special provisions being made for women and children has been resorted to for prescribing special service conditions for women, e.g., that women cannot work beyond certain hours. At times women are considered ineligible for jobs because

[12] 1986 (2) SCC 209.
[13] 1981 (4) SCC 335.
[14] AIR 1979 SC 1868.

of its peculiar requirements. Some such conditions have been challenged in the courts. In the case of *Dothard v. Rawlinson*[15] decided in 1977 in the U.S. the job requirements of a prison guard prescribed height and weight measurements. These were challenged as they would exclude women. The U.S. Supreme Court split three ways over this decision. In another U.S. case, the Department of Water and Power prescribed a larger monthly pension fund contribution by female employees. It argued that women live longer than men and hence must contribute more for pension. This was struck down. We do not have much litigation in this area. The Kerala High Court struck down a requirement of the Cochin Port Trust that port clerks should only be men. The argument was that the job was unsafe for women. But genuine protective measures have been, by and large, upheld. Reservation of posts for women has been upheld under Article 15(3) though Article 16 does not provide specifically for such reservation for women in *Government of A.P. v. P.B. Vijayakumar*[16]. In the case of *Sowmithri Vishnu v. Union of India*[17] Section 497 of the Penal Code under which a woman is not punishable as an abettor of the offence of adultery, has been upheld as protected by Article 15(3) of the Constitution. Similarly in a Rajasthan Case, the provision in Section 497 of the Criminal Procedure Code for granting of bail to women, and children under the age of 16 years in the case of non-bailable offences has also been upheld as covered by Article 15(3).

The principle of equal pay for equal work has not been invoked much in the context of sex discrimination. Perhaps this is because such discrimination is found more in the private or unorganised sector of labour. There is a good possibility of increase in such litigation in future. Similarly, there has not been much litigation on the question of sexual harassment of women at work which is, at the moment, a major area of concern for women in the West. But we cannot live in isolation for long. We have now our own sexual harassment case where the Supreme Court has reversed the High Court order striking down the FIR. Another important case which is pending before the Supreme Court is the case of *Bhanwaribai* a sathin who was raped while she was performing her duties[18]. In the U.S., in a New Jersey case of *Lehmann v. Toys-'R'-us,* the state Supreme Court laid down very interesting norms for determining sexual harassment, departing from the tests laid down by the Federal Court. One important test laid down is: whether a woman would reasonably view the conduct as sexual harassment. The Court said that the conduct is often viewed differently by men

---

[15]433 US 321

[16]1995 (3) SCALE 613

[17]AIR 1985 S.C. 1618

[18]The case has since been decided (cf. *Vishakha v. State of Rajasthan* [(1997) 6 SCC 241]). Relying upon CEDAW and the countries' official commitment to it, in addition to the constitutional mandate, the Supreme Court has laid down guidelines to be followed by employees to prevent sexual harassment of women employees. The guidelines are mandatory till they are replaced by legislation.

and women, and the correct way of viewing it is whether a woman would consider it as sexual harassment, affecting and impairing her ability to perform her duties at the place of work.

Marriage Laws

The marriage laws of the country mould the relief which can be granted in a Court of law. Since we have different laws which apply to different religious groups, the laws are not uniform. It is also not easy to modernise them or harmonise them since they are coloured with religious overtones. As far back as in 1951 in the case of *State v. Narasu Appa Mali*[19] the Division Bench of the Bombay High Court consisting of two very distinguished Judges, Chagla, C.J. and Gajendragadkar, J. said that personal laws were not within the ambit of Article 13(1) of the Constitution under which all laws in force at the commencement of the Constitution, in so far as they are inconsistent with Part III of the Constitution shall be void. The Directive Principles of State Policy do, however, enjoin a uniform civil law for all. The legislature has not been able to carry out the constitutional directive. Recently the Supreme Court has made its pronouncement in support of a uniform civil code to obviate gender bias in different personal laws relating to marriage. If nothing more, it shows the deep concern felt by the highest court of the land for rendering gender justice.

Even within the existing legal framework, in the lower courts which deal with matrimonial matters, often an unconscious gender bias may play a role in granting discretionary orders relating to custody of children or maintenance or relating to attempts which may be made to bring about reconciliation between the parties. Often the impact of domestic violence on a woman's readiness to go back to her husband's house is underestimated or not appreciated. An unthinking insistence either on the part of the marriage counsellor or on the part of the judge on the woman returning to the husband without protecting her in any manner against any domestic violence may cause more harm than good. In the case of custody of children also, often the factor of domestic violence is not taken into consideration or is not given sufficient importance. At times, the Courts have given undue importance to factors such as money and position where women are usually disadvantaged. At times unconscious gender bias comes into play in weighing circumstances which the court takes into account in granting custody, e.g., while there is no hesitation in giving custody to a working father, there is often hesitation on the part of the courts in giving custody to a working mother. Sometimes, as soon as the children become older, the court feels that the mother's role is no longer important, her care and concern for the child notwithstanding. The court often rules that the father being economically stronger should have the custody of the children. In doing so the Court may be ignoring vital emotional requirements of children and the need for maternal support which these children may not be able to express to a court

[19]53 *Bombay Law Reports* 779

of law. A little more sensitivity on the part of the judges on such gender issues would, in my view, help in bringing about more just and humane decisions promoting welfare of the children in these areas of discretionary orders.

The question of maintenance has also found judiciary playing a very progressive role. Even prior to the *Shah Banu case,*[20] the Supreme Court had, in two earlier decisions interpreted Section 125 as giving to a divorced Muslim woman a right to maintenance if the Mahr which she had obtained at the time of divorce was not sufficient to maintain her and, therefore, could not be considered as in lieu of maintenance. Yet when the *Shah Banu*[21] case was decided by the Supreme Court on the same grounds awarding maintenance to a divorced Muslim woman, the legislature thought it fit to enact the Muslim Women (Protection on Divorce) Act, 1986.

Even when the existing law provides for maintenance, it is far from satisfactory and the recovery of maintenance is often a tortuous process. The setting up of Family Courts to provide a speedy redressal for domestic wrongs is a step in the right direction. But the Courts must be set up properly, providing different procedures and a different organisational set up as in Maharashtra where recovery of maintenance has been noticeably speeded up in the Family Courts. A mere additional court labelled "Family Court" cannot achieve anything and may create problems rather than solve them.

None of the laws relating to maintenance expressly refers to the matrimonial home. One of the most obvious and pressing needs of a woman who is driven out of her matrimonial home is the need for shelter. Money is not always a substitute for shelter unless the quantum is adequate for her to purchase or hire a shelter and to maintain herself. The Supreme Court has, in a recent case held that a matrimonial home will have to be considered as a part of a woman's right to maintenance. In the case of *Mangat Mul v. Punni Devi*[22] the Supreme Court said, "Maintenance as we see it necessarily must encompass a provision for residence. Maintenance is given so that the lady can live in the manner more or less to which she was accustomed. The concept of maintenance must, therefore, include provision for food and clothing and the like and take into account the basic need of a roof over the head. Provision for residence may be made either by giving a lump sum in money or property in lieu thereof. The judgement will provide much needed succour to many destitute women.

Women as Law-makers

All over the world the percentage of women in Parliament is decreasing, although there may be more women heads of State or more women in senior positions in the Government. Even senior U.N. officials have expressed concern

---

[20]AIR 1985 S.C. 945

[21]*Ibid*

[22]1995 (5) SCALE 199

over the declining percentage of women in positions of power and law making bodies. The latest constitutional amendment which provides for 33 per cent of seats being reserved for women in Panchayats and local bodies supports women in this vital sphere. It is also now a subject matter of challenge before our courts.[23]

This brief survey of the judicial performance in areas which affect women indicates that out of the various arenas of social conflict, many have been scrutinized by the courts of law. The courts have not, by and large, been found wanting. Where they may have erred, they have shown the capacity to correct their perspective. This is in sharp contrast to the performance of the two other limbs of Government. In many areas the courts have given the widest connotation to laws that help women. What is wanting is the social will to bring about gender justice. One only hopes that the lead which is given by the courts of law will be followed by the common people. It is for them to adopt the principle of gender equality in their daily lives and make it a part of the cultural heritage of this country. Judiciary, by the very nature of its functioning, cannot be expected to act as a social reformer or a crusader for law reform. It cannot, for example, intervene to bring about far-reaching legislative changes, nor can it intervene effectively to provide suitable machinery for redress of social wrongs. But administrative inaction or insensitivity has at times compelled the judiciary to give directions for proper administration. In the long run, for a proper functioning of democracy it is necessary that public opinion is activated and plays its due role to ensure that the administration works for the welfare of the people and the legislature pays heed to the felt need for law reforms. In this context, one can say with some confidence that the judiciary has not been found insensitive to people's aspirations. Its functioning today is severely handicapped on account of overload of work, lack of equipment and lack of suitable man or woman power. But in the area of gender justice, it has handed down decisions of far-reaching consequence. No doubt, it has, at times, failed to live upto expectations, especially in dealing with crimes relating to women. But its growing sensitivity to the issue is reflected in the recent judgements of the Supreme Court. The judiciary should ensure that this sensitivity percolates to the lower judiciary. This will also play a role in social regeneration. Suitable judicial training programmes which make the judges more aware of their social responsibilities and make them sensitive to gender issues can be devised. One hopes that the future training programmes for judicial officers will include this kind of training also.

We have a long way to go before we have anything like gender equality in our society. We are still in the grip of customs and traditions which openly or covertly discriminate against women. While cultural values are important, one must remember that culture, whatever be its description or abode, is not static.

[23]A recent move of the Government to introduce a bill in Parliament reserving 33 per cent seats for women in Parliament was thwarted amidst controversy.

It is ever evolving. Old values have to be sifted, discarding those that no longer harmonize with current universally accepted values. Only then can culture remain alive and throbbing, relevant for the men and women of this time. At times in the name of tradition there are attempts to revive discarded old customs such as Sati which compelled the Government to pass the Commission of Sati Prevention Act, 1987. Sometimes there is an attempt to reintroduce or reinforce old and dying customs like that of a Devdasi. In modern times, young women in search of jobs are sent abroad and may face sexual abuse. Women, in need of supporting a family find it difficult to obtain jobs and earn a living. They still do not have any share by birth in joint family property except in a couple of States. Much of women's work is under-paid or unpaid. There is often a bias-conscious or unconscious against women in professions or in executive positions. Above all there is widespread violence against women reflected in incidents of female foeticide, female infacticide and dowry deaths which have brought to us international attention. There is much in our society that needs change. It is a challenge to the entire society and every part of it. Are we ready to mend our ways and reshape our lives in the light of our constitutional values? One hopes that the support which the judiciary has given to the nation in search of egalitarian values will be utilised by social reformers and law givers and by the ordinary men and women of this country to bring about a transformation in our society so that we can have a just and egalitarian society which was the dream of our founding fathers.

5

International Human Rights and Gender Justice

Justice Silvia Cartwright DBE

I begin with the proposition that as human rights issues have real application and relevance for every citizen, they are the responsibility of Parliament and of the domestic courts and authorities. The affirmation and implementation of human rights' principles form the foundation of a just society. Such issues cannot be dismissed as of concern only to the international community and as such, of academic interest only; they are vital to the peace and prosperity of every society. It has become increasingly apparent that the human rights' issues which affect women in particular, play a critical part in the quest to achieve a just and fair society. Women's place in every community is vital to the well-being of that society; without their work, both in the formal sector and in the family, most communities would not survive. It is now well recognised that enhancing women's status and enforcing their rights on an equal basis with men will do much to achieve the objectives of Equality, Development and Peace adopted at the Fourth World Conference on Women held in Beijing in September 1995.

In 1993 the World Conference on Human Rights concluded that:

> "The human rights of women and of the girl-child are an inalienable, integral and indivisible part of universal human rights. The full and equal participation of women in political, civil, economic, social and cultural life at the national, regional and international levels, and the eradication of all forms of discrimination on grounds of sex are priority objectives of the international community.... The world conference on human rights urges governments, institutions, inter-governmental and non-governmental organisations to intensify their efforts for the protection and promotion of human rights of women and the girl-child."[1]

---

[1]World Conference on Human Rights, the Vienna Declaration & Programme of Action, June 1993 para 18, page 33.

During the World Conference on Human Rights two significant issues were stressed: first, the universality of human rights, described as:

> "the common language of all humanity"[2]

and secondly the importance of including and emphasising the particular nature of *women's* human rights.

Successive United Nations conferences and regional meetings have concluded that issues critical to the future well-being of the world's people, such as resource development coupled with protection of the environment, the pursuit of peace and the improvement of such basic human rights as health and education are all heavily dependent on an improvement in the status of women. And this improvement is needed urgently in all nations, not only in the developing nations and those nations which are torn by years of war and civil disruption. It is now well known that although most nations promise equality of opportunity for women, few come close to delivering it. That failure has a huge impact on the ability of half the world's population to contribute fully to the economic, social, cultural, civil and political spheres of the community's activities. In all nations women earn less from paid employment than men; they have less likelihood of inheriting land and other assets than their brothers; they are more likely to be physically assaulted by members of their own families; they are less likely to serve in governments in senior positions and they are likely to be the sole bread winner for something approaching one third of the world's families. And now they are being infected with the HIV/AIDS virus at a faster rate than men simply because they lack the information with which to protect themselves, or the right or ability to refuse intimate relationships whether with their own husbands or with the rapist.

Women who remain disproportionately represented amongst the world's poorest endure greater health problems than men. Lacking the same access to financial resources and education they also have less ability to participate fully in community and political life. Reform of the law can address some of these inequalities. But even more important is the need to reform attitudes, traditions and beliefs which most nations have developed into an ethic which, upon examination, nonetheless has no ethical basis. These barriers to attainment of equality apply as much in a small but comparatively wealthy country like New Zealand as they do in the great nation of India with its enormously diverse population.

Judges and the courts also have an important role to play in the protection of women's rights. Few women however, would think first of the courts as a means of changing the structural factors which are the real barriers to achieving equality with men. In fact, it is in the making of policy, or in the work of government agencies such as the Police that women's human rights will be implemented or frustrated. The courts therefore have a responsibility to respond

---

[2]Boutros Boutros-Ghali, Secretary-General of the United Nations. Opening Statement to the World Conference on Human Rights.

appropriately to issues which will have an impact on women and to be informed about measures which will assist them in this task.

The Convention on the Elimination of All Forms of Discrimination Against Women

Women's human rights have long been a concern of the United Nations. From 1948 when the Universal Declaration of Human Rights was adopted by the General Assembly, the United Nations has acknowledged that the principle of equality for women and men is a basic human right. However, it rapidly became clear that simply because women were part of the human race, their humanity did not guarantee that their rights would be acknowledged and their dignity as equal human beings affirmed and protected.

As we all know, when a State ignores or tramples on the human rights of its own citizens in times of internal or international conflict, both women and men will suffer. But women will often suffer separately and additionally because of their gender. It was with this understanding that the Convention was developed. The process began in 1967 and what was for its time a remarkable instrument was finally adopted by the General Assembly in 1979. The Convention is a comprehensive charter protecting and promoting the human rights of women, a Convention which as at March 1998 had been ratified by 161 states of the 185 United Nations member nations. While many States do not acknowledge the contribution that women make to the economy, to the family and to society, the Convention emphasises that discrimination in any of these areas of human life will hamper economic growth and prosperity and will detrimentally affect society in general. The Convention is unique in that it recognises the role that education of both men and women has in changing attitudes, so that equality of rights and responsibility becomes accepted, and prejudices and practices based on tradition or stereotype are overcome. Another important feature of the Convention is its explicit recognition of the goal of actual as well as legal equality and of the need for temporary special measures to achieve that goal.

In 1993 India ratified the Convention with declarations or reservations. India has yet to present its initial report to the Committee on the Elimination of Discrimination against Women, but when it does the Committee will undertake the detailed task of assessing how well India's legislation and policies comply with the Convention. The Convention provides a code against which India and other ratifying nations can measure their commitment to human rights and particularly to those affecting women. The obligations assumed are wide ranging. In the Convention the definition of discrimination against women is:

> "...Any distinction, exclusion or restriction made on the basis of sex which has the effect or purpose of impairing or nullifying the recognition, enjoyment or exercise by women, irrespective of their marital status, on a basis of equality of men and women, of human rights and fundamental freedoms in the political, economic, social, cultural, civil or any other field."

Consequently India, in common with all other ratifying States must address its attention to eliminating both direct or intentional discrimination and indirect or unintended discrimination. It is in the area of indirect discrimination that the major obstacles to women's equal participation in both public and private life now lie. And indirect discrimination is undoubtedly the most difficult for a State to address. Hence Article 4 of the Convention encourages States to adopt temporary special measures directed at accelerating *de facto* equality between men and women.

Trends of Discrimination Against Women

The Committee on the Elimination of Discrimination Against Women considers large numbers of reports from States Parties each year. Themes of discrimination against women which are common to all countries emerge and form the basis for detailed examination and analysis. Those which may have application to the work of the judiciary include:

- the low numbers of women occupying positions of influence in public and political life.

In this audience it is perhaps unnecessary to rehearse the reasons for encouraging a far greater participation of women in public life. The work of the late and highly respected Justice Bhandare demonstrates immediately that there is much to gain in ensuring that women take their place alongside men in the judiciary. The community also has much to lose if it does not draw on the talents and education of one half of its population. Moreover every institution which serves the public ought to reflect the composition of the community. In that way it can be and appear to be responsive to the needs of all sectors.

- the low level of literacy among women, particularly in developing countries.

Women or men who are illiterate or have a poor education are more likely to have large families because they are less able to access family planning advice easily. This has an impact on the environment, on the health of the population and on a nation's economy. Women who are educated are better able to provide for their children in a world where about 25 per cent of the families are totally supported by women, (although in Asia this percentage is likely to be less than 20 per cent[3]). Women who are educated and literate can also access public information concerning health and justice to name but two. Legal literacy is of critical importance if women are to know their rights and obligations and how to use them. The work done by this Foundation in providing its "intensive and extensive legal literacy campaign" is an invaluable contribution to the goal of ensuring that women have access to justice.

A woman who cannot read may not know that certain crimes perpetrated against her are forbidden by law; nor will she know that she may have the same rights as men to housing and jobs. Nor will she have ready access to nutrition

---

[3]*The World's Women*, UN Publication ISBN 92-1-16 1313-2 at p. 18.

advice or advice on how to avoid the terrible disease of HIV/AIDS. A literate woman is less likely to figure in the very high maternal mortality figures for this part of the world.[4] In a nation such as India where female illiteracy is greater than male illiteracy and where providing access to an education for the whole population is fraught with almost insuperable difficulty, what limited resources there are ought to be applied vigorously to women's education. The examination of reports to CEDAW demonstrate that in nations where women are educated to a reasonable standard, the birth rate decreases, the health of families improves and the environment and the economy benefits. Women's human rights are also asserted and better protected.

- Structural adjustment programmes.

In many parts of the world economic stabilisation and adjustment programmes have either been imposed by institutions such as the World Bank or adopted voluntarily, such as in my own country. As the analysis of trends and statistics provided in the World's Women[5] puts it:

> "Economic crisis and stabilisation and adjustment programmes have brought increased hardships to many people in much of the developing world, especially in the heavily indebted countries, and these have particularly affected women. With the stabilisation and adjustment process relying heavily on cuts in government spending, women have been disproportionately squeezed out of public sector employment. Cuts in such government services as health, childcare, family planning and education have hit women particularly hard setting back women's earlier gains. Women generally depend more on health services than men because of childbearing, because of their responsibility for their family's health and because they outlive men and require more services in older age.
>
> The burden of inflation has fallen heavily on women who are responsible for procuring staple goods for the household. Often stabilisation and adjustment plans have mandated wage freezes, the resources for obtaining goods have dwindled, and women have had to increase their working hours just to ensure their families' survival. In addition, the costs of imported processed goods or time saving technologies have become prohibitive for many people - and again the increased work burden has fallen mainly on women.

---

[4]"Bangladesh, India and Pakistan - according to WHO - account for 28 per cent of the world's births and 46 per cent of its maternal deaths.

[5]*Op. cit* note 3 at 95.

> Rising interest rates, another result of structural adjustment, also have an insidious effect on women. Because women lack collateral and are discriminated against by formal lending institutions, they have much less access to formal credit than men. So, they must rely on informal lending institutions that charge very high interest rates - pushed up even higher by rising formal rates. An increase in part of women's meagre operating surplus then has to be spent on these payments, adding even more to their work burden."

In countries such as New Zealand where the economic adjustment programme has been coupled with a attempt to reduce the population's dependency on the government for solving health and social problems, women's burden of work has increased as institutions to which those with mental disorders have been admitted are closed or reduced in size. Hospitals are centralised to create efficiencies of size resulting in longer distances to travel for health care. Institutions which held the disturbed or disruptive young person have been closed. The women in the family, or in the voluntary sector in the community have been obliged to assume responsibility for the vulnerable who might otherwise suffer or cause disruption in the community.

- Violence against women.

The nations of the world have become so disturbed at the prevalence of violence against women that a number of important steps have been taken to combat it. The Committee of CEDAW places emphasis when examining the reports of States parties, both on ascertaining the level of violence against women, whether it is condoned or perpetrated by the State and on what measures are in place to combat it. The United Nations has pointed a Special Rapporteur on violence against women and itself has developed a Declaration on the Elimination of Violence against Women[6]. In that declaration the General Assembly adopted the affirmation in the preamble that:

> "violence against women both violates and impairs or nullifies the enjoyment by women of human rights and fundamental freedoms, and [is] concerned about the long standing failure to protect and promote those rights and freedom in relation to violence against women."

Violence against women is defined in the Declaration as:

> "Any act of gender based violence that results in, or is likely to result in, physical, sexual or psychological harm to women, including threats of such acts, coercion or arbitrary deprivation of liberty, whether occurring in public or in private life."

[6]G.A. Res. 48/104 (1994), 1 IHRR329.

Under article 2:

> "Violence against women shall be understood to encompass, but not be limited to, the following:
>
> (a) physical, sexual and psychological violence occurring in the family, including battering, sexual abuse of female children in the household, dowry related violence, marital rape, female genital mutilation and other traditional practices harmful to women, non-spousal violence and violence related to exploitation;
>
> (b) physical, sexual and psychological violence occurring within the general community, including rape, sexual abuse, sexual harassment and intimidation at work, in educational institutions and elsewhere, trafficking in women and forced prostitution;
>
> (c) physical, sexual and psychological violence perpetrated or condoned by the State, wherever it occurs."

It is now widely acknowledged that violence against women prevents them from participating fully in the family, in the work place and in their community. As with those who have a low level of literacy, those whose health is poor, those who earn an inadequate income, this reduced ability to participate in community life is a vast waste of the talents and education of one half of the world's population. The inference to be drawn is that where women are not treated equally not only they and their families suffer, but the community itself loses access to an extremely valuable human resource.

But as contemplated by the definition of discrimination in the Convention equality of treatment does not always denote equality of outcome. Consequently, it is necessary both to address *de jure* the obstacles to women's equality and also to overcome the *de facto* obstacles to achieving that end. It is in this area that the Committee has noted the historic and serious impact of tradition, cultural practices and religion on women's position in society. A contemporary example is the imposition of strict Islamic law on the women of Kabul by the Taleban. Many commentators suggest that the law being imposed is not a true interpretation of the teachings of the Koran. Nonetheless, it is imposed by those who wield authority and the outcome is that women in Afghanistan who must earn a living to support their families will be prevented from doing so. The irony is that many of the women are obliged to earn an income to provide for their families because the long wars in Afghanistan have resulted in the loss of their husbands, fathers or brothers. The impact on society will be immense and will resound for generations. If such strict imposition of one interpretation of Islamic law is accepted there will be much suffering amongst the women and children of Kabul. Many will suffer as access to food and health care reduces, and hidden in their homes women will be unprotected from family violence. The next generation will be poorly educated and unable to contribute fully to their society.

There are many serious examples in other States of the adverse impact of tradition, culture and religion on the lives of women: son preference which condones the aborting of female foetus or the killing of newborn baby girls; the enslavement of young girls as reparation for the crimes or debts of their relations; female genital mutilation affecting the health of millions of women, and strict dress codes which impede women's daily lives. All such traditions, whether based on ancient cultural or religious practices require close re-examination to determine whether they have any validity in a modern society, or whether they are retained because they provide an efficient means of denying women the power to have healthy, fulfilling lives.

The Influence of the Convention on the Work of the Courts

As an international treaty, the Convention has the potential to influence Indian law in several ways. In New Zealand the Law Commission has summarised five major ways in which Courts may take a treaty into account.[7] I suggest that these would equally be relevant to Indian law. They are:

- as a foundation of the Constitution
- as relevant to the determination of the common law
- as a declaratory statement of customary international law which is itself part of the law of the land
- as evidence of public policy and
- as relevant to the interpretation of a Statute.

Perhaps the most likely use of the Convention will be in arguments concerning the interpretation of statute. There is some precedent for this in New Zealand. In *Van Gorkom v Attorney-General*[8] Cooke J employed the (then) Declaration on the Elimination of Discrimination against Women, citing *8 Halsbury's Laws of England*[9], which states that the social rights contained in the United Nations Declaration of Human Rights and the European Convention on Human Rights:

> "[M]ay be regarded ... as representing a legislative policy which might influence the courts in the interpretation of statute law."

It is, of course, well established that an international treaty can influence statutory interpretation. The position was outlined by Lord Diplock in *Salomon v Commissioners of Customs and Excise*[10] :

---

[7]NZLC, *A New Zealand Guide to International Law and its Sources* (Report No 34 1996).

[8][1977] 1 NZLR 535 (SC).

[9](4th ed) para 844.

[10][1996] 3 All ER 871, 875.

> "If the terms of the legislation are not clear [and] are reasonably capable of more than one meaning, the treaty itself becomes relevant, for there is a *prima facie* presumption that Parliament does not intend to act in breach of international law, including therein specific treaty obligations; and if one of the meanings which can reasonably be ascribed to the legislation is consonant with the treaty obligations and another or others are not, the meaning which is consonant is to be preferred."

Similarly, Lord Bridge stated in *Brind v Secretary of State for the Home Department*[11]:

> "[I]t is already well settled that, in construing any provision in domestic legislation which is ambiguous in the sense that it is capable of a meaning which either conforms to or conflicts with the convention, the courts will presume that Parliament intended to legislate in conformity with the convention, not in conflict with it."

The Courts may also be persuaded that in an appropriate case, the common law should be developed consistently with the Convention. In a number of cases in New Zealand the Courts have accepted that the New Zealand Bill of Rights Act is relevant to the development of the common law.[12] There is some support in England for the use of international treaties in this manner; in *Attorney General v Guardian Newspapers Ltd (No 2)*[13] (concerning the *"Spycatcher"* book) the House of Lords was asked to apply the common law/equitable doctrine of breach of confidence consistently with the European Convention on Human Rights. Lord Goff of Chieveley said at pp. 283-284:

> "I conceive it to be my duty, when I am free to do so, to interpret the law in accordance with the obligations of the Crown under [the European Convention on Human Rights]".

The Commonwealth has taken a lead in considering the application of international human rights principles into the domestic jurisprudence. At six

---

[11][1991] 1 All ER 720, 722-723.

[12]Section 3 of the Bill of Rights provides that "This Bill of Rights applies only to acts done - (a) ... by the judicial [branch] of the government of New Zealand ...." See *R v Hufflett* (Unreported CA 453/93 17 December 1993) where the Court said at p. 7 "[T]he Bill of Rights applies to acts done by the judicial branch of the government of New Zealand. There is considerable force in the view that the Courts should accordingly recognise the Bill of Rights protections as and where appropriate in evolving the common law." It was accepted in *Solicitor General v Radio New Zealand* [1994] 1 NZLR 48, 58 that "the New Zealand Bill of Rights Act 1990 applies to ... acts done by the judicial branch of the Government under 3(a)." This was further accepted by Blanchard J in *Duff v Communicado* Unreported HC Auckland CL 20/95 18 December 1995.

[13][1990] 1 AC 109.

separate Commonwealth Judicial Colloquia senior members of the judiciary have affirmed the Bangalore principles[14] reflecting the universality of human rights inherent in men and women and the vital duty of an independent judiciary to interpret and apply national constitutions and laws in the light of those principles. While the general principles were said to apply in all countries, "the means by which they become applicable may differ." From that initial and general approach to the issue of human rights, further colloquia were convened in 1994 at Victoria Falls at Zimbabwe, in April 1996 at Hong Kong and in 1997 at Guyana, all examining the domestic application of international and regional human rights norms as they relate specifically to women. Each declaration emphasised the responsibilities placed on judicial officers. The Victoria Falls Declaration included:

> "Judges and lawyers have duty to familiarise themselves with the growing international jurisprudence of human rights and particularly with the expanding material on the protection and promotion of the human rights of women."

In the Hong Kong Declaration:

> "The participants noted that many opportunities exist for Judges and other judicial officers to draw on the Convention of the Elimination of all Forms of Discrimination against Women and other international human rights instruments so as to interpret and apply creatively constitutional provisions, legislation, the common law and customary law. In so doing, they drew attention to the wealth of decisions from countries which shared jurisprudential traditions where Judges had engaged in such creative interpretation and application. The importance of educating the judiciary and the legal profession with respect to international human rights standards and principles relevant to gender issues was stressed, as well as the need for national judiciaries to carry out studies on gender bias in the judicial process. ... Participants identified a number of areas where there are clear violations of the human rights of women which might be addressed by the utilisation of international norms in domestic decision making. These included, in particular, discrimination in matters of nationality, citizenship, poverty and inheritance, which has serious implications for the exercise and enjoyment by women of either the fundamental human rights. Participants also encouraged the review of legislation to ensure its consistency

[14] Developing Human Rights Jurisprudence, vol 3: "The Domestic Application of International Human Rights Norms" Judicial Colloqium in Bangalore 1988.

> with international human rights obligations undertaken by individual countries."

In the first Justice Sunanda Bhandare Memorial Lecture the Honourable Justice Sujata V. Manohar of the Supreme Court of India, referred to a number of leading cases where the Courts of India have upheld women's human rights.[15] These and like cases demonstrate as Justice Manohar stressed that the Courts will when possible apply human rights standards to the application of statute or common law. In India, as in my country there is a growing recognition of the need to interpret sometimes ancient laws and traditions in the light of evolving social attitudes towards women. In New Zealand women's groups have begun to assist litigants in the process.

In a recent judgement delivered by the New Zealand Court of Appeal[16] the Auckland Women Lawyers' Association applied and was granted leave to appear as *amicus curiae* on the grounds that the case raised issues of considerable public importance. The issue for the Court's determination was whether Ms Ruka lived in a relationship in the nature of a marriage. If she did then she was not entitled to the welfare payments she had received and the convictions for fraud under the provisions of the Social Security Act and the Crimes Act must stand. The Court found that the evidence had established that Ms Ruka:

> "Suffered acute and sustained physical, sexual and emotional violence and abuse at the hands of [her partner] to the point where it properly can be said that she suffered battered woman syndrome. She exhibited the condition of "learned helplessness" and, hence, remained in a violence relationship. The evidence discloses that she was helpless to help herself."

She had been repeatedly raped and beaten and her partner refused to contribute financially to the support of their son or the household generally. The Court held that the phrase "relationship in the nature of a marriage" could not apply to one where there was no mutual commitment and where the facts established that there was no financial responsibility and interdependence. A relationship characterised by such serious violence did not disclose the commitment required.

The Court referred also to the Domestic Violence Act 1995 which came into force on 1 July 1996 which:

> "reflects the legislature's concern about the plight of women who are the victims of domestic violence in domestic relationships by recognising that domestic violence, in all its

[15] *Air India v Nargesh Meerza & Ors* (1981) AIR SC 1829, [1982] 1 SCR 440, *Tuka Ram v Maharashtra,* 1979 AIR SC 185, [1979] 1 SCR 810.

[16] *Ruka v Department of Social Welfare* [1997] 1NZLR 154 (CA).

> forms, is unacceptable behaviour, and to ensure that, where it does occur, there is effective legal protection for its victims.
>
> Initiatives of this kind reflect the extensive work being undertaken at an international level to ensure that violence towards women is recognised as a major barrier to women achieving fundamental human rights and freedoms. [Counsel] elaborated this work at some length and referred the Court to a number of declarations and recommendations which have emanated from various international bodies, including CEDAW (the Committee for the Elimination of Discrimination Against Women). While the importance of this work is recognised, it is not necessary to traverse the reports in this judgement. It is sufficient to acknowledge that they emphasise the disastrous effect of violence against women and the extensive impact which it has on the basic rights of women."

In India, in her book *Kali's Yug*[17] the action brought by Women's Action Research and Legal Action for Women Trust with Dr Meera Mitra and Pramila Dandavate is described. Among other remedies, it sought India's compliance with the principles of CEDAW. It sought:

> "...to highlight and expose the structures of patriarchy and its relationship to gender and justice and subordination of women. Despite the enactment of an egalitarian Constitution which contains comprehensive provisions for empowering women, they have not achieved full equality nor has there been an end to discrimination in the laws. Beneficial legislation pertaining to women has been in the public arena. In the private domain of the family there has been no appreciable change in view of the continuing regime of personal laws. While there is *de jure* equality, women have still to achieve *de facto* equality ..."

Where such proceedings are initiated the judiciary must take a leading role in familiarising itself with and applying universally recognised human rights principles affecting women in their courts. As a sitting Judge, I appreciate only too well how difficult this can be. First, it is necessary to have some understanding of the feminist theory upon which these human rights' norms are based. Then it is necessary, often in the absence of submissions from counsel, to encourage a more broadly-based approach to the resolution of civil disputes and the determination of criminal matters. In a busy court these are added burdens. I would like to suggest that a first step is to become familiar with the Convention on the Elimination of All Forms of Discrimination against Women and apply it where there is a gap in the statute or common law, in the knowledge

[17] at 109, Editor, Rani Jethmalani.

that an international convention that has been ratified by India has real application. Reference to it in judgements will stimulate counsel into a broader human rights-based approach in their submissions.

It must be recognised however that in most countries the majority of Judges have little understanding of the way in which gender bias has become entrenched, not only in the institution itself but more generally in the administration of justice, including the police and the development of public policy. If Judges are to discharge their Judicial Oaths, which in most countries include an undertaking to be fair to all people regardless of race or gender, then as a basic issue of justice we must strive to apply the law more even handedly than it has been thus far. In my own country research has been conducted into judicial attitudes to gender. This research formed the basis for an education programme for all Judges on the impact of gender on judging.

Among the findings the following few are of interest.

- The large majority of Judges believe that it is important that the composition of the judiciary should reflect the community it serves. It must therefore be inferred that the proportions of female to male Judges in New Zealand (at present one to eight) must increase to equality. Not all Judges are enthusiastic about this prospect and women Judges have expressed a concern that increasing numbers might be seen by their male colleagues as a threat. In short, while the number of women in the judiciary remains low, male Judges will advocate increasing their participation. If this is done however, the male Judges may feel their dominant position is threatened.
- 57 per cent of male Judges surveyed considered that there was little or no gender bias against women in New Zealand courts. By comparison, 85 per cent of women Judges felt that gender bias against women is widespread.
- Women Judges observed much more gender bias in the courts than had their male colleagues. Women Judges were twice as likely as men to believe that women as lawyers, witnesses, defendants, court staff or as parties to proceedings might be disadvantaged by their gender.
- Judges were divided on whether they approached the sentencing of men and women differently. A higher proportion of women Judges said that they took women's responsibilities to their children into account as a key factor.

The education programme which was been led by our Chief Justice, Sir Thomas Eichelbaum, thereby demonstrating his commitment to the project held the first, highly successful symposium in 1997. Many Judges commented that the knowledge gained of the reality of women's lives was invaluable to the discharge of their judicial responsibilities.

Conclusion

Ensuring full compliance with the human right's of women has relevance and importance not just to women's status in society, but also to the general health and well-being of the whole community. Without women's full and equal contribution, society will be the poorer and millions of women will continue to suffer personally. It is an issue not only of human rights but of justice and humanity.

The judiciary and members of the legal profession have a role to play in ensuring that women are treated with dignity, that they have equal access to justice and that the outcome for them is one of true equality. This of necessity requires leadership from the judiciary. We must show the way in identifying and refusing to condone violations of human rights and inequality of treatment. If Judges are not aware of the gendered nature of many of our institutions then it is less likely that the legal profession will actively promote measures which will assist women in their objectives of obtaining justice and equality with men. There are many issues in which an approach which recognises women's disadvantaged position can be actively pursued.

So I end with a reaffirmation that human rights issues affecting women are part of the responsibility of the domestic courts, parliament and the authorities. They are also the responsibility for all Judges who have undertaken on appointment to the Bench to do justice without fear or favour, affection or ill will.

Finally may I thank you again for the great honour that you have done me in inviting me to present this lecture dedicated to the memory of Justice Sunanda Bhandare, a woman who lived by the sorts of ideals that I have discussed today. She was a woman who palpably made a difference, not only as a member of the judiciary but to the community in which she lived. I have gained much from studying the information about the work that she has undertaken and I am grateful to you for providing me with this opportunity to learn from her example and to meet with some of her family and colleagues. For her family this occasion may be tinged with sadness. But may I suggest that her example has opened doors for many women and will continue to do so. I will end on an optimistic note exemplified by this well loved Maori blessing:

> *Kia hora, te marino, kia whakapapa pounamu te moana Kia tere, te karo hirohi*

Which translated is:

> *May the calm be widespread, may the sea glisten like the greenstone, may the shimmer of summer dance forever across your pathway.*

6

Gender Justice - Dimensions and Frustrations and the March to the Future

Justice V.R. Krishna Iyer

I stand before you not to deliver an erudite address in scholarly fashion but in a poignant mood to make a lecture in memoriam, with focus on the values sister Sunanda cherished while alive and still loves to promote from afar, even in her incorporeal existence. I knew her closely and shared her passion for gender justice. And now falls the distressing duty on me, at the behest of Murli Bhandare, her life-long loving partner and leading light in the legal profession, to commemorate and hold you here for an hour. To reflect on that gracious lady briefly and expand on the critical issues of our times close to her heart is a personal obligation and a patriotic commitment to womanhood.

Woman's status, empowerment, actual egalite and opportunity for unfoldment of personality have so long dithered, so often been deceived and so treacherously thwarted at the critical point of implementation. Far too long has the truth of this lie been hidden that now comes the hour to call the masculine bluff and battle for feminine success. Sunanda's militant spirit summons me to crusade for the cause and stop not till the goal is reached. But women's dynamic advance is humanity's liberationist challenge, and so I am an integral part of it. It is a categorical imperative which the dialectic of contemporary social forces establishes that no progress for any nation can be stable, sensible or equitable, unless the egalitarian solidarity of sisters and brothers, daughters and sons, husbands and wives, women and men becomes a living reality. Sunanda symbolised this paramount rule of life, fought for its actualisation as an advocate and lent from the Bench adjudicatory support by her presence, persuasion and benign pronouncements.

The watershed of human rights jurisprudence is marked by the epic event of the Indian Constitution coming into force on 26th January, 1950. But the struggle to give meaning to the jurisprudence of justice to women, from foetus to ashes, is still a continuing process resisted at every turn by masculine strategists giving specious reasons and scriptural citations. We must demonetise this die hard blockage by gender-just humanism. I appreciate the vision and mission of women of every stratum in their demand for rightful empowerment, *not* condescending grace, for the birthright to shape their destiny without inhibitions and vulgar, violent and other intimidatory tactics, not charity to a weaker sex treated as a decorated doll at home or an unpaid factotum.

There is a universal principle, a spiritual dimension and a developmental potential implicit in this daring demand for power, remaining unfulfilled *vis a vis* half of Indian humanity even as semi-centennial celebrations are beating deafening drums, concealing the felonious failure to render unto women what is her due.

The current relevance of gender mainstreaming is an obvious global desideratum and so it is that recently 'The Economic and Social Council' on 18th July 1997 recommended that the U.N. General Assembly draw the attention of the United Nations system to the need to mainstream a gender perspective in all areas of work related to, among other things, macro-economic questions, operational activities for development, human rights and peace and security. It recommended that inter-governmental bodies with similar responsibilities in the system should monitor the way in which agencies, funds and programmes implemented mainstreaming in their medium-term plans and programme budgets, including at the field level.

The call came in a set of agreed conclusions adopted following extensive debate on the issue earlier in the session. The conclusions were the first text approved at the current substantive session in Geneva.*

The UNICEF, in its 1997 Progress Report, states that in 15 countries, including India, young children are taken into custody for criminal action by the Police while the little ones have no easy access to justice and legal protection. Juvenile justice, notwithstanding the Juvenile Justice Act, enjoys a long cruel holiday. The high numbers of children held in detention is a global malady. In India the police can apprehend young people if they are likely to be abused or exploited for immoral or illegal purposes or wrongful gains. In short, any child, particularly a girl child, who is poor or orphan is liable to be victimised by the criminal system sometimes in the name of altruism.

Violence against women and girls is on the increase and more than 60 million women who should be alive today are missing because of violence associated with gender discrimination. Millions of women and girls in every country on every continent, and of every class, live under the daily threat of physical abuse.

We live in a diseased world suffering from the misogynist syndrome. True, the U.N. compilation of instruments highlights the right to life, liberty and security of person without distinction of race, colour, sex, religion, national or social origin, birth or other status. But in reality, blue blood and white skin, superior sex and North citizenship are more equal, more blessed, more free to grab because more power belongs to them in the Animal Farm we call the common world.

---

*UN Newsletter - Volume 52 - November 30 dt. 26 July 1997.

In consolatory diction and for popular consumption the General Assembly, thirty years ago, proclaimed the Declaration on the Elimination of Discrimination against Women which, in crimson diction and rhetoric without action, is pleasing to the eye and ear but sans the sword of implementation remains "words, words, words" (if I may borrow from Hamlet). The world's largest assemblage demanding an era of gender unbound and womanhood's empowerment took place in Beijing a few years back and a Platform of Action was announced in stentorian pitch but, judged by the sequelae, these great events and conventions prove to be 'sound and fury' signifying little.

May I, with your leave, turn back, with a nostalgic touch, to the days when Sunanda was at the bar arguing cases with ability and giving a lead to women lawyers as a paradigm of advocacy. (There were a few outstanding women lawyers who did not get just deal). Fighting her way forward and carrying her sisters in the profession to establish an All India Women Lawyers' Organisation, Sunanda Bhandare with other senior colleagues, was an obvious choice for elevation to the Bench. To adorn the Judge's robe is power and prestige indeed. But a bright young lawyer's life has its own charm. The Indian Constitution exalted the office of Judge with abundance of authority but the career at the bar fighting for justice with youthful vigour is happier. In retrospect, when I, a gerontic octogenarian, wistfully cast my eyes to the baby days at the bar, the grey span on the bench, and the aging yet battling decade and more thereafter, Wordsworth comes to mind: 'Bliss was it on that dawn to be alive, but to be young was very heaven!'. Sunanda, smiling and pressing her point undeterred by the hostile judge and winning in the end, must have made her rejoice more in those burgeoning years of professional success than while sitting thro' sour hours and suffering the aggressive and unending 'submissions' in meritless cases not daring to interrupt provokable Counsel. She was too gentle a Judge to be annoyed by audacious advocates, too understanding and sharp, when on the bench, to tolerate repetitions or terrorising lawyering and too discriminating, with her robes on, to be bluffed, bamboozled or browbeaten by pettifogging baloney. Justice Sunanda Bhandare was middle-aged and had golden prospects of spiraling up to highest positions. But the tryst of each soul with its destiny is beyond us to alter. "The moving finger writes; and, having writ, Moves on: nor all thy piety nor Wit shall lure it back to cancel half a Line, Nor all the tears wash out a word of it."

Sunanda Bhandare is no more with us in corporeal form but that is not the end of existence. Robert Ingersoll once observed: "Every cradle asks us whence and every coffin whither". In this subtle dimension of survival after death, waves of thought from the other side may still affect us. May be, that is the reason why I speak today to you on a subject dear to her bosom, namely, Gender Justice and Empowerment of Women.

To treat woman as a subordinated species in unequal gender is a perennial masquilinold malady which 'survives even after statutory death'. The Constitution has abolished it; International Covenants and Declarations have made short shrift of it. Laws have outlawed it. Now it is for humanist activists to bury gender discrimination from the womb to the tomb. How? By empowerment of women and militantisation of youth consciousness into demanding for the sister sector of humanity the fundamental freedom to manifest her faculties and develop her personhood without discrimination. This equalitarian undertaking is a shared concern where a universal human tryst must jointly be redeemed by man as much as by woman. It is not a 'petticoat' struggle but a human liberalisation bugle, since the regeneration of all humanity depends also on man, son of woman, and both sexes must make common cause in this campaign. We have to live down ancient prejudices, masculine arrogance, usurpations of power from the sister sector and accept a New World Human Order where both belong to one World of Equal Dignity. Sita and Panchali are symbolic of the victimisation of women and every community has inflicted injuries on the girl, be its religion what it may. The laws themselves are lawless where women versus men are involved. Look at the Indian Divorce Act passed by the British Parliament to govern Indian Christians. There is obvious discrimination against women and public campaigns to amend or repeal the law have not activised the panchydermic legislatures, even though the courts have frowned upon this violation of equality. The *Cochin Christian Succession Act,* like its *Travancore countepart*, remained on the statute book grossly violating women's equality. When I, as a humble Minister of the Kerala State, moved a bill (1957) to repeal these egregious statutes, a massive ballyhoo was raised by the masculine Christian population, and I had to allow the bill to lapse. A Dowry Prohibition Bill, with teeth, was introduced by me in the Kerala Legislature in 1957. There was noisy opposition and the *men* won the battle since I had to withdraw this pro-gender bill. Long years later, the Supreme Court, in *Mary Roy's Case,*[1] ruled that the Cochin and Travancore Christian Succession Acts had ceased to exist on the Reorganisation of States, thereby automatically making the Indian Succession Act applicable to all Kerala Christians bestowing equal inheritance rights. A Christian Kerala Law Minister tried to bring a bill to undo the effect of the Supreme Court decision. Hindu women, even after Nehru's governance, did not get right by birth in the Hindu co-parcenary and when the Andhra Pradesh Ministry of N.T.R. gave them rights under the law Congress leaders criticised it. Instances are galore a la right to adoption where the bias against women is glaring. No political party or trade union has given fair representation to women activists in the higher echelons of Party or Trade Union or Assembly or Parliament. Man Power dies hard, even the Left parties being indolent in abolishing inequality. The major measure of gender justice is partly manifest in the Panchayathiraj laws but when it came to reservations of $33.^1/_3$ per cent in legislatures, verbal consensus melts away when the hour of actualisation through a bill arrives. The *Dowry Prohibition Legislation* is an exercise in futility even as the anti-rape provisions are writ in water, gang-rape being,

[1]*Mary Roy v/s State of Kerala*, AIR 1986 S.C. 1011; 1986(2) SCC 209

common and police inaction frequent. To multiply this tragic tale is the unnecessary suppression of tribals, illiteracy of damsels and exploitation of the girl child by sale and other forms of female commoditisation.

The Report of the Commission of Enquiry for Women in Pakistan (1997) tells us with candour the unjust social attitude towards women. The recommendations of the Commission indicate that our two countries have much in common when dealing with the pathological disposition towards the fundamental rights of women. Of course, there is a National Commission for Women in both countries. The Indian Commission thunders but because of the inadequacy or ineffective provisions for implementation, its anguish, anger and assertions fail to eliminate anti-women attitudes. Even the Courts, as the Mathura Case[2] shows, and a recent Sathi Case (Rajasthan) indicates, reveal the subconscious adjudicatory allergy. The Muthamma,[3] and Air Hostesses case[4] are exceptions which prove the rule. Judicial guilt, when women's causes claim forensic justice, is a delicate subject where the lie of neutrality, cannot be exposed without risk of punitive contempt. The Indian Judiciary wields great power and prestige but women's presence on the Bench is less than negligible. It is inevitable that the constitutional fundamental of equal power is absent in the courts. We have robed brethren aplenty, but their Lordships being omnipresent, ladies with robes show up on the Bench but once in a blue moon. The sensitivity of the appointing authorities in regard to women as judges leaves much to suspect. Even in the Executive, as officers with power, women are the rarest of the rare. If empowerment is not to be illusory, there must be a reasonable percentage of women in key positions, administrative, police and other.

Women in custody are terribly vulnerable. Lock-ups and jails are horrors of captivity. A high level committee for custodial justice to women reported concrete measures for women's safety and gender shelter but no Central Government nor State Government, Left, Right or Centre, or a brew of all, has bothered to issue a policy statement on women in custody or implemented the recommendations of the Committee (of which I was the Chairman). The blood, sweat, toil and tears of girls in bondage, of women in work houses, of patients in mental hospitals and of old women without means are a matter of no concern to governments, professions and charitable institutions. Thus we need a revolutionary change in conditions of life and a rule of law, sensitised by the rule of life - of women and children with access to social justice.

The girl child is the Cinderella of India. The Convention of the Rights of the Child (Art. 37, 39 and 40) addresses juvenile justice. We have a Juvenile Justice Act which decorates the Statute book but does little yet to improve the lot of the victims. There is a global touch about this neglect, as is obvious from the UNICEF's 1997 Report.

---

[2] *Tukaram V. State of Maharashtra,* AIR 1979 S.C. 185

[3] *C.B. Muthamma V. Union of India* AIR 1979 S.C. 1868

[4] *Air India International V. Nerges Mirza* AIR 1981, S.C. 1829

"Highlighting the effects of denying justice to children and women, this year's Progress of nations report takes stock of topics like water and sanitation, nutrition, particularly infringement of the marketing code for infant formula; health with a focus of HIV/AIDS, education, violence against women and girls, juvenile justice and progress and disparities in growth of cities of the industrialised world."

The Report underscores the plight of dowry victims in India, where over 5000 women are killed each year in dowry related violence. It draws attention to son preference and the prevalence of genetic testing for sex selection which it states has become a booming business in countries like India. According to UNICEF Executive Director, Carol Bellamy, "this chronic condition of violence amounts to the most pervasive human rights violation in the world today. She says, in today's world, to be born female is to be born high risk. Every girl grows up under the threat of violence. The shadows of violence under which girls and women live debilitates them physically, psychologically and socially. It affects the healthy social and economic development of all societies".[5]

The right to life includes the right to livelihood and to dignity. Human dignity can be gained only if education is imparted. Thus free and compulsory education is a component of the fundamental right to life. While Kerala has a high percentage of child education, India has the largest number of children illiteracy. Women's education is the worst casualty, gender violence a grim commonality. Of course, over 140 million of the world's children are out of school. Quality education is a rare commodity, even in Kerala.

Social health is of prime importance, but notwithstanding the constitution, minimum human needs to mother and child are a mirage. Not even drinking water nor sanitation, nor even access to excreta disposal is available to three billion people on earth. In India, to add insult to injury, scavenging women, carrying night soil is a shamefully prevalent practice in some states. The measure of our progress is not fast foods and foreign cars, but the abolition of the pathetic lot of lowly women going to sleep hungry with crying children clinging to them. Breast milk is the best food for the baby but in the name of progress manufacturers of infant formulae still market unwholesome substitutes unethically around the world. The Indian elite consume these substitutes fashionably.

On festive occasions, fine sentiments in romantic phrases are freely expressed, knowing that words are powerless when 'political will flags or lags. For instance, our President in a message to 'RASHTRA MAHILA' on the 50th Anniversary of Independence wrote:

> "After Independence, Indian women have made a mark for themselves in diverse areas of national endeavour. Whether it is in politics, administration, art and culture or social service, their achievements are many and varied. There is today, wide-spread awareness and a deep consciousness in our society that

[5]U.N. Newsletter - Volume 52 - Number 30 - dated 26-7-1997.

> the empowerment of women is vital for the economic and social advancement of our people."[6]

Our Prime Minister oozed optimism in his message when he wrote:

> "We soon hope to adopt the national policy for the empowerment of women to provide an overarching framework for our efforts to bring about gender equality, and eliminate all manifestations of bias against the female sex. We must also rid our country of crime against women so that together with them we can march towards the 21st century."

The distance between assertions and actualisations lengthens and so the vigorous dedication and objective of our *Mahila* masses will be a teasing illusion and promise of unreality until womanhood seizes power from Panchayat to Prime Ministership and Presidentship. Why? The answer is given by Gouri Sen in her poignant article in the 'RASHTRA MAHILA'.

> Denial to a girl child of her right to live is one of the most heinous violations of the right to life committed by society. Gender bias and deep rooted prejudice and discrimination against girl children and preference for male children have led to female foeticide and female infanticide. To eliminate a new born or yet to be born life, just because it happens to be a girl, is the worst kind of gender bias practised by parents and society. As a result sex determination centres and abortion centres are flourishing and expanding in spite of a Government ban. The point to note is that the people demanding foeticide include not only the poorer sections who have socio-economic compulsions but members of the upper and middle classes as well. According to one estimate, between 1981 and 1991 more than four million girl children joined the ranks of India's "missing women" and an estimated 1.2 million lives were snuffed out either through "abortion or postnatal murder".
>
> Even if a girl child is allowed to be born, discrimination and gender bias are evident from day one. She is denied the adequate nourishment and health care given to male siblings. In India, females receive only 88 per cent of the required nutrition intake compared to boys. Therefore, the percentage of undernourished girls and female mortality is much higher than that of boys."[7]

It is shock and shame that the Indian universe of working children strikes horror. Let me give you a mere glimpse of the gory system. Approximately four lakhs of people in Karnataka earn their living through seri culture. A quarter of

---

[6]Rashtra Mahila - August 1997 Special Issue.

[7]*Ibid* page 5.

these workers are estimated to be children, each one of them a bonded labourer stunted for life and robbed of the joy of childhood. Rehabilitation and free education are the statutory recipes on paper. But in this pragmatic world, children are only infants toiling for long hours in tears with none to sympathise or salvage these innocent siblings. Child workers at bangle factories are a sad spectacle. So also the Sivakasi Match Box workers. If they don't go to work under parental pressure they end up in petty crime and smuggling, landing in the hands of the police or sex mafia. Carpet weaving industry uses a very high percentage of child labour. Attempts to bring sunshine in their lives remain symbolic. Sexual abuse of young boys and girls is a routine phenomenon in the streets of Bombay. The remedy for the malady is not in sight. Legislations are impotent. Enforcement of child welfare statutes is unfortunately ineffective.

Rural women do hard labour and backbreaking arduous tasks. They share the same risks and dangers of death and disability as men but are paid much less. Give them a chance to be literate, empower them to share their destiny, we will double our human resources, instead of women being tortured at home, molested through day and nights, becoming the victim sector of society.

What then is the remedy? People's participation in Operation Emancipation, Frustrations and victimisations can be halted only by empowerment social, economic and political. A hundred schemes for women's economic uplift through small scale industries and otherwise can save their dignity and security. This is no dreamy thought but a programme which tomorrow can be put into effect. I can suggest specific projects at once feasible and resource-available. Social equality needs mental, moral radicalism and substantial presence of women in every walk of life. The Constitution, in its equalitarian thrust, must be applied in public and private life in novel ways creatively crafted - a task which can now be rendered easily through Panchayati Raj.

Indian womanhood, to find salvation, in Gandhi's country has to resist many abuses, insist on many legislations and persist in attacking that most colonialist syndrome veneered as the New Economic Policy, Gandhicidal and Nehrucidal in impact and worst of all 'genocidal'. It may seem surprising that when multinational corporations play the *de facto* controllerate of the Indian economy and when Indian industry and agriculture reel under GATTA strophe, the Nation's moghuls should disguise it as an irreversible 'progressive' policy. Permit Raj is bad but has not yet gone. Red-tapism and political corruption are bad but have not vanished. Unemployment is sad but has intensified. Women's lot is lost and destitution is driving them to prostitution. So Bharat must, for resurrection of its heritage and economy, necessarily rekindle its lost vision of Hind Swaraj and for the salvage of that marginalised gender which suffers the most.

There were, of course, also the apparent beneficiaries of NEP, girls who were "lucky" enough to be recruited into sweat shops of export garment industries or electronic goods, sports goods, or toys at a pittance of a wage on a piece rate until, within a very short time, their eyesight falters, their spines cave in, their "nimble fingers" become stiff or their jobs vanish due to bottlenecks in market demand they end up spending their scant savings on a dowry to "settle down" in life to an uncertain future. If less lucky, they may find themselves eking out a living in prostitution, having been "socialised" into it by the sexual harassment of their contractors on the job. In places like Goa large numbers of women have been recruited into the tourism industry which is often a concealed label for sex workers. The Goan women's organization *Bailancho Saad* in a newsletter of 1990 reported that they had been refused loans by Industrial Development Bank of India (IDBI) for employment generation programme for women in distress, as there was enough work available for bar maids and entertainers.[8]

Another instance, among many, is touched upon by Dietrich, the proposition being:

> "At present, hundreds of pavement dwellers and vendors of Chennai are fighting a desperate struggle for their survival after having been evicted from Parry's corner after over forty years of tenancy, nearly the entire period since Independence. There is no place for such people in the schemes for relocation of markets in the city planning under World Bank guidance. Chennai is also under the impact of an Agreement of Understanding with the Japanese government offering to clean the waterways like Coum and Buckingham Canal in the name of ecology. The idea is to build five-star hotels along the waterways and at present the slum dwellers along the canal banks are experiencing an inexplicable chain of "accidental" fires which help to clear them out of the locality to pave the path towards development. There again it is the women who are in the forefront of the struggle as they also have to protect their livelihood as construction workers, vendors, domestic workers and recyclers of waste materials".[9]

There are feminist alternatives through struggle for social transformation as the women of Andhra Pradesh proved in the fight against alcoholism. A common struggle is gradually gestating in the belly of the profiteering global capitalism and the Beijing Conference demonstrates the universal urge of women NGOs to challenge the deplorable status quo. If women are not to be dispensable commodities, a national network with militant nexus is a necessary condition. Indeed, even developmental concepts must receive a Gandhian flavour of 'Small is Beautiful', so that girls can find dignified self-employment and flee male subjugation. In the new policy of macro-industrial - technological development and huge dams and projects, feminine presence will suffer displacement - a process which started in the 80's and 90's and is now a full-blown syndrome. The weakening of the State, under expansion of corporate

---

[8]Dr. Gabriele Dietrich at Fourth M.A. Thomas memorial Lecture in August '97 at Bangalore pp. 7-8.

[9]*Ibid* p. 10.

interests, has led to a situation where accountability is difficult to enforce. Corporations, foreign and native are buying over the civil society. This leads to unprecedented new forms of inequality and social chaos. What are the remedial measures feasible in such Indian conditions? I believe that a series of Conferences of Women N.G.Os of SAARC countries, should be held with a common agenda and platform of action without being mired by or mixed up with controversial politics. The thrust must be women's deliverance, elimination of frustrations and united march to the future.

Women's quest for justice is marching impatiently. The framers of the Constitution have given full scope for the three instrumentalities of the State to swing into gender action. But if a nation is to be tested by how it treats its most vulnerable sections our semi-Centennial is no matter for celebration but for somber introspection. Articles 14, 15 and 16 have mandated equality of the sexes and gone further to validate special provision for women and children. Part IV is rich with provisions to defend the dignity of women and forbid exploitation of childhood and youth. Moral and material abandonment and the abuse of the tender age of children are prohibited. Equal pay for equal work for men and women is assured as a basic proposition. Practices derogatory to the dignity of women are contrary to the fundamental duties of citizens. Within the parameters of the Constitution there is great scope for legislative and administrative amelioration of women's conditions. Of course, an enormous number of enactments and some administrative schemes are available to take care of the welfare of women and children. Even so, exploitation persists as a diehard disease and is far from disappearing, nay, is now on the increase. I do not deny that 50 years of Indian Independence have done some good and removed much injustice. There is a growing awareness amongst the courts and policy makers to take women's rights seriously. Public interest litigation has had an invigilatory effect. Substantial overhauling of procedural laws and providing victims of injustice access to legal aid and assistance is taking shape.

My submission is that the National Commission for Women and the State Commissions must be given more powers, more finances, more authority for studies and researches and issuance of directives to government officers to fulfil the objectives of gender justice. A Women's Tribunal in every district like a Family Court must be set up to try cases for and against women. Investigative agencies under the Commissions with the powers of the C.B.I. must get into action. Women N.G.Os must be given statutory power to visit police lock-ups and, with the aid of the police force, enter any place where women are kept in bondage. The police department must be under an obligation to take action at the Commission's request.

Let us fight for the causes Jesus handed over to us as legacy. Let us with burning conviction, resist commoditisation of human rights. That is the task, the truth. Know the Truth and the Truth shall make you free.

7

Gender Based Violence: The Response of the Sri Lanka Legal System

Savitri Goonesekere

I feel privileged to have been invited by the Trustees to come all the way from Sri Lanka to New Delhi to deliver the Justice Sunanda Bhandare Memorial Lecture. Justice Sunanda Bhandare was, one of those pioneers who had an opportunity to use her own insights as a judge and as a woman to contribute to the important edeavour of providing both men and women equal access to justice through the legal system. For gender sensitivity, as we demand it from judges, is not the capacity to confer unfair privileges upon women, but to ensure that they are not discriminated against through entrenched discrimination in the administration of justice. We remember her and in doing so, pay tribute to all those women and men who have contributed and continue to make a contribution to fairness, objectivity and non-discrimination in the administration of justice.

South Asia is known throughout the world as the continent of 'missing women'. We must be honest and recognise the harsh reality that no other continent denies its female population life chances from birth to death, in the manner that we do, in South Asia. The fact that many of us come from environments where we have been loved and supported to realise our full potential, must not prevent us from recognising the evil of gender based discrimination in our societies. Lawyers and judges have to function and fulfil their responsibilities in the context of this social reality. It is important for us, as legal professionals to recognise that reality, for it is the recognition of a problem that can stimulate us to find solutions.

I propose in my lecture to consider the manner in which lawyers and judges in my own country, Sri Lanka, have responded to a problem of discrimination that is common to all our countries—the problem of gender based or gender related violence.

The theme for this lecture will be 'Gender Based Violence: the Response of the Sri Lanka Legal System'. However, I shall in this lecture refer to comparative developments particularly in other countries in our region. Comparative approaches increasingly demonstrate our own strengths and weaknesses, and help us to find solutions to common problems. India and Sri Lanka like other countries in our region have legal systems which adopt a different approach to international law and domestic law. Governments are permitted to ratify international standards, but retain the concept of national sovereignty, so that international law is not incorporated into national law unless there is legislative intervention. It is only recently that our judges have taken the pathbreaking step of linking our constitutional standards to international standards so as to integrate the international value system in judicial decisions. International law and foreign laws have not yet become a fertile source for developing our domestic jurisprudence. And yet as State Parties to one treaty, the U.N. Convention on the Elimination of All Forms of Discrimination Against Women (CEDAW), our governments and justice systems need to harmonize all our laws with important international norms.

Practically all the countries in South Asia function within the framework of the English Common Law, our common, inherited, and 'foreign' source of law. We have Constitutions with chapters on fundamental rights inspired by international standards as well as the independence Constitution of India. The concept of 'Directive Principles of State Policy' travelled to India from Ireland, and found their way into other constitutions in South Asia. All our countries therefore share a legal tradition that should rely heavily on comparative, international, and regional jurisprudence.

In my own country, judges and lawyers, particularly in the Appeal Courts, refer to a range of judicial decisions from all over the world in deciding disputes that come before their courts. We have a combined Roman Law based civil law, and English Common law jurisdiction. We too have, like our neighbours, systems of personal law based on local customs including Islamic law. Indian decisions have been used in our courts in practically every branch of our legal system, together with cases from England from the beginning of the colonial period. We have also relied heavily on South African case law for decades. More recently our courts are citing decisions from the United States in fundamental rights cases, and citing international law and decisions of the European and Inter-American Courts.

Nevertheless it is, I believe very rarely that our own judicial precedents travel overseas. Leading Privy Council decisions like *Attorney General v Reid* (1964)[1] find their way into an occasional Indian case[2]. Article 39(1) of South Africa's Constitution (1996) requires the courts in that country to consider international law, and they may consider foreign law. Indian cases are already being cited in constitutional cases in South Africa[3]. We may therefore witness a new interest in constitutional jurisprudence, from all

[1]67 NLR 25 (P.C.): (1965) A.C. 720.

[2]*Sarla Mudgal & Others v Union of India,* (1995) 3 SCC 635.

[3]*Soobramany v Minister of Health* (Kwazula Natal) case CCR 32/97 (1997).

countries of South Asia, particularly with the new information technology that is becoming available to research institutes and even private lawyers.

The Constitutional Environment

Sri Lanka's present Constitution does not recognise a 'right to life.' However, unlike the Indian Constitution, it recognises a fundamental right to freedom from torture and inhuman degrading treatment[4]. Since either the torture article or the right to life is being interpreted as a constitutional basis for protecting people, and women in particular from violence, it is important to understand the space that this provides for responding to gender based violence.

The celebrated *Vishaka* case in India[5], recognised that sexual harassment and violence constitute a denial of the right to life. The 'right to life' is a civil and political right in the European and Anglo-American legal tradition, and refers to denial of life without due process of law. The Indian Supreme Court has made a major contribution to international human rights jurisprudence by interpreting this right not merely as a negative duty of the state to prevent infringement, but a positive duty to ensure an environment conducive to the sustenance of life and human dignity[6]. The *Vishaka* case gives this development a gender sensitive dimension by suggesting that a woman has a right to live in a violence free society, where her bodily integrity is respected. The case pronounced guidelines in regard to creating a sexual harassment and violence free working environment. Sri Lanka cases have adopted a similar approach and recognised that sexual molestation in police custody and any acts of assault and physical violence infringe the right to protection from torture[7]. However there is an unfortunate tendency to trivialise mental harassment that has no sexual connotations, and does not involve threats of violence. A woman who was humiliated and treated with 'gross incivility' in her working environment was therefore considered by the Supreme Court not to have been a victim of a violation of the fundamental right guaranteed by Article 11. The court held that the threshold of violence necessary for an infringement of her rights had not been established[8]. Unfortunately the Court did not address the obvious dimension of gender based, though non-sexual, harassment that took place in this case.

While the public sector is covered by the Constitutional safeguards, consistent with current jurisprudence on human rights, Sri Lanka Courts require that a violation should be by an executive or administrative act. Yet many infringements

---

[4]Art 11.

[5]*Vishaka v State of Rajasthan* (1997) 6 SCC 241.

[6]*Unni Krishnan v State of Andhra Pradesh* JT 1993 474; *Mohini Jain v State of Karnataka* (1992) 3 SCC 666 (right to education) *Samity & others v State of West Bengal* AIR 1996 SC 24, 26 (emergency health care).

[7]*Saman v Leeladasa* (1989) 1 Sri LR 1, *Velmurugu v Attorney General* (1989) 1 Sri LR i.e. (1989) 1 Sr, LR 406 (physical violence) *Kumaradasa v S.I. Sriyantha* SC Appl 257/93 SCM 23 May 1994 (sexual harassment of girl in police custody).

[8]*de Silva v Ceylon Fertiliser Corporation* (1989) 2 Sri LR 393.

of the right to life and bodily security take place because of the conduct of non-state or private actors. Abusive male spouses, siblings, or partners, inflict serious injuries, but legal relief for that conduct is through a system of punishment under criminal law, or financial compensation through criminal or civil law remedies. Yet in all our countries law enforcement is the responsibility of the State. In Sri Lanka women of all classes complain to the police when there is violence in the family. They see the police as the agency that will protect them and provide some personal security. However, it has been found that in family violence in particular, the police see their role as mediator and conciliator. Their ideology of 'preserving family harmony' rather than 'promoting family breakdown' influences the police to undermine the very laws that they are expected to enforce to punish acts of violence. Labour authorities are expected to play a role in monitoring and preventing acts of violence in the workplace. However they too do not see their role as a pro-active one.

It is in this situation that the extension of the Constitutional remedy to cover private conduct can be useful to promote accountability on the part of public law enforcement agencies. Sri Lanka courts have like the Indian Courts responded to this need by developing a concept of 'State inaction'. There are two important appeal court decisions that reflect an approach similar to Indian cases[9] that have decided that inaction or failure to prevent an assault by a private person in a police station, is State action. Thus, inaction by administrative authorities and law enforcement agencies can be considered to constitute 'State action' in Sri Lanka today[10]. Sri Lanka's new draft Constitution reflects this jurisprudence in using the broader expression 'State action'[11] rather than administrative or executive action, for 'State action' can also constitute inaction. In addition the new draft Constitution makes it possible to challenge judicial action of courts exercising original criminal jurisdiction in narrow circumstances where there are orders on arrest, detention and punishment, and in specified aspects of administration of criminal justice. It would seem that decisions on sentencing and aspects of criminal procedure that deny women access to justice in cases of violence may now be challenged.

In *Aery v Ireland* (1979)[12] the European Court on Human Rights decided that the State could be responsible for not taking positive steps to ensure that a woman had access to courts to obtain a separation from a violent husband. Sri Lankan courts may not go so far, but the present approach does suggest that the police and law enforcement authorities can be liable for an infringement if they fail to intervene and take action on complaints resulting in further acts of violence by private actors. Besides certain developments in regard to the liability

---

[9]*Saheli Women's Resource Centre v Commissioner of Police Delhi* AIR 1990 SC 513, *Padmini v State of Tamil Nadu* 1993 Crim L.J. 29641.

[10]*Faiz v Attorney General* (1995) 1 Sri LR 372 *Upaliratna v Tikiri Banda* (1995) 1 Sri LR 165.

[11]Draft Constitution Oct (1997) Art 30 (a) (a).

[12]32 Eur. Ct. H.R. (Ser A) 1979.

of the State for the acts of violence and abuse of state officials under cover of authority have re-enforced these developments that extend the scope of state action.

In the case of *Velmurugu v Attorney General* (1981)[13] Sharvananda C.J. said that: 'the sweep of state action.... will not cover acts of officers in the ambit of their personal pursuits, such as rape by a police officer of a woman in his custody; such act has no relation to the exercise of state power vested in him—the officer had taken advantage of the occasion, but not his office for the satisfaction of a personal vagary. His conduct is totally unconnected with any manner of performance of his official functions'. However, Sri Lanka courts are using their power to 'grant such relief or make such directions as it may deem just and equitable' to order compensation to victims of torture, and these orders are made against both the state and the individual public officer[14]. They are also recognising that acts of violence under cover of authority create both state and individual responsibility for abuse of power. It is in a sense an adaptation of the 'respondent superior' concept of tort liability. We know that this liability was the English common law's response to the need to make both employer and employee liable for harm they cause in the community, and an effort to promote accountability on the part of both. This view challenges the assumption that gender based violence in custodial situations is a private act which in the words of Sharvananda C.K. 'has no relation to the exercise of power vested in him'. Acts of custodial violence in police stations as in the *Mathura* rape case in India[15] or in hospitals and other state institutions, may now become justiciable as an infringement of the fundamental right to protection from torture and inhuman and degrading treatment.

In the *Vishaka case,* sexual harassment in the workplace was also perceived as a violation of the fundamental right to equality and non-discrimination on the ground of sex. Several cases in the Sri Lanka courts that have questioned the exercise of a discretion by a public authority on the basis of the constitutional guarantee on equality, interpret the concept of equality as a broad requirement that protects against all discriminatory arbitrary and capricious actions of the state. The courts view discretionary powers as a 'public trust to be used to promote public welfare[16]. This would mean that an act of gender based violence which constitutes discrimination and arbitrary treatment can be perceived as in the *Vishaka case* as a violation of the right to equality. There is an unreported

---

[13]1981 1 Sri LR 406 at 422.

[14]*Kumaradasa V S.I. Sriyantha* supra, *Podiappuhamy v Liyanage and others.* SC APP 446 / 96 SC M.31 May 1994. *Ratnasiri v Basnayake and others* SC Appl. 4/94 SC Minutes 3 Nov 1995 cited in Amerasinghe *ARB Our Fundamental Rights of Personal Security and Physical Liberty,* Sarvodaya Colombo (1995) Ch. II.

[15]*Tukaram & Another v State of Maharashtra* AIR 1979 SC 185.

[16]*Gunaratna v Petroleum Corporation* (1996) 1 Sri LR 315 at 324-325; *Premachandra v Jayawickrema* (1994) 2 Sri LR 90; *William Silva v Shirani Bandaranayake* (1997) 1 SRLR 92 (Presidential discretion to appoint a judge of the Supreme Court is not absolute).

case in Sri Lanka in 1993 where a woman doctor challenged a prejudicial administrative decision in regard to medical internship and transfer, made against her when she made an allegation of rape against a male colleague in the hospital where they both worked[17]. Her allegation of gender bias and discrimination seems to have been accepted when the case was settled out of court.

The capacity to use the jurisprudence on the right to life, freedom from torture, and equality in response to violence, can, however, be undermined when the right to freedom of religion and cultural practice is used to justify acts of violence and gender based discrimination. There is here a potential for conflict of rights and interests.

In certain jurisdictions, the courts engage in what is described as 'purposive interpretation' where they try to balance fundamental rights so as to ensure that the overarching purpose of the Constitution to protect human rights is not undermined. They use the concept of lawful limitations placed on rights that is recognised in many constitutions to arrive at such 'purposive' interpretations. Thus, the concept of 'public order or respect for the rights and freedom of others' has been used to prevent rights of freedom of speech or religion undermining the right to non discrimination and equality. There is judicial authority in Canada that 'hate speech' directed at an ethnic or religious minority which undermines the right of non-discrimination and equality cannot be accepted as a legitimate exercise of the right of freedom of speech[18].

There are decisions in our own jurisdiction which have adopted this 'purposive' approach in judicial decision making, and tried to balance conflicting interests in areas outside constitutional jurisprudence. In the *Mudgal* case for instance[19], the Supreme Court of India recognised that a man who had contracted a monogamous marriage under a statutory marriage law, could not unilaterally decide to contract a polygamous marriage on the ground that he had become a convert to Islam. This judicial approach was followed recently in Sri Lanka. In *Abeysundere v Abeysundere* and *Attorney General* (1988)[20] the Supreme Court overruled the decision of the Privy Council in *Attorney General v Reid* (1964), and held that a man who had contracted a monogamous marriage under the General Marriages Ordinance which applies to the majority of Sri Lankans could not unilaterally convert to Islam and exercise the right of polygamy conferred on a Muslim minority. The *Mudgal* case was cited with approval in the Sri Lanka case. The controversial *Shah Bano* case[21] in India represented a similar effort to balance the rights of Muslims under a uniformly applicable

[17]*Fernando v Director General Medical Service*, news item *Daily News* 3 July 1993.

[18]*R v Keegstra* (1990) 3 SCR 697 cited Hogg P.W. Constitutional Law of Canada Carswell (1992) 818-819.

[19]Note 2 supra.

[20]S.C. Appeal No 70/96 (1996).

[21]*Mohd. Ahmed Khan v Shah Bano Begum* 1985 2 SCC 556.

maintenance law, and the conflicting right to be governed under Muslim personal law. This balancing of interests is also seen in the early legislation that introduced restraints on the age of marriage, or permitted all members of a plural society to dispose of their property by will, or adopt children. Similarly the colonial Penal Codes in all our countries tried to reinforce laws on restraint of marriage by recognising an offence of statutory marital rape, where a married man had intercourse with a girl below a specified minimum age of marriage[22].

Sustaining this 'purposive' approach has become difficult in all our countries today because of the pressure for recognising ethnic and religious identities in the name of pluralism and tolerance, freedom of religion and conscience. The Indian experience on the Muslim Women's Protection of Divorce legislation after the *Shah Bano* case is replicated in a recent experience in Sri Lanka. When the Penal Code amendment was enacted in 1995, and the age of statutory rape was increased to 16 years, the Muslims were excluded from the scope of this reform. The National Committee on Women however insisted that the protection of the earlier Penal Code should remain, and so the age of statutory rape was retained as 12 years for Muslim girls. This restraint, therefore, applies to Muslims even though Muslim law, unlike other systems does not recognise any minimum age for marriage[23].

A recent decision of the Supreme Court of India on the legality of unilateral repudiation and "talak" divorce refused to question the validity of personal laws on the ground of conflict with constitutional guarantees on fundamental rights[24]. The fear that constitutional norms may result in challenges to the personal laws has contributed to the Sri Lanka Constitution (1978) as well as the new draft Constitution containing a provision that existing laws cannot be subject to judicial review. However the new draft Constitution (1997) makes provision for the President to appoint within 3 months of the commencement of the Constitution, an expert committee to review and make recommendations in regard to laws that violate the Constitution[25].

It seems important for all our countries to develop a jurisprudence in regard to purposive interpretation of the Constitution, in order to prevent the overall objectives of the Constitution on non-discrimination and gender equality being undermined by arguments based on the need to protect freedom of religion and manifestation of religious practice. We need to distinguish between freedom of conscience and religion, and manifestation of religion in practice, and use the tool of public order and respect for rights and interests of others to prevent the recognition of policies and practices that sustain and encourage violence and denial of life chances to women. No cultural or religious practice should be permitted to undermine the core value of gender equality and non-discrimination.

---

[22]Child Marriage Restraint Act (1929) India, Bangladesh, Pakistan (now amended) General Marriages Ordinance Sri Lanka (1907) and Penal Codes definition of rape.

[23]See discussion on Penal Code Amendment Act (1995) infra.

[24]*Ahmedabad Women's Action Group v Union of India* (1997) 3SCC 573.

[25]Constitution. (1978) Art 16(1), Draft Constitution (1997) Art. 28(1)(2).

The Indian courts have given the lead in South Asia in expanding the concept of *locus standi* to enable individuals and organisations other than the victim to file an action for violation of fundamental rights[26]. Some effort were made to introduce the concept of 'public interest' litigation into international human rights law in the draft Optional Protocol to the Convention on Women's Rights (CEDAW). This was a recognition of the reality that women whose human rights have been infringed, are not always able or willing to identify themselves as victims of infringement, to pursue legal remedies. Even large scale violations may occur, and the person or persons best equipped to bring an action will be a third party activist or organisation. The Optional Protocol to CEDAW has not yet been adopted, and proceedings before international tribunals with jurisdiction to hear complaints can still be initiated only by the victim of an infringement[27].

Sri Lanka Courts have restricted capacity to allow public interest litigation because Article 126(2) of the Constitution requires the victim of a violation of fundamental rights to be before courts. However, our judges too have been influenced to some extent at least by developments in the Indian Supreme Court. In *Somawathie v Weerasinghe*[28] Kulatunga J, dissenting from the majority who interpreted Article 126 as denying a spouse a right to file a petition said: 'Having regard to Article 126 (2) this court cannot entertain complaints having the character of public interest petitions (as in India). However in circumstances of grave stress or incapacity, particularly torture, ... next of kin such as a parent or a spouse may be the only people able to apply to this court.... this court may entertain such applications, notwithstanding the failure to effect literal compliance with the requirement of Art 126(2).'

The impact of the concept of widened standing in the Indian Courts was clearly seen in the willingness of the Sri Lanka Supreme Court to entrain the applications of persons in prolonged detention for violation of fundamental rights, on the basis of letters written to the court. It is also seen in the rules of the Supreme Court permitting an allegation of an infringement to be brought to the notice of the court so that the court may direct an attorney at law or the Legal Aid Commission to submit a petition on the matter[29]. This initiative has broadened the interpretation of standing, but the Supreme Court rules nevertheless require a victim of infringement to be at least identified in an application. The current procedure on standing therefore continues to impact negatively on women. Thus, a discriminatory regulation in regard to visa applications of male spouses of Sri Lankan women married to foreigners has not been challenged for many years because the affected women have been unwilling to petition the

---

[26]*SP Gupta v Union of India* AIR 1982 SC 149; *Bandua Mukthi Morcha v Union of India* AIR 1984 SC 802.

[27]*Ameeruddy Cziffra et al v. Mauritius, Communications of Human Rights Committee* No. 35/1978 UN Doc. A/36/40 (1981).

[28](1990) 2 Sri LR 121 at 1310132.

[29]*Boosa Applications discussed in Gomez M* Emerging Trends in Public Law. Vijitha Yapa Colombo 1998 p. 30; Rules of the Supreme Court (1992) Gomez *ibid* 32-33.

courts, even when free legal aid has been offered, in fear of further adverse action by immigration authorities. It is only recently that a woman has taken the initiative to challenge the regulation, and obtained relief. In *D'Souza v Attorney General* (1997) the Supreme Court of Sri Lanka decided that as long as the petitioner was married to the (alien) husband, the immigration authorities shall grant him a visa to live and work in Sri Lanka[30]. Consequently government officials have been ordered to follow the same liberal policy to applications by foreign wives and foreign husbands, implicitly recognising that having a family unit within the country of birth is important for both men and women.

The pressure for broadening standing has come from academics and human rights organisations familiar with Indian jurisprudence. Government has responded with a widened proposal on standing in the new draft Constitution (1997). Thus the new proposal incorporates the present position reflected in the Supreme Court rules. In addition 'an application may be made' for violation of fundamental rights 'in respect of any person or persons affected, in the public interest, by any person or by any incorporated or unincorporated body of persons acting *bona fide*[31]. This has indeed widened the scope of standing, bringing Sri Lanka's Constitutional jurisprudence in line with landmark cases in India like *S.P. Gupta v Union of India* (1981). We know that such cases have helped to develop the concept of public interest litigation, moving forward from the Anglo American or European jurisprudence which requires a victim of infringement to petition for relief.

In Sri Lanka, like many other countries in our region with a common law tradition, treaty based international law does not apply at the national level unless it is incorporated into domestic jurisprudence by legislation or by judicial interpretation. Consequently international human rights standards that our countries have ratified operate as a separate system, unless there has been legislative or judicial interventions, locally. This means that the standards of CEDAW or the U.N. Convention on the Rights of the Child (CRC) 1978 are not relevant in general in national jurisprudence. The *Vishaka* case cited and used the standards of CEDAW on non-discrimination, and also the standards of the non-binding UN Declaration on Violence against Women (1993) in interpreting the Indian Constitution. Yet in a recent case on citizenship in Bangaladesh which challenged the gender discriminatory Citizenship Act, the Supreme Court failed to use CEDAW standards in interpreting the right of equality, even though counsel cited it in argument. There is no case in Sri Lanka too that has cited either CEDAW or CRC, though the country is a State Party to both these Conventions. This is partly because Sri Lanka lawyers even when they are familiar with international human rights standards, prefer to refer to rights in the Covenant on Civil and Political Rights. They are not sensitised to using CEDAW or CRC in the same way. However, international human rights

---

[30]*D'Souza v The Attorney General SC* Appl. No. 712/96 3.10.1997 (unreported). (3.J.)

[31]Art 30 (1) (b) and (c).

standards on civil and political rights are increasingly being cited and used to interpret the Sri Lanka Constitution's guarantees on fundamental rights[32].

Both CEDAW and CRC have been ratified by a large number of countries. CRC indeed has been ratified by all countries except the USA and Somalia. CRC contains a core Article 2 which recognises the rights of all children to non-discrimination on the ground of sex, and thus endorses core standards of CEDAW. Lawyers and judges must focus on treaty based law in national jurisprudence. Besides the time may have come to argue that non-discrimination on the ground of gender is as much customary international law, binding on all nations, as the norm of freedom for discrimination on the ground of race. This should encourage courts in our countries to constantly link our Constitutional interpretations to the international human rights standards on gender.

Criminal Law

The Sri Lanka Penal Code and the Evidence Ordinance which define the core norms in this area are based on the Indian Penal Code which travelled in colonial times to many countries of Asia and Africa. Nevertheless, there are some key differences in the area of violence against women. The most recent amendments to the Sri Lanka penal Code (1995) however, have borrowed to some extent from the amendments to the Penal Code introduced in India in 1983.

Sri Lanka's 100 year old Penal Code was amended in 1995 to reflect substantive change in the laws that can have some impact on violence against women[33]. These changes originated from a Technical Committee set up to examine the issue of law reform in the area of child labour and child abuse. Proposals of this Committee combined with proposals of another ad hoc committee set up by the Minister of Justice to examine the law on rape, led to common proposals for reforms being accepted by the previous government. The draft legislation was placed before Parliament after consultation with the National Committee on Women (NCW).

The legislation as it emerged under this government was somewhat different from the original draft that was approved by NCW. It demonstrates the inability of women's groups to sustain lobbying efforts and support for change to carry a bill through in parliament. It also indicates how sectarian and perhaps minority views can prevail with politicians even without evidence that they represent a larger constituency.

The Penal Code Amendment Act (1995) in Sri Lanka redefined the offence of rape, so as to delete the reference to the words, 'against her will.' Rape is now defined essentially as 'non-consensual' sexual intercourse. An explanation to the newly defined offence, indicates that evidence of resistance such as physical injuries will not be considered essential to prove absence of consent[34].

---

[32]*Leela Violet and Others v Inspector General of Police* CA 2.12.1994 (unreported), *Gamini Athukorale and others v Attorney General* S.D. No. 1/97-15/97 5.5.1997 (unreported).

[33]Penal Code Amendment Act No. 22 of 1995.

[34]Amended S. 363 and Explanation (11).

This reform was a response to the argument that the focus in adversarial cross examination on the need for evidence of physical injuries, made it impossible to defeat the defence of consent in the absence of evidence that the victim engaged in a physical struggle with her attackers.

The new offence of rape is different from the comparable section 375 of the Indian Penal Code, as amended in 1983, despite the fact that the statute has borrowed several provisions from the Indian Code. The Sri Lanka Code's concept of minimum sentences for rape, higher sentences for statutory rape (raised to 16 from 12 years) and heavier sentences for gang rape, rape of a pregnant woman and custodial rape are modelled on provisions in the Indian Code[35]. Sri Lanka's statute adopts an approach that seeks to impose a higher sentence for rape of a minor child (under 18 years) unlike the Indian Act, which for some reason, only provides for a higher sentence in the case of rape of a girl under 12 years[36]. Was the reference to 12 years an omission in a context where the earlier age of statutory rape was, as in Sri Lanka, 12 years? The Sri Lankan code has an additional situation where a higher sentence is imposed for rape of a mentally or physically disabled woman[37].

The Sri Lanka legislation does not go so far as to create separate offences that cover consensual sex in custodial situations, in the manner indicated in Sections 376B to 376D of the Indian Penal Code. However, it has confined the offence of marital rape in the same way to situations of judicial separation. In addition, it has introduced a broad offence of sexual harassment in place of the original offence of using criminal force to offend the modesty of a woman[38]. This offence covers sexual harassment in the work place as recognised by the guidelines in the *Vishaka Case*. It would also cover sexual harassment that does not constitute rape, which is covered by the Indian Code's provisions on consensual sex in custodial situations.

The Indian Code's definition of marital rape, covers cases of *de facto* separation, because of the reference *to separation under 'custom or usage.'* The Sri Lanka Penal Code refers only to marital rape in situations of legal separation. This is restrictive and unrealistic as this remedy is hardly used even by those who file matrimonial actions. However, both the Sri Lanka Code and the amended India Penal Code retain the concept of British Colonial law when they continue to recognise a concept of statutory marital rape. In otherwords a man commits rape if he has sexual intercourse with his wife below a specified age. This provision is relevant in Sri Lanka today, only in relation to the Muslim community, since age of marriage is not regulated in that community. The Indian Code refers to the offence of statutory rape of a wife under 15 years, because Indian legislation does not make a union below the minimum age of

---

[35]S 363, 364; c.f. Indian Penal Code S. 376.

[36]Sri Lanka code S.364 (2) (e) Indian Code S.376(2)(f)

[37]S. 364 (2) (f).

[38]Sri Lanka Code S.363 (a) c.f. Indian Code S. 376 A (marital rape); sexual harassment, Sri Lanka Code S.345.

marriage void. In Sri Lanka by contrast the marriage of non-muslims is void when they violate the current minimum age of marriage of 18 years. Consequently the concept of statutory rape of a wife under the age of 12 years in the Penal Code amendment cannot apply to non Muslims[39].

The Penal Code amendment in Sri Lanka introduced several new criminal offences that cover sexual conduct, which are not found in the amended Indian Penal Code. For instance the Indian Penal Code continues to follow the English Common Law tradition which regarded incest as a matter that should not come within the realm of public criminal law. Only a religious or ecclesiastical court originally had jurisdiction in cases of incest, which was considered a 'private' crime in the Common law. Consequently incest was recognised as a minor crime only in British colonial statutes of many countries, which regulated prohibited degrees of marriage. Sri Lanka's 1995 legislation rejected this idea and criminalised incest. However, the Attorney General has a discretion in regard to whether to prosecute or not[40]. This was an attempt to take into account considerations that may warrant non-prosecution. However, no guidelines have yet been developed for the exercise of the Attorney General's discretion.

Another new sexual offence in Sri Lanka covers 'grave sexual abuse'. This refer to non-consensual sexual violence, that can be committed without constituting the conventional offence of rape[41]. When reforms were introduced there was reluctance to expand the familiar offence of rape to cover other acts of sexual abuse. This was the rationale for retaining the offence of rape, and creating a new offence to cover other acts of sexual violence. The qualification to the concept of consent, in situations of intimidation etc. have been introduced into this new offence. However, the proposal on introducing a concept of 'statutory grave sexual abuse' by which consent of a person below the age of minority would not be deemed to be consent, was not accepted. This creates an unsatisfactory situation where unless the exceptions apply, a minor girl's consent will be a complete defence to the offence of grave sexual abuse.

The amendment also has several new offences on child pornography, child prostitution, prostitution in general, and trafficking, repealing the earlier provisions in the Penal Code. Nevertheless a proposal to repeal the colonial Vagrants Ordinance that was introduced into many colonies in the British period has not been accepted as yet. Consequently police continue to prosecute children and women considered street sex workers under the Vagrants Ordinance, without prosecuting the pimps and procedures under the new law. Victims of sexual abuse or underage girls who have sex are also often committed to

---

[39]Sri Lanka Penal Code S.363(e); Indian Penal Code S. 375 exception; amendments to the General Marriage Ordinance and Kandyan Marriage Act (1995) in Sri Lanka raised the minimum age of marriage for both sexes to 18 years.

[40]S. 364 (A).

[41]S. 365 (B).

certified schools, because they are perceived as 'accomplices' to the sexual offence rather than victims[42].

Proposals to make adult homosexuality legal and repeal the old offences on 'acts of gross indecency between males' and 'unnatural offences' were not accepted. They were, however, modified. Fears by the legal draftsman that the redrafted provision would be challenged because it referred only to males, led to use of the term 'person' instead. Consequently female homosexuality that was not an offence in either English law, or the Penal Code, which introduced English law, now becomes a criminal offence in Sri Lanka![43]. This is an anomoly that is yet to be rectified.

The Penal Code Amendment repealed the earlier law and strengthened the law on physical assault as a crime[44]. The pressure for this change came from those who argued that the earlier definition was so narrow and technical as to prevent effective prosecution for acts of physical violence. A new definition of an offence of cruelty to children[45] also strengthens the law on criminal sanctions for acts of gender based violence against girl children.

Sri Lanka has as high incidence of back street abortion. Unlike India which introduced Medical Termination of Pregnancy legislation two decades ago, Sri Lanka like other countries in South Asia has very stringent laws on abortion. The proposals that preceded the Penal Code Amendment suggested that medical termination of pregnancy under regulated conditions such as mandatory requirement of medical certification, should be legal in cases of rape and incest, or in situations of gross foetal defects at the request of parents[46]. This proposal was accepted by the Cabinet of the former government and the present government, and indeed went into the draft bill. However, the Minister who presented the Bill, appears to have been lobbied to withdraw these particular provisions. He promised to 'decriminalise abortion' and introduce it as part of health legislation, but Sri Lanka has failed as yet to introduce legislation on the lines of India to deal with this difficult subject.

Family Planning Organisations are deeply concerned at the misuse of abortion as a contraceptive measure, and by abortions on victims of sexual violence in poor conditions, resulting in maternal deaths from septic abortion. Nevertheless the Minister who introduced the Sri Lankan amending legislation on the basis of the government's duty 'to protect' women and children against violence, did not refer to the anomaly of prohibiting medical termination of pregnancy after acts of violence such as rape and incest. Most of the speeches in parliament on the amending legislation supported the Minister's decision to withdraw the provision on abortion, with strong expressions of support for 'right

[42]The majority of inmates of the Ranmuthugala Certified Home for girls are known to be victims of sexual abuse or girls under the minimum age of marriage.

[43]S.365 and 365(A).

[44]S.311 repealed and new section introduced in 1995.

[45]S. 308 (A).

[46]Penal Code Amendment Bill (1995), and debate in parliament on the bill.

to life' views. Only one member of parliament raised the issue of the violence perpetrated on women by forcing them to bear children in circumstances of rape, incest or gross foetal defects. He referred to the absence of support services for child care, particularly in regard to non-marital and disabled children, which added to the injustice of forced pregnancy in these circumstances.

The changes in the substantive law in Sri Lanka have not been followed by changes to the law of evidence. Sri Lanka's Evidence Ordinance (1895) like the Indian Evidence Act (1872) reflects norms of British colonial law on Evidence. These statutes contain a provision that in a prosecution for rape or attempted rape 'it can be shown that the prosecutrix (i.e. the victim) was of a generally immoral character'[47]. This provision is well known to encourage adversarial cross examination and is a disincentive to women making a complaint of rape. Yet this provision still remains on our statute books. Though the Evidence Ordinance itself does not contain a rule in regard to corroboration of the evidence of a prosecutrix in a rape case, the Sri Lanka Courts have followed the English Common law approach that in sexual offences the complainant is regarded as an accomplice. Independent corroboration of her evidence is therefore considered a legal requirement. There are at least two important cases of the Superior Courts that have stated that a jury may convict on the uncorroborated testimony of the prosecutrix[48]. Nevertheless the warning to juries regarding the fact that it is unsafe to do so continues to be administered. Besides, the courts focus on the need to prove evidence of physical injuries to prove resistance or unwillingness[49]. Evidence of resistance and physical injuries is regarded as evidence that corroborates the victim's evidence. The warning as well as the emphasis on resistance may now be considered to conflict with the Sri Lanka reforms of 1995, which have made proof of resistance unnecessary to establish rape. There is, however, likely to be confusion in the interpretation of the new definition of rape, in the absence of supportive changes in the law of evidence.

Separate and distinct statutes in Sri Lanka also create important criminal offences that can be used to prosecute for acts of violence. The Torture Act (1994) which seeks to integrate the international standards Sri Lanka has accepted by ratification of the Torture Convention (1984), covers private acts of public officers who commit torture. There is some duplication with the expanded remedy that the courts have recognised for violation of the fundamental right to freedom from torture. A recent important decision in a high court has interpreted the Bribery Act so as to consider soliciting for sexual intercourse from an employee, an act of bribery, which attracts penalties under this statute[50].

---

[47]Sri Lanka Evidence Ordinance (1895) S. 155(d); Indian Evidence Act (1872) S. 155 (4).

[48]*Karunasena v Republic of Sri Lanka* (1975) 78 NLR 63; *Rajaratna v Attorney General* CA 13/94 23.1.1996 (unreported).

[49]*Karunasena, ibid.*

[50]*Republic of Sri Lanka v Kuthubdeen High* Court Colombo B 839/93 3.3.1994.

Civil Law

The Sri Lanka legal system has a Roman Dutch legal tradition which provides a source of law for awarding compensation in cases of violation of fundamental rights or acts of violence.

In the Roman Dutch law of delict (tort), an act done wrongfully and intentionally which causes either physical harm or an interference with dignity can confer a right on the victim to claim damages. The Roman Dutch law concept of compensation for interference with 'dignity' thus creates a right of action in the event of physical assault, sexual harassment, or rape. In an important decision in the Supreme Court[51], *Saman v Leeladasa* (1989) Justice Mark Fernando stated that the limitations of public law in providing relief for fundamental rights only against state actors could be overcome by recognising that the Roman Dutch law concept of 'wrongfulness' in the law of delict refers to violation of fundamental rights. If this interpretation is followed in cases of violence against women, it is possible to argue that violation of fundamental rights as well as criminal acts of assault and violence can give a right to financial compensation. The civil remedy and the fundamental rights action can be of practical use in situations like the *Vishaka case* where a criminal prosecution by the standard of proof beyond reasonable doubt may not be successful.

There are, however, intrinsic problems in the use of the civil remedy. Civil litigation is very time consuming and expensive. Besides Roman Dutch law also contains outmoded principles such as the husband's 'marital power' which may surface, and be used to trivialise violence against women. For instance, a leading case in the Supreme Court of Sri Lanka recognised that a violent husband could claim compensation for an attempted rape on his wife, on the ground that this was an interference to *his* dignity[52]. The inaccessibility of the civil remedy has led the legislature to introduce payment of compensation to the victim in criminal cases as an additional sanction. Thus the Penal Code Amendment Act (1995) provides for payment of compensation as an additional sanction to fine or imprisonment.

Matrimonial laws also provide some relief in situations where matrimonial actions for divorce can be filed on grounds of constructive malicious desertion or gross cruelty, or an order for judicial separation can be obtained on the ground of cruelty. When such litigation is brought under the general law there is procedure for obtaining a restraining or exclusion order from court to address a problem of violence and harassment pending proceedings. However, the personal laws provide for divorce by mutual consent, through administrative procedures, and this can be used to obtain a dissolution of the marriage without adversarial litigation. Muslim law in Sri Lanka recognises the right of a woman to sue for a *fasah* divorce on the ground of cruelty or illtreatment[53]. A recent

---

[51]*Saman v Leeladasa* note 7 supra.

[52]*Nadaraja v Obeysekere* (1971) 76 NLR 268.

[53]General Marriage Ordinaces (1970) (fault divorce) Kandyan Marriage Act 1952 (consensual, marriage breakdown and fault divorce); Muslim Marriage and Divorce Act (1951) [Islamic law and *fasah* and *talak* divorce].

court decision which diluted the legislative procedures for conciliation prior to divorce has strengthened the husbands power to pronounce *talak*, and unilaterally repudiate his wife[54].

The most serious acts of violence are committed against women and children pending a divorce or a separation. Since violence constitutes some offence under the Penal Law, a woman who decides to use the legal system and resist acts of violence, must either initiate matrimonial proceedings or complain to the police in order to be able to use this system. It is only by initiating this process that she can obtain a 'binding over' order against the husband, restraining further harassment.

Law Enforcement

Some steps have been taken in Sri Lanka to strengthen law enforcement. The setting up of women and children's bureaus in police stations has been one measure introduced recently to ensure that the police takes action on complaints by women, and these cases are prioritised. However, lack of training of women police officers and the weak infrastructure hampers effective use of the law. In particular, the absconding accused and the intimidation of witnesses present a problem for effective law enforcement.

The advantage of setting up of the 'Police Desks' is that the male police service is now being moved in the direction of recognising that their task is not to conciliate, when there are gross acts of violence. There has been some effort to sustain training for police officers, since the new law was introduced, and there seems to be much more commitment in prosecuting offenders, even in cases of domestic violence. The setting up of a Presidential Task Force on Child Abuse chaired by the President has suddenly given the agenda of violence against women and girl children a higher profile within the police service. The Sri Lankan experience shows that connecting the issue of violence against children to violence against women, creates a supportive environment for law reform and enforcement.

The Supreme Court has in a recent case held that legislation that mandates minimum sentences and removes or restricts judicial discretion, is an interference with the judicial power[55]. Scrutinising the very heavy minimum sentences introduced in recent ragging legislation, the court held certain penalties to be excessive, and therefore in infringement of the right to protection from inhuman and degrading treatment. Interestingly the ragging legislation, was itself modelled on similar legislation in Tamil Nadu on ragging. Ragging in Sri Lanka universities and schools places students of both sexes at risk of extreme violence. Ragging women students invariably constitute acts of gender based violence, and the Ragging Bill attempted to set norms and deter these acts by imposing very strong penalties.

[54] *Khan v Moomin* (1995) 1 Sri LR 107.

[55] Case in Supreme Court on *Ragging Bill*, S.C. Determination No. 6/98 SD 7.4.1998.

It is fortunate that the Penal Code Amendment which also provided for minimum sentences was not challenged before it was enacted, and it is now a past law, that cannot be challenged! The concept of minimum sentences has certainly encouraged greater awareness among law enforcement authorities of the need to avoid trivialising acts of violence against women. Courts are now imposing heavy sentences of fine, and imprisonment and also making more significant awards of compensation. This represents a dramatic change from an earlier practice of allowing plea bargaining, making minimal awards of compensation, and suspending sentences[56].

A major development in the last few years is the reliance on medical evidence in torture cases, and the focus on strengthening the forensic aspects of investigation. Many more medical professionals, particularly in the universities are researching in the area of medicine and human rights violations, child abuse, torture and domestic violence. The shortcomings and the lack of coordination between medical personnel, the police, the Attorney General's department and the judiciary has surfaced, and efforts are being made to revise existing procedures including the form which is routinely used for the medical report in cases of sexual violence. There has also been some focus on training and sensitisation of lawyers, judges and police, and including the issue of violence in courses in medical schools. The Supreme Court is also recognising the importance of medical evidence in torture cases. Judges sometimes pass strictures on medical reports of injuries filed by the police as respondents, denying an allegation of torture. They are scrutinising these reports and stress high professional standards from doctors[57].

I have tried in the course of this lecture to indicate the manner in which Sri Lanka jurisprudence respondes to the problem of violence against women, and the links that we continue to have to legal thought and ideas in India. These links of scholarship go back to early centuries when scholars from Sri Lanka like Buddhagosha travelled across South India and made their contribution to a cross fertilisation of thought and ideas. I cannot also fail to mention the activism of those Indian women of antiquity such as Mahaprajapathi Gothami, who travelled on foot across India demanding from Gauthama, the Buddha, that they be admitted as nuns to the Buddhist clerical order.

India and Sri Lanka share an intellectual tradition, and have drawn from common roots of law and jurisprudence, even though we do not seem to have sustained the link to judicial activism. Perhaps we need to be inspired by the blend of intellectual thought and activism that represents the best that India has to offer to all people of the region and the world. We need to commit ourselves

---

[56]News paper clippings, *Daily News*. 21 August 1998, 3 Aug. 1998, 4 August 1998, (reports of cases in trial courts). Goonesekere Savitri, *Realising Gender Equity Through Law: Sri Lanka's experience in the Post Nairobi Decade*, Centre for Women's Research. CENWOR Colombo (1995) p.6.

[57]Cases cited in Amerasinghe *op cit* at p. 48-49.

to sharing the best, rather than the worst dimensions of our cultures and traditions. That is perhaps the most difficult challenge for South Asia as we enter the next millennium.

There are those who will argue that laws and legal processes have no meaning in the context of the problems of poverty and economic deprivation in our region. We in Sri Lanka have strived for over four decades to commit recourses to human development, even when we rank as a poor developing country. That concept of human development in our country has always had a place, for law, governance, the rule of law and human rights, even in the darkest periods of our contemporary history. The manner in which all sectors of our population have sought justice through the courts in cases of disappearances killings and custodial rape indicate their determination to use legal processes.

It is important to recognise that we cannot achieve conflict resolution in our countries in an environment where our societies continue to tolerate violence against a large portion of their population—women and children. How can we expect conflict resolution by peaceful means, when we give legitimacy to violence against women and children in our families and communities? We must retain faith in norms and standards on human rights, laws, legal strategies and institutions and not succumb to the cynicism that would reject them in the name of 'Asian' values, economic development, or cultural purity. Countries like India and Sri Lanka like all other countries need laws, regulations, rights and accountability in governance. It is for us to develop those abiding values in the context of our third world realities and ensure that through change, adaptation and dynamism, we use our laws and legal institutions to bring justice and equity. Comparative experiences from India which show how the courts have tried to achieve change, have strengthened our own legal system, particularly in the area of constitutional jurisprudence. We must ensure that this continues and is re-inforced by the willingness of professionals and activists in both our countries to recognise that the legal system can and must be a strategy for achieving justice and human development.

8

Gender Sensitization of the Judiciary

Justice Leila Seth

Women in India normally exist either as a part of their parents' or their husbands' home. After their husbands die they live in their son's home dependent on him. Consequently their freedom and right to equality are dependent on these families and their attitudes, which normally treat them as subservient. The question of independence and having a home of their own, where they can express themselves in the manner of their choice, rarely arises. But equality is what they are entitled to.

The Indian Constitution has clearly indicated that equality is a fundamental right. Article 14 guarantees equality before the law and equal protection under the law. Article 15 prohibits discrimination on the grounds of religion, race, caste, sex and place of birth and Article 15(3) permits the State to make special provision for women. Article 16 provides for equality of opportunity in matters of public employment.

Equality is not defined and is perhaps undefinable. Equality means different things at different times and to different people. In legal parlence, there is a formal approach that is, those similarly situated are to be treated equally; further one cannot treat unequals as equal. So, it means, if persons are different then differential treatment is justified. But substantive equality requires that inequality of disadvantaged groups in society be eliminated. The shift is from those alike and those different to disadvantaged groups. How is the change to be brought about so that disadvantaged groups become equal to others? By reservation? But the dilemma is that reservations violate equality in that everybody must be treated equally; but are not reservations fundamental to equality since equality requires disadvantaged groups to be treated differently? But will reservations result in equality or perpetuate a disadvantaged group? Who never learn to walk well and become dependent on their crutches.

Constitutional law and Supreme Court judgements hold that equality does not require the law to treat all individuals in the same manner. But if classifications are made between individuals these should be reasonable, that is founded on "intelligible differentia" and that differentia must have a "rational relation" to the object sought to be achieved.

Looking at gender equality the approach normally taken is that women are different from men because they are weaker and subordinate and consequently need protection. Women are basically thought of as wives and mothers and as such allocated the role and responsibility of looking after the home and the children. Because of this role they are economically dependent on men. But the protectionist approach reinforces this difference and continues it. On the other hand, taking into consideration that women bear children, an attempt must be made to examine the difficulties faced by women because of this difference and give them special treatment, i.e. a working woman be given proper and adequate maternity leave, and not penalised promotionally for this, thus treating them equally. This compensatory approach acknowledges that pregnancy and child bearing and taking care of a small child make a women's life different and this difference must be clearly recognised and its relevance acknowledged. Thus, this historically disadvantaged group needs compensatory and corrective treatment, because failure to appreciate the difference only serves to reinforce and perpetuate the differences and not improve the position of women.

As Judges and lawyers we are required to do justice and justice requires an even hand. Without equality there is no justice. Justice has to be done without fear or favour, affection or ill-will or taking into consideration such factors as race, caste, sex etc. In a model society one would expect every individual to have equal opportunity and equal chances and be able to lead a life of dignity so that one can realise his/her aspirations.

Today carrying the historical baggage it is difficult to understand and appreciate what is true equality. We face difficulties because they are no definite parameters. What might have looked just and fair 50 years ago no longer looks just and fair in the manner of treatment of women. 70 years ago, Sudhansu Bala Hazra, a young woman in Calcutta was refused the right to practise on the ground that women were not fit for the "hurly burly of the legal profession". But today, there are women in the legal profession both as practising lawyers and as judges, though the number of judges is comparatively few. In the higher judiciary there are about 10 women judges out of approximately 500 judges and a small percentage in the subordinate judiciary.

However, there cannot be any hard and fast rule, but it is a matter of approach. We as lawyers and judges have to think equality before we can write equality. Writing judgments is an art but the thought process is made up of our background and upbringing. And if this thought process or language of the mind is not right, we have to re-educate ourselves. The forces that make us what we are, lie in our consciousness. The way your father treated your mother or how they dealt with you and your siblings as a child are all part of the sum total of that consciousness. But so is the way that you treat your mothers, wives and daughters. And if you are made aware that you don't treat them fairly or equally, you can try and learn the language of equality. For as Gandhiji said "Every home is a University and the parents are its teachers".

Since law and the needs of society are constantly changing, the knowledge of law requires constant refreshing. Similarly attitudes and approaches that influenced one in youth, have to be re-examined. It is a continuous process of educating oneself. The effect of re-educating oneself cannot be over estimated especially in bringing about true equality and justice. The function of the judiciary is to provide justice, that is, it's primary goal. How do we educate ourselves to be a good judge, that is, a judge to whom integrity and impartiality and a judicious temperament are of paramount importance. A judge is always on display and it is not only his judgments but his manner of dealing with the public and people that is important. He has to conduct himself with dignity and decorum and without prejudice. There can be no dichotomy in his thought process while writing judgments and his other behaviour or reactions outside court. He must recognise a woman's rights.

A judge in his dealings with the public has to be doubly careful, extra circumspect, because like Caeser's wife no one should be able to point a finger at him. The public comes in contact first with a Magistrate or Subordinate Judge and that is the impression of the judiciary which he carries. I will tell you a small incident. When I was appointed a Judge of the Delhi High Court in 1978, a lady who was a neighbour asked me, whether the Judicial Magistrate of the area was my boss. "He is all powerful", she said. So you can see from this incident that for the public, the Subordinate Judge or Magistrate is the most visible rung of the judiciary and the one with which the public is most concerned. So his attitudes are most important.

Once a matter has been heard in court, the judge has to take a decision after assessing the arguments and the position of the various parties. The ultimate decision is contained in the judgment. "It is a reasoned pronouncement by a judge on a disputed legal question which has been argued before him." It is not an essay and stands in a class by itself. "The judge speaks with authority and what he says should therefore be spoken with befitting dignity. He should not affect a grand eloquence but he has to be impressive. The strength of a judgment lies in its reasoning and should therefore be convincing. Clarity of exposition is always essential. Dignity, convincingness and clarity are exacting requirements but they are subservient to what, after all, is the main object of a judgment, which is not only to do but to be seen to do justice". In writing a judgment, first the material facts have to be marshalled in a logical way, leaving out the unessential. The next step is to formulate and apply the law to them. This generally involves a critical examination of principles and precedents and is the core of the judgment. The conclusion follows.

It all sounds very simple, but is an extremely exacting exercise, because, in order to do it well, one has to master the facts and the law. The fact finder's perceptions and prejudices affect the decision. The judge has to be sensitive to the realities in the context of each case and not be influenced by his own predilections. Objectivity is the need of the hour in order to ensure equality. Equality will be a hollow concept if it were subordinated to every other value a court feels, is constitutionally pressing. It is important to have equality without discrimination as they are inextricably linked. As Hon'ble Justice Claire L'Heureux Dube of Canada has observed, "equality is not simply about equal treatment, and it is not a mathematical equation waiting to be solved. It is about human dignity and full membership in society. It is about promoting an equal sense of self worth. It is about treating people with equal concern, equal respect and equal consideration. *Those* are the values that underlie equality. Those are the values that are offended when we discriminate consciously or not."

It appears to me that the manner in which the judge treats a woman lawyer, a woman petitioner, a woman respondent, a woman witness and his attitude in trying to understand the problems of a woman litigant and his dealings with the female members of his family and friends and acquaintances, all add upto the sum total of his approach to gender and his objectivity and his sense of fairness. Because that is what equality and justice are all about. As Lord Diplock said law is about man's duty to his neighbour. And I say, that should make no difference if his neighbour is male or female."

I think everyone is agreed that integrity and impartiality are the real essentials of a judge. That is why the judges' oath says that he will decide without fear or favour, affection or ill-will. In the case of race relations, Lord Devlin said the social service which judges render, was the removal of a sense of injustice and for this both impartiality and the appearance of impartiality were essential. This can truly also be said with regard to cases pertaining to women and the girl child.

It is clear that the judicial function is not always automatic and therefore it is necessary to recommend and train intellectually able men and women to serve as judges who will decide cases as objectively as possible. Judicial independence means that judges are not dependent on governments in ways which might influence them in coming to a decision in individual cases. But judges are human with human prejudices. A judge is conscious that his reputation as a judge is likely to be adversely affected if he decides one way and favourably affected if he decides another way. Such pressures do exist. Judges are the product of a class and have characteristics of that class dependent on the family and the type of schools and universities they attended. As such there is a perceptive difference between the lower and the higher judiciary.

This difference is clearly illustrated by various decisions of the courts. The sensitivity recently displayed by the Supreme Court of India in rape cases is often lacking in judgments of the trial Courts and as has been observed "presents a rather disquietening and disturbing feature".

In *State of Punjab vs. Gurmit Singh & Others*[1], where the charge was of abduction and rape of a young girl of 16, the trial Court acquitted the accused. Dr. Justice A.S. Anand speaking for the Supreme Court of India observed in paragraphs 13, 14 and 15:

[1]AIR 1996 SC 1393.

"13. The trial Court not only erroneously disbelieved the prosecutrix, but quite uncharitably and unjustifiably even characterised her as a girl "of loose morals" or "such type of a girl".

14. What has shocked our judicial conscience all the more is the inference drawn by the Court, based on no evidence and not even on a denied suggestion, to the effect:

'The more probability is that (prosecutrix) was a girl of loose character. She wanted to dupe her parents that she resided for one night at the house of her maternal uncle, but for the reasons best known to her, she does not do so and she preferred to give company to some persons."

15. We must express our strong disapproval of the approach of the trial Court and its casting a stigma on the character of the prosecutrix. The observations lack sobriety expected of a Judge. Such like stigmas have the potential of not only discouraging an even otherwise reluctant victim of sexual assault to bring forth complaint for trial of criminals, thereby making the society to suffer by letting the criminal escape even a trial. The Courts are expected to use self-restraint while recording such findings which have larger repercussions so far as the future of the victim of the sex crime is concerned and even wider implications on the society as a whole–where the victim of crime is discouraged–the criminal encouraged and in turn crime gets rewarded. Even in cases, unlike the present case, where there is some acceptable material on the record to show that the victim was habituated to sexual intercourse, no such inference like the victim being a girl of "loose moral character" is permissible to be drawn from that circumstance alone. Even if the prosecutrix, in a given case, has been promiscuous in her sexual behaviour earlier, she has a right to refuse to submit herself to sexual intercourse to anyone and everyone because she is not a vulnerable object or prey for being sexually assaulted by anyone and everyone. No stigma, like the one as cast in the present case should be cast against such a witness by the Courts, for after all it is the accused and not the victim of sex crime who is on trial in the Court."

After convicting the accused, the Supreme Court observed that such matters must be dealt with utmost sensitivity. I can do no better than quote the words of the learned Judge "a murderer destroys the physical body of his victim, a rapist degrades the very soul of the helpless female. The courts, therefore, shoulder a greater responsibility while trying an accused on charges of a rape."

Let us compare these sentiments with those of the District and Sessions Judge, Jaipur, who decided Bhanwari Devi's case. The case of Bhanwari Devi indicates how the prejudices of a judge are displayed in a judgment. Bhanwari Devi was a Sathin in a village called Bhateri and was working under the Women's Development Programme of the Rajasthan State Government. She carried out a vigorous campaign against the evil of child marriage. She and her husband allegedly received several threats and were subjected to severe beatings by vested interests. When she succeeded in preventing the marriage of the one year old daughter of Ram Karan Gujjar, she was allegedly gang raped by five men on 22nd September, 1992. It is alleged that her husband was tied to a tree and beaten up. The victim's efforts to seek justice was futile because it appears that the culprits could influence the local police. Her medical examination was delayed.

The National Commission for Women, at the request of a voluntary organisation visited the village to investigate the case. They held discussions with medical experts, police officers and officers of the Women's Development Programme. They met the Chief Minister and asked him to take stringent action. Women's organisations were naturally agitated about the efforts to shield the culprits and the inertia of the state law enforcement machinery. The Commission took up the matter with the Union Home Minister and the Minister of Human Resources Development. On the basis of the Commission's Report a sum of Rs. 10,000/- was sanctioned from the Prime Minister's Relief Fund as relief to the victim. Subsequently, the case was entrusted to the Central Bureau of Investigation for investigation and a case registered.

After trial, the District and Sessions Judge, Jaipur, acquitted the accused. Women's organisations were indignant. The judgment delivered by the District and Sessions Judge shocks me, not so much for the acquittal of the accused, but, for some of the grounds on which they appear to have been let off; that they were middle-aged men of good social status and well placed in the caste hierarchy. An editorial in the *Pioneer* on 27th November, 1995 called this judgement morally repugnant and says that the righteous indignation of women's organisations is certainly not misplaced. On the contrary, it would be surprising, if the sensibilities of right minded and responsible citizens had not been hurt by this judgement. "The track record of India's judicial system in dispensing justice in rape cases has been anything but exemplary. To that extent the acquittal of the five persons accused of having gang-raped the Sathin working with the Women's Development Programme of Rajasthan is by itself neither historic nor even remarkable. If anything, it only further underlines the fact that rape victims in this country have only a faint hope of seeing justice being done."

What is historic, however, is the view taken by the judge in this case that the accused by virtue of their age and social standing are necessarily incapable of a crime like rape. The judgment suggests that rapists are usually teenagers. This may or may not be statistically true, but extending that to mean that all those who are not teenagers cannot rape is really stretching the point. If this were to be accepted, all cases of rape should be dropped the moment it is established that the accused have crossed their teens. Equally astonishing is the claim that since the alleged rapists were middle-aged, they must necessarily be "respectable", a contention supported neither by statistics nor by elementary logic. The most astounding reason given for acquittal, however was that the accused were fairly highly placed in the caste hierarchy, and one of them was a Brahmin and this ruled them out as possible rapists of a lower caste woman. Such caste characterisation of crime, apart from being morally objectionable, betrays an entire perspective. It is no secret that down the ages while upper caste men may have treated those at the bottom of the social ladder as untouchable for most other purposes, this has never constrained them when it comes to using the female body for their carnal pleasure. Why then should they be expected to make an exception when it comes to rape?

Such a judgment would have been reprehensible in any rape case, but the specific circumstances of this case make it more so. What is alleged in this case is not just that Ms. Devi was raped to satiate a few men's lust but that humiliation was inflicted upon her because of her campaign against child marriage, which went against the feudal set up. It is therefore of paramount importance that justice be done and be seen to be done. It remains the duty of the judiciary and the State to ensure that this does happen if others working for social reforms are not to lose heart and believe that they are not only fighting the feudal order but also a supposedly modern State.

I am told that it had been suggested to Bhanwari Devi after the rape to leave the village. However she said, "I have not done anything wrong and I will continue to stay in Bhateri." She was socially boycotted and her community ostracised her, her in-laws and neighbours despised her and called her a shame to the village as if she had committed a crime. A lesser woman would have given up but she fought it out. During her in camera trial, she had to testify in front of 17 men. It was virtually a re-enactment of the rape. She went through hell and even after the judgment she was not ready to give up. She said "I will continue my fight till I get justice... How can I ask people to fight for justice when I am unable to get justice from the State even though I am a Government servant". She is an exceptionally courageous woman.

But this case raises many questions: How does an international covenant like the Convention on Elimination of Discrimination against Women (CEDAW) help the Bhanwari Devis of this world? How can one prevent violence being used on women, especially rape which is a terrible trauma? How can one prevent harassment of this nature to a person who is doing her work conscientiously? How are the feudal attitudes to be changed so that discrimination and domination ends? Where is equality and justice, development and peace?

Despite the Constitution of India being in existence for almost 50 years and providing for equality of women and men and despite the Convention on the Elimination of Discrimination against Women having been ratified by India in

1993 and despite the special Rapporteur on violence against women being in place, the societal change is very slow....Gender sensitisation of the judiciary is a must.... They must be made aware of international conventions like CEDAW and Declaration on the Elimination of Violence against Women (20.12.1993). The study done by Sakshi, N.G.O, found that most judges were not even aware of these Conventions or Declarations and 64 per cent felt that women must share the blame for violence committed against women.

We have to strengthen international accountability, make provision for advisory services and adequate funding, improve the efficiency of the review bodies and bring about increased awareness of human rights by information and education and establish national institutions for promotion and protection of rights—and make "more fluid the interface between international and domestic law".

The Supreme Court in *Vishakha vs. State of Rajasthan,*[2] has held that it is now an accepted rule of judicial construction that regard must be had to international conventions and norms for construing domestic law, when there is no inconsistency between them and there is a void in the domestic law. In the absence of domestic law occupying the field, to formulate effective measures to check the evil of sexual harassment of working women at all work places, the contents of international conventions and norms are significant for the purpose of interpretation of the guarantee of gender equality, right to work with human dignity in Articles 14, 15, 19 (1)(g) and 21 of the Constitution and the safeguards against sexual harassment implicit therein. Any international convention not inconsistent with the fundamental rights and in harmony with it, must be read into these provisions to enlarge the meaning and content thereof, to promote the object of the constitutional guarantees. This is implicit from Article 51 and the enabling power of the Parliament to enact laws for implementing the international conventions and norms by virtue of Article 253 read with Entry 14 of the Union List in Seventh Schedule of the Constitution.

It is pertinent to mention that the immediate cause for filing of this case was Bhanwari Devi's case above mentioned, that is the rape of a social worker, which revealed the hazards to which the working woman is exposed and the depravity to which sexual harassment can degenerate. The Court held that the gender equality and the right to life and liberty contained in Articles 14, 15 and 21 of the Constitution were clearly violated as also the right to practice a profession as contained in Article 19(1)(g). It was of the view that the fundamental right to carry on any occupation, trade or profession depends on the availability of a "safe" working environment. The right to life means life with dignity. The primary responsibility for ensuring such safety and dignity through suitable legislation and the creation of a mechanism for enforcement is of the legislature and the executive. However, since the matter had been brought before the Court indicating that instances of sexual harassment resulted in violation of the fundamental rights of women workers under Articles 14, 19 and

---

[2]AIR 1997 SC 3011.

21, the Court was of the view that for effective redressal required guidelines be laid down for the protection of those rights to fill the legislative vacuum.

Consequently the Court proceeded to lay down the guidelines and requested the Central Government/State Governments to adopt suitable measures including legislation to ensure that the guidelines are observed. It further states that the guidelines would not prejudice any rights available under the Protection of Human Rights Act, 1993. It also directed that the guidelines and norms laid down be strictly observed in all work places for the preservation and enforcement of the right to gender equality of the working women. It further observed that these guidelines would be binding and enforceable in law until suitable legislation is enacted to occupy the field.

As is apparent from what is outlined above, the Supreme Court of India is trying to teach a new language of equality and bring about a change in the consciousness....of the lower judiciary, employers and others.

Lord Justice Scrutton said, "the habits you are trained in, the people with whom you mix, lead to your having a certain class of ideas of such a nature that when you have to deal with other ideas you do not give as sound and accurate judgments as you would wish". That is why one group of people with certain commitments can say to another group, "where are your impartial judges? They all move in the same circle as the employers and they are all educated and nursed in the same ideas as the employers. How can a labour man or a trade unionist get impartial justice?" Consequently, it is clear that it is very difficult "to be sure that you have put yourself into a thoroughly impartial position between two disputants, one of your own class and one not of your class". This could easily be read as one of your own sex and one not of your sex. In a country where a criminal offence is perpetrated on women every seven minutes, a woman raped every 53 minutes and one murdered for dowry every 110 minutes, impartiality in decision making is a must.

So can a woman get impartial justice from a man? Or conversely, can a man get impartial justice from a woman? The answer is.... "Yes" .... in both cases. But judges have to learn the language of equality and be impartial and try and place themselves alternately in the shoes of the two disputants and appreciate the problem and give an objective decision. This process of learning the language of equality is slow—but has to be encouraged. Otherwise there will be no equality and no justice. As one learns a new language when one goes to a new country, so must we learn the language of equality as we enter a new century, with hope and with desire to remove injustice.

BIBLIOGRAPHY

1.	The Writing of Judgments	Lord Macmillan
2.	Gender Justice— Paper read on 5th December, 1995 at Patna, at the Seminar on Gender Justice organised by the National Commission for Women.	Leila Seth
3.	Constitutional Challenges and Contesting Discourses: Equality and Family In *Subversive Sites,* p. 173.	Ratna Kapur and Brenda Cossman
4.	Guaranteeing the Rights of Women and Children: International Protections Paper read in August 1996 at the Seminar on Human Rights, an International Legal Perspective at Salzburg, Austria.	Leila Seth
5.	Indian Women: Victims of the Indian Constitution In *Women-March Towards Dignity'* p. 81.	Krishan Mahajan
6.	Social Action Litigation in India In *The Constitution of South Africa from a Gender Perspective;* edited by Sandra Liebenberg, p. 97.	Leila Seth
7.	Rape in India: An Empirical Picture In *Rape in India,* p. 196.	Sohaila Abdulali
8.	Durgabai Deshmukh Memorial Lecture 1997 on the Girl Child and Social Development.	Leila Seth
9.	Night Duty for Women: Protection or Discrimination? In *the Indian Women's Search for an Identity,* p. 165.	
10.	Making Equality Work In *The Indian Advocate,* Vol. VXXVII 1996-97 - Journal of the Bar Association of India, p. 22.	Hon'ble Justice Claire L'Heureux Dube

11. On The Rights of the Child In *India International Centre Quarterly,* Winter 1995, p. 79.	Leila Seth
12. Sexual Harassment: Moving Away from Discrimination—*Modern Law Review,* 1995 Vol. 58, p. 343.	Janet Dine and Bob Watt
13. Gender and Judges: A Judicial Point of View–Report by Sakshi (1996).	Convenor: Naina Kapur

9

Women and Education

V. Mohini Giri

The emancipation of women in the western countries had its effect on the movement in India as it developed during the latter half of the nineteenth century and the early twentieth century. In India the feminist movement did not take the aggressive and militant form which it took in some European countries, for it did not meet with much opposition. In the latter half of the nineteenth century, the struggles and agitations carried on by women were purely reformist in nature and emphasized the needs of women of a particular class - the small class of the educated and privileged women. But the mass of women in the villages and the workers in the field and the factories suffered many disabilities which were legally removed only by the Constitution of the Indian Republic, adopted in January 1950.

Education has long been one of the most decisive of our life-choices, the key to equal opportunity and the ladder to advancement. Without education, and especially without equal educational opportunities or skills and qualifications, men and women alike of certain classes and social groups have over the years been condemned to inferior status, women specially in their personal development, in their choice of work, as citizens, and in their power to influence government leadership, and decisions.

Widening access to education has been a major policy goal in most developing countries for the past three decades. This reflects a broad recognition that education is essential to economic and social development. The evidence is overwhelming that education improves health and productivity and that the poorest people gain the most. When schools open their doors wider to girls and women as well as to boys and men, the benefits multiply. Indeed, failing to invest adequately in educating women can reduce the potential benefits of educating men. This failure exacts a high cost - in lost opportunities to raise productivity, to increase income, and to improve the quality of life. Yet women's education still lags far behind men's in most developing countries, with far-reaching adverse consequences for both individual and national well-being.

Several indicators - including measures of literacy, enrollment, and years in school, reveal important patterns and trends in women's education in developing countries. Each of these indicators leads to the same conclusions: the level of female education is low in the poorest countries, with just a handful of exceptions and, by any measure, the gender gap is largest in these countries.

Education conceived as organised instruction is part of the development process. Theoretically, education must enable persons to acquire knowledge and necessary skills. This knowledge and skills should further enable them to compete for and acquire better occupational status or higher social status in life. Thus, education should lead to social and economic productivity of the individual and, as a corollary, of the society. These are some basic assumptions about education in an open and competitive society. Fair competition requires equality in the initial social status or situation affecting the person or one's community. Hence there is a need for protection or support by the State to those lacking such initial advantage or those who suffer from social and economic disabilities. It is universally recognised that "mother is the first school of the child", yet the formal educational system keeps her out of the school because of socio-economic reasons, foremost among them being the bias towards girls' education, primarily because of patriarchal attitudes. Thus, the society is deprived of 50 per cent of human power for human development. No doubt, in the course of history, the status of women in our country has changed for better in some spheres and for worse in some others. In particular, education has come to be considered more important for women than men at least in theory.

The University Education Commission (1949) remarked:

> **There cannot be educated people without educated women. If general education had to be limited to men or to women, that opportunity should be given to women, for then it would more surely be passed on to the next generations.**

As elsewhere, there is good deal of discrepancy between the idealistic notion of the Indian women and the actual life situation in which she finds herself. As Linsay Mackie and Polly Pattalo pointed out:

> **The education of women has ever been a matter of great debate. Opinions expressed about it have often been reactionary, sometimes absurd and occasionally extraordinarily insulting. It comes as no surprise that Dr. Johnson said that a man is better pleased when he has a good dinner upon his table than when his wife talks Greek.**

In particular, the Working Group on Higher Education of Planning Commission for the Ninth Five Year Plan has specifically examined the issue relating to higher education of women. Dealing with access and equity, the Working Group observed:

> **The major issue concerning higher education is expansion versus consolidation, access and equity versus means to maintain quality of education. While the issue has been highlighted in plan after plan, it has not been addressed squarely. Hence, even the increased plan outlays have not made visible impact on expansion of programmes and the development of infrastructure with the large percentage increase in student enrolment.** ***Unless, in the Ninth Plan, this is redressed, the system will continue to be paralysed by the sheer numbers entering it.*** **Both conventional and non-conventional solutions will have to be addressed in the Ninth Plan. These would include a leap forward for open education, not only as separate institutions, but also within conventional universities offering the dual mode to both separate student populations as also to the same student.**

There is also a need to be concerned about access and equity for groups in the system which remain marginalised. These are women who form almost half the country's population, the reserved categories, the minorities, and the differently disabled.

Social Inequity

In terms of horizontal segregation, women are concentrated in low-paying positions such as secretary, typist, beautician, nurse, caregiver and assembly-line worker. "Equal work but unequal pay" is still a common practice in India's private sector, Statistics have shown that in 1995 women on average received only 3 p. for every rupee earned by men.

If one analyses the women's education scenario, one would find that women's education is an area cluttered with contradictory complexes, opposing theories and tremendous emotions. In brief:-

1. On the one hand, India has a large mass of people either disinterested in or ignorant of the problem of education for women; on the other hand, a few enlightened women alone express deep concern about the problem.
2. The area of education for women is at cross roads between intellectual rationality and social conservatism. It is often emotional and ends in negativism.
3. Some people believe that education cannot be different for males and females. Hence, men and women should have the same curriculam content. But, there is another school of thought which believes that there are inherent differences between girls and boys. Therefore, the content of education should also be different. However, there is consensus of the common general objectives of education, namely, character formation, personality development, increasing employability competence and inculcation of civic sense.
4. Since education needs to be geared to the needs of individuals, one of its objectives for boys is employment, while the twin objectives of employment and home-making hold good for girls.

The women aspiring for higher education could broadly be classified into four categories:

(i) Employment oriented

(ii) Marriage oriented

(iii) Employment cum marriage oriented

(iv) Unspecified others

In taking up higher education and choosing a subject of specialisation girl students have in mind one or the other specific objectives. Where a professional subject has been chosen and then later on, in life they do not opt for a career of specialisation then, I need not emphasise, there is both waste of human resources and lack of national objectives. I have had occasions to discuss with experts about the non-availability of services of women agriculture graduates. After spending much time, energy and funds they do not utilise the knowledge they have acquired for the development of the society. Realising the importance of women's higher education *vis-a-vis* utilisation of their professional knowledge and skill NCW sponsored at the National Academy of Agriculture Research Management, Hyderabad, a Workshop on "Issues of Professional Women in Agriculture". The need is to evolve a system by which higher education resources are so channelised as would meet the demands of women, both in rural and urban settings. Women have generally been engaged in such traditional areas like teachers, nurses etc. A shift in a substantial manner, not in tokenism is needed.

The growth in the number of women students in higher education since independence has been phenomenal. While women constituted only 9.3 per cent of all students in institutions of higher education on the eve of independence the percentage of women students enrolled in all colleges and universities was 34.1 in 1995-96.

The pace of growth has been particularly faster in the last two decades, or so. The number of women enrolled, per hundred men, registered a four fold increase during the period 1950-51 to 1995-96. Noteworthy factor of the general increase in the number of girl students in higher education is the uniformity in their enrolment at all levels of education. Faculty wise, Arts stream accounts for the highest, followed by Commerce, Science, Education, Law, Engineering and Technology. The number of women colleges in the country has recorded substantial increase. It increased from 780 in 1986-87 to 1146 in 1995-96. It is significant that the University Grants Commission has a programme for promoting women's studies wherein it gives assistance to universities for setting up Centres/Cells for women studies. As on 31st March, 1996 the UGC had provided assistance to 33 Universities and Colleges for setting up such Centres/Cells (22 Centres and 11 Cells).

At the time of Independence in 1947 we had only 20 Universities and 500 Colleges. The number of students and teachers in higher education system was very small. At the beginning of 1996-97 we have 209 Universities and there is a tremendous increase in the number of colleges i.e. from 500 to 9278 in which the number of women colleges is 1146.

The annual report of the Ministry of Human Resources Development (1996-97) proclaims:

> **Women's education has always been a priority area and NEE envisages the entire educational system to work for women's education and empowerment. It has been emphasized that gender concerns must be built into all educational process. Emphasis has been laid on enrolment and retention of the girl child in formal and non-formal schooling, recruitment of rural women as teachers and removal of gender bias in the curriculam.**

One aspect of unequal relations of society, the world over and in our country, is the disadvantaged and marginalised position of women and girls in education, and specifically in higher education. While women form fifty per cent of the population, in higher education they form only about 34 per cent in graduate and post-graduate studies and 26.6 per cent in Diploma and Certificate Courses. The issue is even more of social justice and gender equality. One of the main reasons for the majority of the girls not being able to take up higher education is the weak base i.e. at the school stage, particularly in the rural areas. Added to this are, economic deprivation, lack of motivation and strong patriarchal attitudes against girls education.

I would very much like to draw the attention of women's universities to the needed flexibility in women's educational package. Creativity has to be an inalienable part of the educational content; Innovation has to be encouraged. Literally adhering to the knowledge of the past may not hold good to-day and for tomorrow. A periodic review of educational packages is very important. Unless girls and women are enabled to identify their needs with the education offered, the purpose of education will not be achieved.

The women universities in the country (5), the number is very small, could take a lead in this matter in association with the UGC and the women study centres. They could specifically examine the issues and recommend to the government and the corporate sector the needs of girl students, desiring and deserving, and to atleast render financial and motivational assistance to those who go in for higher education.

10

March of the Human Rights of Women

Halima Embarek Warzazi

In dealing with this issue which today is a major preoccupation of the international community, we must go back to history in order to be able to evaluate the progress in the promotion of women all over the world.

We know that thousands of years ago, in the societies ruled by the patriarchal system, man personified the power inside and outside the family.

According to the Egyptian sociologist Nawal El. Saadawi, as long as the matriarchal system was in rule, women through their contribution to agriculture were equal to men and their supremacy in the family structures was ensured. In that period people lived in communities where hierarchy and classes, masters and slaves were unknown.

But with the introduction of new techniques of production the common property of lands was gradually transformed into private property. The notions of property and inheritance put an end to the foundations of matriarchy and have led to the introduction of repressive systems against women. Consequently women were deprived from the predominant role they had been playing in the family and the community. They were converted to objects belonging to the father, the husband and the family. They were even excluded from the religious fields where they had enjoyed equality with men.

So, it is not surprising to learn that centuries ago the theologists in Europe contributed to the degradation of the condition of women accusing them of all sins including the original one. Women were considered animals whose value was determined by their usefulness. In other parts of the world, the same discriminatory treatment was reserved them. Manu, who brought the tables of law to the Indian people said: "Child, the female must depend on her father, young on her husband, widow on her sons, a woman must never be independent". Confucius had defined the role of women in one verb "to obey" and for Buddha: Women were the personification of evil.

In pre-Islamic societies, the birth of a girl was considered a curse. It was the tradition to bury girls, alive as soon as they were born. The father or the man of the family did the job. This tradition was abolished by Islam which condemned severely the practice. One verse of the holy Koran said to those who were justifying it for reasons of poverty: "Don't kill your children because of fear of poverty. We will secure their nutrition as well as yours. The murder you are committing is a horrible sin". Islam was the first religion which at the seventh century dealt with the condition of women in the Arabic peninsula to combat the discrimination against respect for life and the dignity of women and girls as well as their rights. The prophet had campaigned against women's discrimination by even saying: "All those, who ensured security, education and married their daughters, will be entitled to go to paradise".

This didn't prevent men from interpreting some verses of the Holy Koran according to their own interests and retrograde mentality. Their subjective interpretation had negative consequences on the condition of women in most Muslim countries.

Women all over the world, with very few exceptions, have, during long centuries endured their segregation, their oppression and their sufferings in silence accepting their unfortunate fate with resignation. It is only at the end of the 19th century and at the beginning of the present one, that changes began to happen. Through education of girls, access to work outside in the absence of men mobilised by the second World War and the flow of information even in the most remote places, women discovered their own existence as human beings entitled to be considered as members of their community.

However, in order to be recognised as such, their societies ruled by men had to put an end to discriminatory preconceptions. The move that followed this discovery by women was an impressive one in its apparent aspects but less impressive in fact. The world has certainly realised what a French author wrote in the 19th century while commenting on the situation of women in his country: "access of women to a perfect equality will be the biggest manifestation of civilisation and will double the intellectual strength of the human gender".

In Egypt, at around the same time, an eminent writer, Kaseem Amin, campaigning against the discriminatory status of women, said that it was impossible for a nation to be developed as long as it was deprived from the contribution of half of its population composed of women. But, it took a long time for this conclusion to be accepted at the national level.

In fact, the United Nations has worked very hard since 1945 when its Charter, provisions are mandatory for all state members, was the first international instrument to advocate the principle of equality between men and women. It proclaims in its preamble the determination of the people of the United Nations to "reaffirm faith in fundamental human rights, in the dignity and worth of the human person, in the equal rights of men and women."

In 1946, the Commission on the Status of Women was established with the task of preparing recommendations for the ECOSOC dealing with the promotion of women's rights in political, economic, civil, social and educational fields. However, it is after 1960 that the General Assembly of the U.N. and its specialised agencies gave more and more attention to all aspects of the discrimination against women. This attention given to women's problems all over the world was primarily due to the increasing participation of women in the work of the United Nations and other international forums..

Besides, in 1960, three important factors contributed to the awareness of international public opinion.

(1) The right of vote acquired by women in a number of countries.

(2) The awakening of the coloured people.

(3) Decolonisation.

This third factor led to the presence at the U.N. of African women, who brought their enthusiasm and innovative ideas to the Committee of the General Assembly dealing with world's social, cultural and humanitarian issues.

Their genuine indications supported along the years, by other women coming from Asia and Latin America led to a great number of declarations, conventions and resolutions aiming at the recognition and achievement of equality between men and women. Yet, even with the establishment of the Commission on the Status of Women, the international community did not look at the real issues of women as declared by Article 1 of the Charter, which declares that .... "one of the purposes of the United Nations is to achieve international cooperation.... in promoting and encouraging respect for human rights and fundamental freedoms for all, without distinction of race, sex, language and religion".

It is true that the first texts adopted by the U.N. dealt with the political rights of women, the nationality of married women and the minimum age for legal marriage. In fact in the U.N. and its organs, viz the ECOSOC the Commission on the Status of Women, the Commission for social, cultural and humanitarian questions, the problems of women were considered in their social aspect. They were registered along with vulnerable groups such as children, handicapped and elder persons.

Indeed for many governments, women were considered as minors and were dealt with as such. How would it be otherwise, when women, in their majority, were seriously handicapped by ignorance, the weight of backward traditions and prejudices? When women delegates arrived at the U.N., they found themselves obliged to face this *fait accompli*. Besides that, they had an obligation to act with due respect of their governments' instructions. Moreover, coming from countries where the living conditions were hard, these delegates did not hesitate to share the general opinion concerning the problems of women as social ones.

I was, at that time, one of them. While I had followed the trend for many years, I found one day myself trying to understand why western women delegates never reacted against that unfortunate position which in my opinion, was the main reason of the extended delay registered by the international community in recognising effectively human rights as inherent rights of women. Only recently, I found the answer to my question in a speech delivered by the delegate of New Zealand on the 12th February, 1946, at the first General Assembly Session of the United Nations on the occasion of the creation of what was to be the Commission on the Status of Women. "There is no need to stress the necessity for pushing on the practical work in connection with the parts of our Charter which emphasised the equality of women.... But there is something more than the intellectual battle and something more than winning a *political victory* in various countries and that is *economic and the social status of women....* During the course of the General Assembly meeting and the meetings of the Committees, the women delegates have been very busy in endeavouring to see what was the best way in which the questions of economic and social equality in respect of women could be pushed ahead. This declaration left me both astonished and indignant."

In the first Assembly of the United Nations in 1946, 17 women representatives and advisers took part, representing eleven member states, most of them from western countries. Consequently, they were only thinking of women from their part of the world, speaking of the progress they had made during the war, evaluating the kind of responsibility they had to accept in order to participate in the reconstruction and improvement of the standard of life of their countries, totally ignoring the question of human rights of hundreds of millions of women in the rest of the world which unfortunately were not represented at that time.

We had to wait until the admission of the newly independent countries to the United Nations, to hear and deal with all the issues concerning their people and women. By the end of the sixties, the United Nations began to adopt a new attitude towards women of the developing countries for whom the problem of development was a priority. In 1969, the declaration on progress and social development was adopted after long negotiations with developed countries which were not enthusiastic about it. This Declaration was a happy discovery for women delegates because they realised that they could, through the issue of development, breach the wall of discrimination raised by men.

The efforts deployed, since then, aimed to draw the government's attention on the interest of mobilising and integrating women in the progressive development process of their countries. This question was among the major preoccupations of U.N. institutions.

The first International Conference on women took place in Mexico in 1975, under the title "Equality, Development and Peace". One of the conclusions of this Conference was that women should and could contribute to the progress of their country as well as any man. In one word, women were recognized as a factor of development. Later on, a new step was taken, after the decision of the member states of the United Nations to recognise the necessity not only of the full participation of women in the development process but also to guarantee them the enjoyment of this development. They were, from now on, the factor and the beneficiary of that development.

In this respect, the prospective strategies of the third world Conference on Women in Nairobi (1985) stipulate: "It is necessary to recognise that women contribute equally with men to the orientation of efforts for development and must benefit from the advantages generated by that development".

This conclusion was very important as the notion of development has evolved in a positive way. It was finally admitted that development has to be evaluated not only by figures or statistics dealing with the income and economic growth but rather by a global development of women in the economic, social, cultural as well as civic and political field. Inspite of an increasing interest on that matter, a satisfactory concept in dealing with the problems of women was to be agreed upon only in 1992.

One year before the celebration of the second world conference on Human Rights, whose initiative was taken by my country, Morocco in 1989, I had to submit the draft agenda directly to the General Assembly of the U.N. for adoption. While I was preparing the draft I decided to pay tribute to women by dedicating to them its point 11, which read: "Examination of actual tendencies and new obstacles preventing from the complete realisation of men and women's rights including those of persons belonging to vulnerable groups." In doing so, not only did I take women off the vulnerable groups and consequently off the social framework, but for the first time in the history of the United Nations, women were able to occupy their place in the human rights field. From now on the status of minority was forgotten, compassion had no place and social assistance programs were established under gender equality, while paternalism shown towards women's promotion was over.

The World Conference on Human Rights in 1993 was a success for women, when it recognised them in the same manner as men.

The World Conference, in its chapter on the declaration and the program of action entitled: "Equality, dignity and tolerance", urges the full and equal enjoyment by women of all human rights which has to be a priority for governments and for the United Nations. It also underlines that the equal status of women and the human rights of women should be integrated into the mainstream of the U.N's system.

The fourth World Conference on Women of Beijing in 1995 was, in my opinion, the most successful one, amongst the four conferences held since 1975. There was no ambiguity in the declaration and the platform of action. All the problems were analysed and dealt with. Nothing was left out. The clash between North and South had, this time, little to do with politics. Women came to defend their rights. Once again, the stand was very clear: "Women rights are Human rights".

Those reading the declaration and the plan of action of Beijing will have no doubt about it. Inspite of all these fruitful events registered during the past decade, we have to be lucid to realise that much more progress has to be achieved imperatively. In fact, not all that glitters is gold. Many of the decisions taken during the conferences of Vienna and Beijing will require a long time for being really implemented.

The majority of women in the world suffer from poverty and even extreme poverty. Women are exploited, abused, raped, forced to prostitution and new forms of slavery. They are the first agonising victims of wars as well as of internal conflicts caused by ethnic, nationalistic and religious intolerance.

Recently, the horrors witnessed by the world in Bosnia have confirmed that men can be converted to terrible beasts capable of committing collective and massive rape of innocent women. This inhuman behaviour must effectively be punished as a crime against humanity. We found the same behaviour in Liberia, Burundi, Rwanda, the Congo, where men kill, rape and destroy for the success of their ugly cause. Furthermore, there are countries where women's dignity and lives have no value. Fanatic religious and opposed armed groups slaughter women, girls and proceed to torture children in the presence of their parents. They kidnap young girls and kill them after having raped them.

In Afghanistan, women have been forced to go back to the dark ages in flagrant violation of Islam. The doors of schools, hospitals and work have been closed for them. They cannot move freely. They are under constant threat for just being women.

Violence against women is widely expanding in all parts of the world. Women and girls are battered by their husbands, raped in the street or abused at home by the father or a close relative without any recourse.

Today there is a wide campaign against this world phenomenon through condemnations and sensitivisation of governments and public opinion. The Human Rights Commission has appointed a Special Rapporteur who, each year, discloses to the international community all kinds of violence against women.

The United Nations is also scrutinising the attitude of various governments toward traditional practices which are harmful to the physical and mental health of girls and women. A plan of action has been adopted at the international level in order to condemn and put an end to these practices including female genital mutilation which is affecting more than 130 million women and girls in thirty countries, mostly in Africa.

The preference accorded to the male has also a serious effect on the health and the level of education of girls. This tradition is the cause of female infanticide and pre-natal sex selection in some Asian countries.

Dowry related violence, the burning of the widows, and forced sterilisation are other serious violations committed against women. As reported by UNICEF, in its last report this violence "is the most pervasive form of abuse of human rights". It exists not only in our part of the world but in the developed countries also, which means that till today "to be born a woman is to be born at risk".

The present situation of women justifies a constant mobilisation of the international community, governments and all members of society.

The promotion of women and their access to the full enjoyment of all human rights as provided by the international instruments rely primarily on three factors:

(1) The political will of governments to comply with their international obligations in implementing the programmes of action in favour of women.

(2) The extension of education, to all women which represent actually the majority of the illiterate people in the world.

(3) The cooperation and the solidarity to be brought to women deprived of their rights or not able to defend themselves when exposed to a situation of violation of their dignity, their security and their freedom.

Concerning the first factor, the government should adopt what is known as "affirmative action" to prove its political will in the field of women's promotion. This policy can ensure the access of women not only to universities and employment but to political and governmental posts as well. Recent statistics show that only nine per cent of women in the world are represented in Parliament and four per cent occupy high posts of decision and national responsibilities. Some governments and political parties have decided to fix a quota in order to guarantee greater women participation in the political life of their countries.

In France, the Prime Minister decided recently to incorporate in the Constitution the principle of the parity between men and women in all fields. This is a real way of expressing the political will of a government. Moreover, it will be nonsense to think that any positive evolution concerning the status of women can be achieved without men's support. It is absolutely necessary to associate them to such as enterprise.

Sensibilisation, dialogue and ability of persuasion generally lead to success. Politicians must play the game with realism and sincerity because they cannot keep using women as voting tools only. Authority and power must be shared with those who represent often more than half of the electorate. On the other side, the women who have successfully acceded to high posts of responsibility should not sleep on their laurels and forget the others who are victims of discrimination.

Women who are organised can play a very important role in the defence of human rights of women. In my country, the mobilisation and the motivation of famine organisations and N.G.Os have widely contributed to the amelioration of women's image and consequently their status. This movement found its foundations on an event which had a big influence on the future of our women. In 1946, the late King Mohammed V asked his elder daughter to deliver an official speech with her face unveiled. In that period all women in Morocco were wearing a veil. She did so and the Royal decision was a clear encouragement to women to enter the political arena considered then, as a traditional male prerogative. In doing so, the monarch, in his capacity as Head of State and Commander of the Faith, showed thus, that he considered Moroccan women as full fledged citizens. In 1992, the Constitution adopted stipulates in its article 5 "all Moroccans are equal before the law".

Today we find women in all fields of national life: engineers, doctors, pilots, professors, diplomats, artists, who have won gold medals in sports etc. But it took a very long time to finally see women acceding to ministerial posts and to Parliament.

The progress is very slow in this field. Political parties have not yet really shown their readiness to contribute to the promotion of women. Power is still difficult to share. Besides as indicated in one of the numerous studies done on the condition of the woman in my country: "Inspite of all the progress, she sails in ambiguity among several reefs such as poor knowledge of the law, anachronism in the law, in particular, family law, male resistance, the paradox of female censorship and most importantly, insufficient education especially in rural areas. However, it is said that "the Moroccan woman knows what she wants". What she wants is to put an end to all forms of discrimination and violence particularly family violence affecting her. She also wants to be able to occupy a legitimate place in male dominated careers and in political activities in order to contribute fully to the well being and prosperity of her country. Women all over the world have expressed the same will and purpose. However, to reach their objectives, women should occupy also strategic positions like the one offered by the information and the communication through the mass-media. Studies have proved, that if the public opinion does not constantly put pressure on the government, the implementation of bye-laws aiming to the elimination of all factors of discrimination will be slow.

I would like to conclude by saying that time has come for the women to face the future, with determination. A future where there is no place for ignorance, prejudices, discrimination and segregation. The coming century shall be the century of ultimate progress and technology, as well as out and out competition.

A country which will neglect half of its population will be condemned to extinction.

Women have a vital role to play in favour of the progress of their societies, in the strengthening of peace and security at the national and international level, in the promotion of human rights and in the protection of the environment.

There are roles successfully assumed by women because they always have handled carefully their families where the society have confined them.

It is true, that life will not always be easy for those women who will choose to assume responsibilities of that kind. Discriminations, inequalities, injustice and harassment of all kinds will not disappear overnight. But as an author George Mathew Adams has said: "In this life, we shall get only the things we look for, for which we are ready to fight and we are able to sacrifice ourselves."

11

The United Nations and Gender Justice*

Nitin Desai

The advancement of women in economic and political life is perhaps the single most important change in our social systems in the course of this century. In the second half of the century the United Nations has played a central role in this advance by providing a platform for dialogue where a shared consensus would evolve, a consensus shaped not just by governments, but by an active women's movement. Besides raising awareness at the national and global level, this United Nations process has had an impressive range of outcomes in the form of specific conventions, culminating in the Convention on the Elimination of Discrimination Against Women, in action programmes and strategies from four high-profile global conferences and in the establishment of inter-governmental bodies, and institutions for research, advocacy, coordination and technical assistance.

From 1945-1962 the focus was on securing women's legal equality. The starting point was the creation of the Commission on Human Rights and the Commission on the Status of Women in 1946 and the Universal Declaration of Human Rights in 1948. To codify the legal rights of women and to ascertain the extent of discrimination as it existed in law and in practice worldwide, a vast global research and pulling effort was undertaken. Findings became the basis for global standards incorporated into international law through a series of treaties and conventions.

From 1963-1975, as more Governments responded to the standard setting by adopting national laws and programmes to protect women's rights, the focus broadened to encompass the economic and social realities of women's lives. Stress was placed on policy formulation, attitude change, political commitment and institution-building. In 1975, International Women's Year, the first World Conference on Women was held in Mexico City. Out of this conference came the three-part theme—equality, development and peace—which became the basis for the Organization's work for women in the years to follow.

The 1976-1985 phase coincided with the United Nations Decade for Women. During the Decade, the focus shifted from women's development needs to the recognition that women are essential contributors to the development process. Statistics collected by the United Nations made evident that women's equality

*The work of the United Nations for gender justice has been described in detail in *The United Nations and the Advancement of Women 1945-1995* (United Nations 1996).

and rights were key to the well-being of societies. In 1979 the General Assembly adopted the Convention on the Elimination of all forms of Discrimination against Women, an international bill of rights for women which came into force in 1981. And in 1980, a Second World Conference on Women, held in Copenhagen, adopted a Programme of Action for the second half of the UN Decade for Women which emphasized education, employment and health.

In 1985, the Third World Conference on Women in Nairobi reviewed achievements made and obstacles encountered during the Decade. The Nairobi Forward-looking Strategies for the Advancement of Women to the Year 2000, adopted by consensus, provided a framework for action at the national, regional and international levels to promote the empowerment and advancement of women.

From 1986 to 1995, support for women was woven into the development efforts of all the Organization's agencies and bodies. Women's issues were well reflected in the outcomes of the continuum of United Nations Conferences on education, children, the environment, human rights, population and social development during this period.

In September 1995 the Fourth World Conference on Women was held in Beijing, China. This was an epochal event involving the participation of 20,000 government delegates and over 30,000 representatives of non-governmental organizations and civil societies in the Conference itself and the parallel NGO event. The outcome of this Conference was a Platform for Action that emphasized the human rights of women and the need to mainstream a gender perspective in all sectors and at all levels of policy-making and planning to achieve gender equality. The Commission on the Status of Women was charged with the responsibility for monitoring the implementation of the Platform. In June 2000, a special session of United Nations General Assembly will assess the follow-up and propose further actions and initiatives.

As part of this review, the Committee that monitors the Convention on the Elimination of all Forms of Discrimination against Women (CEDAW) will provide information reported by the 182 State Parties of the Convention on follow-up actions to the Platform of Action as they relate to their obligations under the Convention.

The work that the United Nations has done for the advancement of women is the result of the empowerment of women that has taken place at the national level. This in turn has been driven by women themselves organized in activist groups, in human rights movements and in national political processes. A great deal has been achieved, but much more remains to be done to ensure that women have their rightful place in economic, social and political life.

Justice Sunanda Bhandare was a firm advocate for and also an embodiment of gender justice. Her commitment to human rights, women's advancement and social justice reflected values that lie at the very heart of the work of the United Nations for the advancement of women. The best tribute to her memory would be to ensure that these values are given full and effective expression at the national and global level.

12

Indian Women's Search for Gender Justice: Towards a Historical Framework

Vina Mazumdar

I

Historians of modern India have, by and large, tended to view the social reform movement of the 19th century as the foundation of the notion of gender justice and later, of the women's movement's active struggle for this goal in India. Some of us on the other hand, have been struggling through the last two decades to seek our roots in much earlier periods of India's history. This search has sought to counter the long held belief that Indian women's right to justice and equality was essentially a contribution of men - reformers, jurists and political leaders. It is not the intention of this paper to undervalue the contribution of such great men, but to introduce - in any historical exploration into this theme - the concept of women's *agency* which can only come by recovering women's lost history, which remained mostly unrecorded. One method used successfully by some anthropologists, and a few others is through re-interpretation of our myths and legends - preserved through oral tradition-sometimes recorded at a later date, with all the risks involved of distortion and biases of the recorders of different periods. To cite a few examples, one can take the contrasting views of many nationalist historians of the early 20th century[1] who projected a very high status for women in ancient India, which was succeeded by gradual decline in later periods. They were also the first generation to recognise the 19th century social reform movements as a new beginning to improve women's position in society. A few of them also started the argument that the transformation of Indian nationalism into a mass movement subsumed the reform thrusts, and consigned the 'women's question' to a low priority back seat, from which it went into oblivion.[2]

In contrast to the historians, who drew mainly on Sanskrit texts as their sources - I would like to cite the recorded views of Ishwar Chandra Vidyasagar

[1]Cf. R.C. Majumdar, A.S. Altekar, etc.

[2]S. Natarajan, Social Reform Movement in India.

- who was by training a product of the traditional system of Sanskrit education and a master of all the texts which many of the 20th century historians had to read with the help of translations, or interpreters. Vidyasagar claimed that:

> "mother India has always been unkind to her daughters, and I wonder why these unfortunate beings continue to be born in this country"[3]

Half a century later another 'reformer' - Mahatma Jyotibha Phule - from another corner of the country - boldly stated

> "the subjugation of women has been the basic instrument of maintaining Brahmanical dominance in Indian society.[4]

This contrast - between the views of recorders/analysts of a later period, and 'social activists' - who struggled not only for but also with women, to ensure some justice for them, has not, in my opinion, been adequately explained by contemporary analysts. Another unexplained coincidence, or fact - is that both Vidyasagar and Phule were 'dissenters' - who rejected the sanctity of much of our cultural heritage - especially the caste system.[5]

To turn to another doyen of modern social sciences in India - M.N. Srinivas - one finds two simultaneous theories of social dynamics in Indian society, as contradictory responses to hierarchical Indian social system which has demonstrated its resilience, and capacity for survival through thousands of years of our history and recurring movements of opposition and dissent. The first of Srinivas' theory, which has been accepted as valid not only in the context of India but elsewhere as well, is that of the sanskritisation process. Put in simple language - it projects a continuous struggle for upward mobility by groups classified as 'the lower orders/castes/communities' to climb the social ladder by emulating the behavioural norms and cultural values of the upper orders/castes/ communities. One of the major instruments of the sanskritisation process - in Srinivas' words, is 'the immurement of women' represented by controls over their mobility, seclusion from persons outside the family and kin network, denial of many basic human rights i.e. of divorce or remarriage after widowhood, and finally complex methods of appropriating women's labour, sexuality, identity, and their basic freedoms, including those of belief, worship, and values. Srinivas however was careful to explain that this process was manifested only among those groups which had already attained a degree of upward mobility through wealth, power, or education.[6]

---

[3]Translated from a tract written during the controversy over widow remarrige in *Vidyasagar Rachana Sangraha*, Niraksharata Durkaran Samiti, Calcutta. See also Vina Mazumdar, *Education and Social Change*, Indian Institute of Advanced Studies, Shimla, 1972.

[4]Translated from Marathi and cited in V.P. Vohra, *Liberal Thought in Maharashtra* (Ph.D. Thesis, Pune University, 1974, unpublished).

[5]M.N. Srinivas, *Social Change in Modern India*, Orient Longman, 1972.

[6]M.N. Srinivas, *Changing Position of Indian Women*, OUP, 1981.

He has however often complained to friends[7] that the other half of this theory has hardly been taken note of by his contemporaries or succeeding generations. This latter half put forward the thesis that the struggle for equality and justice by all those who are denied these basic rights is as old as India's hierarchical social system.

Sometime in the mid-1970s I asked Srinivas how he would interpret the response of women to the Bhakti movements of the medieval period. His immediate answer was that the very depth and extent of women's response to these movements (which he viewed as challenges to the caste/social/religious hierarchy, espousing human equality as their basic value), as evidence that women found the hierarchical system extremely oppressive. Hence their response - not only as followers but as 'leaders' of these movements.

My original question had been "were people like Akkamma Mahadevi in the South, and Meera or Lallan in the North basically saints, as we have been led to believe, or rebels?". I have, for nearly three decades come to recognise the great capacity of the Indian civilisation to contain social rebellions by deifying the leaders of such movements, Mahatma Gandhi's case being the latest.[8] Srinivas was inclined to agree with me but being a careful scholar - prompted me to get more research done on these figures. He, however, offered a very strong argument in favour of my half-baked theory.

> "All the movements that began as anti-caste hierarchy end up by being turned into yet another caste within the system".[9]

Some additional support for my tentative hypothesis I received from my late cousin Ashok Majumdar who had done a considerable amount of research on the Vaishnav movements. I never had a chance to get him to elaborate his cryptic comment—

> "All these movements were supported by the lower orders and were initially propagated in the language of the common people. But somewhere down the line the Brahmins captured the leadership and thereafter the texts began to be formulated in high flowing sanskrit.[10]

Further support came from the late A. R. Desai, to whom I had posed the same question as I had done to Srinivas. He remembered that his own father had written a book on 'The Childhood of Meera'[11]. He kept his promise to look it up and after some months informed me that there was enough evidence in the

---

[7]Personal conversation with the author.

[8]Vina Mazumdar, *Education and Social Change,* op.cit., p. 2.

[9]Personal conversation.

[10]On my insistent request he had written a short note on the position of women in the Vaishnav movement which the Committee on the Status of Women in India drew on in its attempt to portray the position of women in different religions (Chapter 3, *Towards Equality)*

[11]Novel by R.V. Desai - *Bala Yogan;* See also Neera Desai, Women and the Bhakti Movement, *Samya Shakti,* p. 92-99, Vol. 1, No. 2, 1984.

book to support my hypothesis - of Meera having been a rebel first. Recent work of Parita Mukta indicates that Meera's elevation to saint possible took place - because the 'lower orders' would not allow her memory to die down.[12]

Since I can not claim any expertise on ancient or medieval Indian history, let me now turn to the modern period, and my contention that the 19th century social reform movements never had gender equality on their agendas but basically sought to improve women's position within the family - primarily with the objective of countering the spread of Western religion, culture and values has not provoked either opposition or rejection. Women were projected as the 'custodians of traditional values', and to enable them to retain some control, particularly over the young men who were going astray, excited by the new ideas coming from the West.[13]

One grave mistake made by earlier historians of our freedom struggle was to see the pre-independence women's movement and the acceptance of gender equality in the Fundamental Rights Resolution of the Indian National Congress in 1931 as linear progressions from the 19th century reform movements.[14] Recent work by women's studies scholars, on the other hand, contend that the women's movement during the freedom struggle drew its inspiration from many sources. While the earlier phase owed a great deal to demand for education, and better legal rights thrown up by the Indian reformers and Western women's movements, the later phase undoubtedly drew heavily on the revolutionary ideas of Mahatma Gandhi's brand of anti-imperialism as well as the anti-imperialist or socialist ideologies of some sections of the International women's movements.[15] The outcome of these multiple inspirations was the emphasis on gender equality in social, economic and political rights. It is this demand that was accepted in principle and then reflected in the Constitution of the Indian Republic.

II

The Preamble to the Constitution of the Indian Republic posits five major principles as the foundation and aim of the Indian political system:

---

[12]Parita Mukta, *Upholding the Common Life: The Community of Mirabai*, Delhi, OUP, 1994.

[13]Vina Mazumdar, *Social Reform Movement - From Ranade to Nehru in B.R. Nanda (ed.)*, Radiant, 1990; *Indian Women: From Purdah to Modernity*, Vikas, Delhi, 1975.

[14]Vina Mazumdar, Women, Development, and Public Policy, *in* Women and Development Perspectives from South and South East Asia, ed. by Ronaq Jahan and Hanna Papanek, Dacca, Bangladesh Institute of Law and International Affairs, 1979; Vina Mazumdar, *Emergence of Women's Question and the role of Women's Studies*, CWDS, Occasional Paper No. 7, 1985; *An Unfulfilled or a Blurred Vision? Jawaharlal Nehru and Indian Women*. CWDS, Occasional Paper No. 30, 1998.

[15]Maithreyi Choudhury on the Sub-Committee Report, Leela Kasturi, Development, Patriarchy and Politics: Indian Women in the Political Process, *in* Patriarchy and Economic Development: Women's Position at the End of the Twentieth Century, ed. by Valentine M. Moghdam, WIDER, Oxford, Clarendon, 1996. Vina Mazumdar and Leela Kasturi - *Introduction to Women and Indian Nationalism*, Vikas, 1994.

> "We, THE PEOPLE OF INDIA, having solemnly resolved to constitute India into a Sovereign Socialist Secular Democratic Republic and to secure to all its citizens:
>
> Justice, social, economic and political;
> Liberty of thought, expression, belief, faith and worship;
> Equality of status and of opportunity;
> and to promote among them all
> Fraternity assuring the dignity of the individual and the unity and integrity of the Nation;
> IN OUR CONSTITUENT ASSEMBLY this twenty-sixth day of November, 1949, do HEREBY ADOPT, ENACT AND GIVE TO OURSELVES THIS CONSTITUTION.

The key words in this Preamble, in my view, are 'to secure to all its citizens', irrespective of their caste, class, creed, or gender. Though justice, liberty, equality and fraternity have been listed as separate principles, again the key to their interpretation is provided by the phrase 'assuring the dignity of the individual'. Thus without using the words 'human rights', the Preamble subsumes its meaning. During the debate after the publication of the Report of the Committee on the Status of Women in India,[16] Justice Krishna Iyer said, *rethinking the separate terms from the perspective of women who, despite the constitutional guarantees had not achieved real justice, or liberty, or equality, or dignity, - came up with the holistic concept of gender justice which united all the principles into one, to challenge the persistent denial of these promised objectives to the overwhelming majority of the women of India within quarter of a century after the birth of the Republic.*

The Committee on the Status of Women in India had, to an extent, tried to suggest the same sense by incorporating, at the end of the Approach Chapter of its Report, the following guidelines and criteria:

1. that equality of women is necessary, not merely on the grounds of social justice, but as a basic condition for social, economic and political development of the nation;
2. that in order to release women from their dependent and unequal status, improvement of their employment opportunities and earning power has to be given the highest priority;
3. that society owes a special responsibility to women because of their child-bearing function. Safe bearing and rearing of children is an obligation that has to be shared by the mother, the father and society;
4. that the contribution made by an active housewife to the running and management of a family should be admitted as economically and socially productive and contributing to national savings and development;

[16]Towards Equality: Report of the Committee on the Status of Women in India, Government of India, 1975, p.8.

5. that marriage and motherhood should not become a disability in women's fulfilling their full and proper role in the task of national development. Therefore, it is important that society, including women themselves, must accept their responsibility in this field;

6. that disabilities and inequalities imposed on women have to be seen in the total context of a society, where large sections of the population - male and female, adults and children - suffer under the oppression of an exploitative system. It is not possible to remove these inequalities for women only. Any policy or movement for the emancipation and development of women has to form a part of a total movement for removal of inequalities and oppressive social institutions, if the benefits and privileges won by such action are to be shared by the entire women population and not be monopolised by a small minority;

7. that if our society is to move in the direction of the goals set by the Constitution, then special temporary measures will be necessary, to transform *de jure* into *de facto* equality.

These guidelines testify that to the CSWI, the concepts of equality, justice or dignity were absolute values, and that unless they were achieved for all citizens equally, the promises made to the women of India by the founding Fathers (and a few Mothers) of the Indian Republic could never be translated into reality. *Equality, therefore, did not mean 'equality among equals.*[17] *but equality across the vertical and horizontal divisions of our plural society. Since women cannot be separated from their community, caste, religious group, class, occupational segments, they have to be perceived as a category among all these sections.* It is obvious that their status *vis-a-vis* men in their own section or *vis-a-vis* other women in our plural and hierarchical society, could not be analysed or defined without reference to the position of that particular group within the Indian socio-economic and political system. *Efforts to define or pursue gender equality or gender justice without this contextual setting would be futile.*

III

The contemporary Indian women's movement draws its strength from a wide range of diverse ideologies, class, sense of identity and understanding of the sources of women's oppression as well as priorities for struggles. This diversity is reflected in the movement's attitude to the state, law making and its enforcement, the concept of the rule of law and state policy - because most sections of the movement have sought to use law and state policy as instruments of social, economic and political change in gender relations and the dominant social construction of gender. They have sought to protect rights already conceded-and bring these within reach of all sections who have so far been denied access. They have sought amendments, or new laws and policies to counter some of the macro processes of change—economic, social, political or

[17]As stated by a Union Law Minister, commenting on the controversial Muslim Women's (Protection of Rights in Divorce) Bill, 1986 - in the documentary *"In Secular India"*, Mediastorm, 1986.

cultural — which constitute not only obstacles but also threats to gender equality/justice. In doing so however, the movement's position has not been static, nor has it been influenced only by women-specific issues or problems. The movement has been compelled to respond to the changing political, social, economic and other national and global realities - altering its strategies and positions at different points of time on the same issues. As a political movement the women's movement generates its own political dynamics which has to respond to the changing historical context of which it is a part.

The women's movement has never viewed the Constitution as complete or perfect, but only as providing: (a) the basis for a new identity for women as full citizens of the Indian republic; and (b) a source of their rights to equality, dignity and justice in all spheres.

The Constitution's radical departure from inherited social values represented to women of that generation its greatest intrinsic quality. For the women of my generation, with definite memories of pre-independence society and of the freedom struggle, the acceptance of gender equality in the Constitution was the fulfillment of a dream - of women's entitlement to an independent identity. For those of us who entered various professions of that period, the exhilaration of being accepted as equals by our colleagues and our families was a living reality. But we came from progressive families, had received the best education that this country could provide, and had little experience of communities or institutions which did not agree with the implications of the constitutional guarantees or remained unaware of them.

The first shock was from the investigations, and publication of the Report of the Committee on the Status of Women in India (1972-75) and the second shock with the declaration of National Emergency (1975-77) with the suspension of fundamental rights of citizens. The impact of these two was to reawaken the women's movement from its passivity and substantially determined its political ideology in the coming decades. New or renewed consciousness about the responsibilities that came with political rights drove the movement into questioning (i) the 'invisibility' of women's economic and social contributions and problems in state policies; (ii) the validity of wide-spread social beliefs that denied the real life experiences and aspirations of the majority of women-reflected within state policy, some legislation and the role of the judiciary in interpreting them.

Drawing on existing social science research as well as its extensive field interviews with women of different classes, occupational, social and educational backgrounds across the country, as well as the official data provided by the Census, National Surveys and the Election Commission etc. the CSWI's report demolished the validity of most of these widespread social beliefs e.g.

(a) that Indian cultural traditions did not permit women to work for a living;

(b) that Hindu society did not traditionally permit either divorce or remarriage of widows;

(c) that polygamy was mainly confined to Muslims because of Islamic law;

(d) that dowry was a practice deep-rooted in traditional culture, and would disappear with the spread of education and employment among women;

(e) or that uneducated women's 'backward consciousness' kept them away from political participation.[18]

Internationally, the 'adverse impact' of modernisation/development on the majority of women in third world societies was the great discovery in the first half of the International Women's Decade (1975-85). The Indian Report preceded this discovery and provided an alternative analytical framework to the dominant economic model and theories of women's economic participation. Indian women also played a key role in the global debates in challenging theories of economic growth or stereotypes of the sexual division of labour, and also in the search for alternative strategies to achieve gender justice at least in the economic sphere, forcing the UN system to rethink its mandate by the second half of the women's decade, by taking cognisance of third world women's perspectives on international development strategies.[19]

Within the country the movement struggled to change policies and laws that permitted, promoted or aggravated both invisibility and devaluation of women's labour—as violations of constitutional guarantees, and removed from the realities of most women's economic identities. 94 per cent of women workers received no protection from the labour laws modelled on ILO Conventions. To the Indian movement, this denial of workers' status and rights to the majority of Indian women became a priority in struggles against the state, because in the movement's understanding they represented issues of survival and justice.

Identifying itself with the problems, perspectives and priorities of the majority of women - as distinct from the earlier phase, was a deliberate choice to assert a new identity for the resurgent women's movement - to break out of the inherited class and cultural norms and dominant perception of women's issues as mainly social - not political or economic - a distinctly patriarchal as well as colonial legacy. This particular preoccupation also pushed many in the movement into organising educational, economic, legal literacy and other activities to empower women from below. Such exposure led to closer interaction and a widening mass base of the movement and the adoption of new issues and priorities from the perspectives of poor rural and urban women[20] - of environmental degradation, livelihood insecurity, deprivation and discrimination against girl children, disappearance of customary rights of access

[18] *Towards Equality* - Chapters 3, 4, 5, 6, & 7. Alternatively, see Status of Women in India: Summary of the Report of the National Committee, ICSSR, and Allied Publishers, Delhi 1975.

[19] India's intervention led to the NAM mobilisation on this issue (Delhi 1977, Baghdad 1979, Delhi 1985); and persuaded the UN Commission on the Status of Women to Employment, Health, Education as sub-themes for the Mid-Decade Review Conference (Copenhagen 1980). The final Programme of Action adopted at Copenhagen, owed a great deal to the new perspectives/strategies offered by India.

[20] See *Shram Shakti:* Report of the National Commission on Self-Employed Women and the Women in the Informal Sector, Government of India, 1988.

to basic productive resources and the non-penetration or deliberate failure of the legal process to provide justice to the majority of women. Struggles for peasant women's rights to land, water and forest produce, for minimum and equal wages in the informal sector, for legislative protection for home based producers, for child care services, for all women in low income groups as a basic right, and for earmarking resources and mandatory quotas for women within all anti-poverty programmes - also represented the movement's assertion of democratic citizenship - women's right and responsibility to correct and redirect the State policies for national development and to insist on the fulfillment of the Directive Principles of State policies. The movement adopted a fundamentalist position that India is a welfare state and refused to subscribe to the theology of the free market or globalisation as the remedies of India's mal-development, unemployment, inequality and poverty. On the other hand, it has persistently opposed all moves to dilute the democratic, socialist and secular ideologies that provide the underpinnings of the Indian political system.

Its opposition to centralised authoritarianism during and after the emergency was manifested in its refusal to view the late Indira Gandhi as a symbol of women's power; its support for decentralisation of governance sought by the 73rd and 74th Constitutional Amendments and its insistence on giving priority to reservations for women in these local self government bodies as leaders of the women's movement pointed out in 1988, while making this recommendation— "we need a new leadership to emerge from below".[21]

Its absolutist position on secularism has brought it into confrontation with the right wing of the Hindu majority and Muslim and other minorities. The movement recognises the deep sense of religiosity of most Indian women, and the identity conflict experienced by many, especially in minority communities, when communal relations worsen. The initial mistake - of campaigning for the Hindu Code Bill in the 1950s, leaving the other personal laws intact—to be amended only when the 'community' asked for it, has crippled and haunted the movement in its current phase. The movement recognises that India's strength lies in its cultural heritage of the religio-ethnic diversity and it has been firm and active in opposing all communal conflicts but it has not yet resolved to basic critical issues. How does it achieve human rights for women while protecting the rights of minorities in general? Where the particular minority groups are also historically exploited (as in the case of the Scheduled Castes) or other backward classes or feel threatened by cultural and ethnic extinction (as in the case of Scheduled Tribes) - they tend to adopt regressionary attitudes with regard to their women's basic freedoms and customary rights for survival. How should the movement respond to such women's appeals for solidarity in their struggles to improve their own status?

[21]National Perspective Plan for Women to the year 2000, Government of India: Perspectives from the Women's Movement: Report of a National Debate organised by national women's organisations, Delhi 1988.

Secularism per se, though it provides a basic premise, cannot ensure human and social development for all India's communities, just as liberal representative democracy does not provide *defacto* equality of opportunities or justice for all. Nor does the pursuit of human rights in the form being loudly advocated by the wealthy nations of the North prevent fragmentation and alienation of individuals from their social environment.

Especially in the context of globalisation in its current form - with a weakened Nation-State system, and the increasingly unrestrained and unaccountable power of trans-national entities representing international capital—the Non-aligned Movement, the United Nations and the International Women's Movement are themselves crippled and divided by the same forces.

At the beginning of its new resurgences in the late '70s, the Indian women's movement had to face the rising wave of violence against women—both within domestic boundaries, and outside—as a new social phenomenon that threatened not only women but the culture and civilisation of India. In its persistent struggle against this phenomenon it has brought about many legislative changes, introducing new concepts like custodial or power rape in jurisprudence and some sensitisation of the judiciary but has failed to improve the state of law enforcement or justice delivery, especially to women from the weaker sections.

Recognising the flaws in our educational system which has increasingly been influenced by

(a) the dominance and hegemony of international knowledge systems; and

(b) the continued legacy of 'monoploy of knowledge power inherited from our own past' buttressed by the hierarchical elitism of colonial education.

The movement has struggled to make the system more responsive to women's perspectives and priorities as well as the values proclaimed by the Constitution. To this end it fought to incorporate a section on Education for Equality within the National Policy on Education (1986), ensuring thereby the inclusion of the section on Scheduled Castes/Scheduled Tribes as well as minorities within the policy. The large number of women within the education system as administrators, teachers, researchers, and students has encouraged the growth of women's studies as an instrument and a strategy—to question dominant views/theories/curriculum pedagogy—which reflect values/attitudes that are opposed to the principles of human equality and justice and welfare for all (*Bahujan Hitaya),* thus trying to arrest the educational system's current role as the most powerful instrument of the sanskritisation process.

This brief record of the movement's efforts and struggles during the last two decades, in my opinion, proves that its roots and vitality are drawn from India's historical evolution which is unfairly challenged very often as western inspired. The current unseemly and unjust criticisms of the proposed Women's Reservation Bill for State Assemblies and Parliament has to be evaluated in the light of this record of the women's movement, rather than preconceived notions and ignorance of the activities, priorities and ideologies of the women's movement.

Justice Krishna Iyer had observed that without the inclusion of gender, the promise of justice—social, economic and political—would remain impossible and unrealisable. According to the ideologues of the women's movement,[22] much of the present maladies of the Indian political system and the growing political violence within the country requires a far more active participation of women in larger numbers in the governance of the country. The proposed Bill will not solve all of India's political problems including the problem of achieving a just system of representation for a multi-culturalist, multi-ethnic and highly inegalitarian society. But that is a problem facing most democracies today.

We do not think that the present is an appropriate time to tamper with the basic framework of the Constitution. The movement has, therefore, specifically mentioned quotas within quotas for only the constitutionally recognised underprivileged, historically exploited groups, the Dalits and the Adivasis. Devising a more just and balanced system of representation will have to be faced as major challenges in the 21st century. But at the fag end of five decades of the Indian republic we need to ask a question—who among India's multiple 'peoples' are more civilised, humane and more socially developed—the Adivasis who do not destroy their daughters either before or just after birth, or the rest of us who seem to be increasingly becoming prone to these inhuman practices despite all the hue and cry against them for the last decade and a half?[23]

---

[22]Backed by a galaxy of concerned constitutional and politically concerned scholars, and citizens e.g. Upendra Baxi, P.M. Bakshi, Rajni Kothari, the late Prof. Iqbal Narain, Prof. V.M. Sirsikar, D. Bandyopadhyay and many others.

[23]Dr. Satish Agnihotri's (IAS - currently Secretary, Department of Women and Child Development, Government of Orissa) path-breaking analysis of juvenile sex-ratios indicates this. It also suggests that juvenile sex-ratios are tending to become more adverse to females in the more prosperous districts, which have lower female work participation, and absence of significant tribal population (Forthcoming, Sage, Delhi, 1998-99).

13

Women and Employment

Sarala Gopalan

Introduction

The role of women at the work place is not as recognised as their reproductive and other roles in the family. Many societies expect women to be by the hearth, cook, care for the family, and uphold the dignity of the family. This basic belief in the cultures of many societies influences the upbringing of girls and their exposure to education, skills and work outside the home. These societies do not expect women to work and earn a wage. This framework moulds the social attitudes to the status of women. The structures in the society also do not provide for substitution for the work of women either within the household or outside. The security afforded by the family, particularly by the men for the women in the household, is the return for the exertion made by the women for the care of the family.

The document of the World Bank on Gender and Poverty in India highlights the invisibility of women in the labour force owing to the definitions of work and methods of measurement of that work that ignores work done by women in the household and for the household.

The concept of the status of women has undergone a great deal of change over the last few decades. Globally, there has been acceptance of a role for women outside the household. Until very recently, it was not so honourable for women to work for a wage or remuneration outside the household. Work with remuneration has since become a symbol of economic empowerment for women. Unfortunately, women all over the world are yet far from realising such empowerment.

Global Situation

The situation of women is well summarised by James Gustave Speth in his "foreword" to the Human Development Report of 1995 referring to disparities in societies. I quote:

> "The most persistent of these (disparities) has been gender disparity, despite a relentless struggle to equalize opportunities between women and men. The unfinished agenda for change

> is still considerable. Women still constitute 70 per cent of the world's poor and two-thirds of the world's illiterates. They occupy only 14per cent of managerial and administrative jobs, 10 per cent of parliamentary seats and 6 per cent of cabinet positions. In many legal systems, they are still unequal. They often work longer hours than men, but much of their work remains unvalued, unrecognized and unappreciated. And the threat of violence stalks their lives from cradle to grave".

Analysing the global situation, the Report recognises that the opportunities open to women have remained limited despite higher female enrolments at all levels in developing countries and rising women's paid employment in industrial countries. The Report emphasises the following:

* Poverty has a woman's face - of 1.3. billion people in poverty, 70 per cent of them are women. The increasing poverty among women has been linked to their unequal situation in the labour market, the treatment under social welfare systems and their status and power in the family.
* Women's labour force participation has risen by only 4 percentage points in twenty years - from 36 per cent in 1970 to 40 per cent in 1990. Compare that with a two-thirds increase in female adult literacy and school enrolment.
* Women receive a disproportionately small share of credit from formal banking institutions. They are assumed to have no collateral to offer - despite working much harder than men.
* Women normally receive a much lower average wage than men, because they hold low-paying jobs or work in the informal sector and because they are sometimes paid less than men for equal work. The average female wage is only three-fourths of the male wage in the non-agricultural sector in 55 countries that had comparable data.
* All regions record a higher rate of unemployment among women than men.

A lot of work that women do is unpaid. A substantial part of this work is at the household level for the care of the family. The HDR 95 estimates that women's economic contributions of the order of $11 trillion a year is grossly undervalued or not valued at all. The Report links the undervaluation of women to the undervaluation of their work and non-recognition of the economic contribution they make. The following scenario emerges based on data on time use by women and men for a sample of 31 countries:

* Women work longer hours than men in nearly every country. Of the total burden of work, women carry on average 53 per cent in developing countries and 51 per cent in industrial countries.
* On average, about half of the total work time of both men and women is spent in economic activities in the market or in the subsistence sector. The other half is normally devoted to unpaid household or community activities.
* Of men's total work time in industrial countries, roughly two-thirds is spent in paid activities and one-third in unpaid activities. For women, the situation is reverse. In developing countries, more than three-quarters of men's work are in

market activities. Therefore, men receive the lion's share of income and recognition for their economic contribution - while most of women's work remains unpaid, unrecognised and undervalued.

Elimination of Gender Disparity

Women do not hold wealth or titles to assets in patriarchal societies where only men hold these. Religions and social beliefs preach dignity for all persons without any kind of discrimination. Unfortunately, in a materialistic world, hierarchical superiority and power to make decisions is associated with wealth and titles to assets; consequently social status gets inter-linked with economic status. Women holding no wealth and titles to assets, therefore, do not become equal in status to men in the society. This is the crux of the struggle of women to achieve equality in society.

In the past few decades, gender disparities have come to critical notice. The United Nations has brought emphasis on the elimination of gender disparities through its various agencies and associated organisations. The greatest contribution has been the intensive research on prevailing situations which has led to the Convention on the Elimination of all forms of Discrimination against Women (CEDAW) and a Commission to review the status of women in different member countries of the United Nations. The Human Development Report of 1995 brought out by the UNDP pointed out "investing in women's capabilities and empowering them to exercise their choices is not only valuable in itself but is also the surest way to contribute to economic growth and overall development".

There is no rationale for the exclusion of women. Women are essential agents of political and economic change. Globally, societies have to act towards replacing old concepts on the role of women and their status in society to achieve the goal of equality for women in all spheres of activity including social, economic and political. The message to the world is that "human development, if not engendered, is endangered". The three cardinal principles laid down in the Human Development Report, 1995 are the following:

* Equality of rights between women and men must be enshrined as a fundamental principle. Legal, economic, political or cultural barriers that prevent the exercise of equal rights should be identified and removed through comprehensive policy reforms and strong affirmative action.

* Women must be regarded as agents and beneficiaries of change. Investing in women's capabilities and empowering them to exercise their choices is not only valuable in itself but is also the surest way to contribute to economic growth and overall development.

* The engendered development model, though aiming to widen choices for both women and men, should not predetermine how different cultures and different societies exercise these choices. What is important is that equal opportunities to make a choice exist for both women and men.

The Fourth World Conference on Women held at Beijing, China, in September, 1995 discussed gender issues and gender relationships between men and women for achieving equality, peace and development. At the end of a two week deliberation, it came out with the Beijing Declaration and a Platform for Action by Governments, international organisations and non-government organisations. Clause 16 of the Beijing Declaration relating to women's role in economic development stated as follows:

> "Eradication of poverty based on sustained economic growth, social development, environmental protection and social justice requires the involvement of women in economic and social development, equal opportunities and the full and equal participation of women and men as agents and beneficiaries of people-centred sustainable development".

This led to the determination in clauses 26 and 27:

> "26. Promote women's economic independence, including employment and eradicate the persistent and increasing burden of poverty on women by addressing the structural causes of poverty through changes in economic structure, ensuring equal access for all women, including those in rural areas, as vital development agents, to productive resources, opportunities and public services;
>
> 27. Promote people-centred sustainable development, including sustained economic growth, through the provision of basic education, lifelong education, literacy and training, and primary health care for girls and women".

It is now the responsibility of all Governments, international bodies and non-government organisations to intensively pursue action on the basis of these decisions/recommendations to create an environment of equality for women in the society, in the interest of social justice and social development.

Women's Contribution to the Economy Invaluable

Based on the analysis in the Human Development Report, 1995, two broad conclusions are that men's work in the market place is often the result of "joint production, and not a solo effort", as much of it might not be possible if women did not stay at home looking after the children and household. Secondly, if women's unpaid work were properly valued, it is quite possible that women would emerge in most societies as the major bread winners or at least equal bread winners - since they put in longer hours of work than men. It is worthwhile to reproduce the following summation from the report on women's contribution to the economy:

"The monetization of the non-market work of women is more than a question of justice. It concerns the economic status of women in society. If more human activities were seen as market transactions at the prevailing wages, they would yield gigantically large monetary valuations. A rough order of magnitude comes to a staggering $16 trillion - or about 70 per cent more than the officially estimated $123 trillion of global output. This estimate includes the value of the *unpaid* work performed by women and men as well as the value of the *underpayment* of women's work in the market at prevailing wages. Of this $16 trillion, $11 trillion is the non-monetized, invisible contribution of women.

"Such a revaluation of women's work will thoroughly challenge the present conventions. For husbands to share income with their wives will become an act of entitlement rather than benevolence. The basis of property rights, divorce settlements, collateral for bank credit - to name only a few areas - will have to change completely. Men will also have to share more of the burden of household and community work.

"If national statistics fully reflect the "invisible" contribution of women, it will become impossible for policy-makers to ignore them in national decisions. Nor will women continue to be regarded as economic non-entities in market transactions. The starkest reflection of the low status accorded to women is the discrimination against them in the law. In many countries, women still are not treated as equal to men - whether in property rights, rights of inheritance, laws related to marriage and divorce, or the rights to acquire nationality, manage property or seek employment".[1]

Comparative Situation in India

The percentage of women participating in economic activity at the global level ranges between 8 per cent and 77 per cent. It is about 43 per cent, 60 per cent and 37 per cent for all high, medium and low human development countries respectively. It stands at 28 per cent for India. Females as per cent of male labour force ranges between 12 per cent and 81 per cent. The percentage of women is high in countries where the female participation is high as in China and low as in the Arab States where female participation in the labour is very low. South Asia and India occupy the lower ranges, while Sub-Saharan Africa, South East

[1]HDR 1995 page 6.

Asia and the Pacific have higher female participation rates and higher proportion of female workers, but much lower than China as shown in the table below.

Table - 1
Participation of Women in Economic Activities

Region / Selected Countries	Female Participation % (1994)	Female as % of Male (1994)
All developing countries	50	55
Industrial countries	46	61
Arab States	18	21
East Asia	69	80
Latin America and the Caribbean	30	37
South Asia	29	35
South East Asia and the Pacific	49	56
Sub-Saharan Africa	52	58
Least developed countries	53	57
European Union	40	52
Nordic countries	56	76
OECD	44	57
China	70	81
USA	50	65
Japan	50	64
United Kingdom	46	60
Brazil	31	38
Egypt	9	12
Nigeria	45	51
Ghana	51	63
India	28	34

Source: Human Development Report 1995 (UNDP)

Women in the Indian society are still looked upon as "housewives". The culture of work outside the home is more a symptom of economic backwardness and social backwardness. The comparatively low participation rate for women is indicative of this cultural bias in India. The 1991 census recorded a higher work participation rate for women at 22.27 per cent over the 1981 census at 19.67 per cent. This left some wondering whether this was a symptom of greater impoverishment of the society.

"Work" is defined in the census as "participation in any economically productive activity. Such participation may be physical or mental in nature. Work involves not only actual work but also effective supervision and direction of work. It also includes unpaid work on farm or in family enterprise". Such work has to be during a reference period of one year preceding the date of enumeration. The census also makes a distinction between *Main Workers* i.e., those who have worked for major part of the year that is six months (183 days or more) and *Marginal Workers* who have worked for less than this period.

It would be worthwhile to mention here that special efforts were made to capture women's work in the census by introducing specific questions in the census questionnaire in the household schedules and training the investigators to ask "probing questions" regarding the work done at any time at all last year. Reports were that respondents in some of the states were reluctant to admit that women in the households were economically active. To some extent, this social attitude has depressed the work participation rate for women in these states. Women's work participation is the lowest for Punjab at 4.40 and highest for Mizoram at 43.52 per cent in India. Generally, work participation is high in Andhra Pradesh, Arunachal Pradesh, Himachal Pradesh, Madhya Pradesh, Maharashtra, Manipur, Meghalaya, Mizoram, Nagaland, Sikkim ranging between 30 and 44 per cent. It is between 20 and 30 per cent in Assam, Goa, Gujarat, Karnataka, Orissa, Rajasthan and Tamil Nadu. It is between 10 and 20 per cent in the other States. Punjab is the only State with even less than 10 per cent work participation for women. There is a relationship between proportion of scheduled caste, scheduled tribe population in a state and the women's work participation rate in that State. Another factor that influences women's employment is the type of agricultural operations prevalent in that state. For example, labour intensive operations like rice cultivation employ a larger proportion of women than wheat cultivation.

The reflection of women's work participation is based on the definition of work in any system. The definition of work is based on the concept of work brought out in resolution No. 1 of the 13th International Conference of Labour Statisticians 1982. Normally, this definition describes economic activities as those involving production of goods or services for pay or for profit (classified as market activities) and production or processing of primary commodities for own consumption or own account production of fixed assets (classified as non-market activities). The census of India excludes non-market activities completely except cultivation of cereals, millets, and sugarcane. All other cultivation for own consumption is not considered as economic activity. Consequently, a great deal of work done by women on their family farms or households is excluded from economic activity. The National Sample Survey Organisation (NSSO) have a slightly wider concept of work and include market activity and any non-market activity relating to the agricultural sector. Both census and NSSO do not consider attention to household chores as economic activity. Similarly, earnings by beggars, prostitutes and gamblers are not considered as economic activities even though they generate incomes. It is estimated that the economic contribution to the Net Domestic Product (NDP) by the unpaid work done by women at home and on the farm would push up the NDP by 49 per cent and the contribution only on the farm by 33 per cent (Contribution to and Use of Social Product by Women - 1988 - ILO Report on Economic Evaluations of Unpaid Household Work: Africa, Asia, Latin America and Oceania - Women, Work and Development - 14, [1989]).

Table - 2[2]

Percentage of Total Female Workers to Population by States/Union Territories (Rural, Urban, Total), 1981 and 1991

State/Union Territory	1981			1991		
	Total	Rural	Urban	Total	Rural	Urban
India*	19.67	23.06	08.31	22.27	26.79	09.19
States						
Andhra Pradesh	33.54	40.03	11.81	34.32	42.48	11.94
Arunachal Pradesh	45.67	47.64	11.62	37.49	40.86	11.95
Assam	NA	NA	NA	21.61	23.27	07.52
Bihar	13.50	14.65	04.78	14.86	16.26	05.11
Goa	21.88	24.89	15.13	20.52	23.92	15.46
Gujarat	20.66	26.85	06.52	25.96	35.60	07.22
Haryana	10.60	12.29	04.45	10.76	12.62	05.08
Himachal Pradesh	31.86	33.37	11.26	34.81	36.61	14.08
Jammu & Kashmir	31.31	37.08	09.38	NA	NA	NA
Karnataka	25.33	30.66	11.83	29.39	36.60	12.90
Kerala	16.61	17.72	11.76	15.85	16.86	13.02
Madhya Pradesh	30.64	35.78	09.63	32.68	39.27	10.24
Maharashtra	30.63	40.85	10.14	33.11	46.06	11.44
Manipur	39.48	43.39	28.61	38.96	43.22	27.88
Meghalaya	37.49	42.05	16.12	34.93	38.85	17.23
Mizoram	37.72	42.81	21.88	43.52	47.11	39.37
Nagaland	43.20	48.30	10.93	37.96	42.78	12.09
Orissa	19.81	21.09	09.49	20.79	22.62	08.10
Punjab	06.16	06.90	04.20	04.40	04.37	04.48
Rajasthan	21.06	24.99	05.88	27.40	33.25	07.22
Sikkim	37.61	41.37	15.58	30.41	31.47	18.75
Tamil Nadu	26.52	33.55	11.97	29.89	38.50	13.10
Tripura	12.78	13.28	08.73	13.76	14.58	09.27
Uttar Pradesh	8.07	9.04	3.46	12.32	14.16	04.78
West Bengal	08.07	08.89	05.59	11.25	13.07	06.21
Union Territories						
Andaman & Nicobar Islands	10.78	12.01	07.20	13.13	14.36	09.60
Chandigarh	9.10	03.57	09.46	10.39	05.34	10.89
Dadra & Nagar Haveli	41.33	42.31	26.84	48.79	51.05	22.10
Daman & Diu	22.62	26.39	16.15	23.17	29.46	16.40
Delhi	06.84	08.75	06.69	07.36	05.46	07.57
Lakshadweep	09.16	11.29	06.65	07.60	06.96	08.10
Pondicherry	13.48	18.10	09.30	15.24	22.85	10.99

[2]Figures for India exclude Assam for 1981 and Jammu & Kashmir.

Source: Census of India 1991, series - 1 India, Paper - 2 of 1992, Final Population totals: A brief analysis of Primary Census Abstract, Registrar-General and Census Commissioner, India, New Delhi.

Micro level studies on women's work have established that nearly 55 per cent of the female population above age five would be included as workers if domestic work is included in the concept of work.

The definitions adopted by the NSSO are more representative of the nature of work in an agricultural economy like that of India. The NSSO has usual status approach which incorporates two categories on the basis of time spent namely principal status or subsidiary status. This nets in women who perform some gainful activity during the year along with their household chores. The phrase "family gain" in the definition of "economic activity" by NSSO helps to include unpaid work at the household farm or household/non-farm enterprises performed mostly by women and children. This focuses on certain special but marginal activities performed by women alongwith or in addition to their household chores such as free collections of goods (vegetables, roots, firewoods, fish, cowdung, cattle feed etc.), maintenance of kitchen garden, orchards etc., work in poultry or dairy, sewing, tailoring, weaving etc. for household use, collection of water and tutoring of children.

The NSSO looks at reference periods of a year, a week and days within the week. This approach helps assessment of employment, unemployment and under employment. It has been held that the NSSO methodology for the measurement of employment/unemployment rates are the scientifically best available for estimating the rate of unemployment that reflects the structure of the Indian economy. However, even the NSSO methodology does not do justice to women's work, as most of the activities of women are non-market activities such as dairying, poultry, weaving, etc. The existing definitions tend to under-estimate the economic role played by women according to the Socio Economic Research Centre, New Delhi.

Nature of Female Employment in India

The work participation rate for women in the rural areas is far higher than in the urban areas. As mentioned earlier, it was 22.27 per cent in the rural areas and 19.67 per cent in the urban areas according to the 1991 census. According to the NSSO survey 1993-94, the share of females in the rural work force was 35.9 per cent against 21.2 per cent only in the urban areas. The work participation rate for the females was 32.8 per cent in the rural areas against 15.4 per cent in the urban areas. The work participation rate for men was 55.3 per cent in rural areas and 52 per cent in urban areas in the same survey. The marked differential between rural and urban work participation rates is owing to the predominance of women's work in agriculture, which is largely in the rural areas.

The growth of employment is currently not keeping pace with the growth of population. The rural population growth rate between 1971-91 was around 1.77 while the increase in the rural employment rate was 2.52 during 1972-78, 1.74 during 1978-83 and 0.95 during 1983-88. The urban population growth rates during 1973-91 was around 3.80 and 3.10 against urban employment growth rate of 4.31, 4.10, 3.79 and 3.58 during the four interquinquennial NSS survey periods. The conclusion is there was increase of employment in urban areas and decrease in employment in rural areas. Since there has also been migration of unemployed from rural areas to urban areas, the urban unemployment situation and the backlogs of unemployment do not get completely wiped out. The NSSO surveys have analysed that (a) agriculture and manufacturing contributed to general decline of growth; (b) construction and mining sectors experienced steep growth: and (c) transport, storage, communication and services experienced no clear trend.

Table-3[3]
Number (in 000's) and Proportion of Main Workers by Industrial Categories and Sex - 1991 (India*)

Industrial Categories (1)	Persons (2)	Males (3)	Females (4)	%age of Females to persons (5)
Total Main Workers (I-IX)	278,940 (100.00)	216,018 (100.00)	62,922 (100.00)	22.56%
I. Cultivators	107.143 (38.41)	85.610 (39.63)	21,533 (34.22)	20.10%
II Agricultural Labourers	73,752 (26.44)	45,482 (21.05)	28,270 (44.93)	38.33%
III. Livestock Forestry, fishing, hunting etc. and allied activities.	5,306 (1.90)	4,298 (1.99)	1,008 (1.60)	19.00%
IV. Mining, Quarrying	1,717 (0.62)	1,504 (0.70)	213 (0.34)	12.41%
V. Manufacturing Processing Weaving and repairs				
(a) in household industry	6,743 (2.42)	4,523 (2.09)	2,220 (3.53)	32.92%
(b) in other than household industry	21,649 (7.76)	19,210 (8.89)	2,439 (3.88)	11.27%
VI. Construction	5,434 (1.95)	5,015 (2.32)	419 (0.60)	7.71%
VII. Trade and commerce	20,818 (7.46)	19,398 (8.98)	1,420 (2.26)	6.82%
VIII. Transport, storage and communications	7,843 (2.81)	7,639 (3.54)	204 (0.32)	2.60%
IX. Other services	28,535 (10.23)	23,339 (10.80)	5,196 (8.26)	18.21%

*Excludes Assam & Jammu & Kashmir.

[3]Note: Figures in parenthesis denote per centage distribution.

Source: Census of India, 1991 Series-1, India, Paper-2 of 1992, final Population Totals: Brief Analysis of PCA, Office of the Registrar-General and Census Commissioner, Government of India, New Delhi.

Distribution of Women Workers

The 1991 census highlights the predominance of women's work in agriculture as agricultural labourers and cultivators, which accounts for 79.15 per cent of all women workers. The highest proportion of workers amongst women (44.93 per cent) are agricultural labourers and the next highest is of cultivators (34.22 per cent). The remaining are scattered in the other industrial categories of the census with 8.26 per cent in category IX "other services". In all the nine industrial categories, female workers are less than 50 per cent of total workers, the largest being 38.33 per cent as agricultural labourers and the second highest in household industry at 32.92 per cent. Cultivators (category I), Livestock forestry, fishing, hunting etc. and allied categories (category III) and other services (category IX) have 18 to 20 per cent of women workers to total workers. They are comparatively less significant in the other categories.

Trends in Employment of Women

There has been a high rate of growth of employment of women between 1971 and 1991, much higher than the rate of growth of employment for men, both in the organised and unorganised sectors of employment as shown in Table-4.[4]

Table-4
Employment in the Organised and Unorganised Sectors during 1971 to 1991

Year	Male		Female		Total	
	Organised sector	Unorganised Sector	Organised sector	Unorganised Sector	Organised sector	Unorganised Sector
1971	10.43%	89.57%	6.16%	93.84%	09.69%	90.31%
1981	11.00%	89.00%	6.13%	93.87%	10.03%	89.97%
1991	10.23%	89.77%	4.21%	95.79%	08.51%	91.49%

The number of women workers in 1971 census was 31.35 millions. In 1991 census it increased to 89.77 million which is nearly a 200 per cent increase as against a 50 per cent increase for men from 149.18 millions to 224.36 millions. The proportion of women workers in the organized sector also increased from 11 to 14 per cent during this period as against men. The increase in the unorganised sector was much larger and consequently the proportion of women in the unorganised sector increased to 96 per cent from 94 per cent in 1971.

There is scope for a higher rate of increase in employment in the organised sector for women considering a higher rate of unemployment of educated

[4]Source: DGE&T, Ministry of Labour, Government of India, New Delhi; See also SAARC guide book on Women in Development p. 245; Status of Women in India-A Synopsis of the Report of the National Committee, ICSSR, New Delhi - 1975, p. 160; Towards Equality - Report of the Committee on the Status of Women in India, Government of India, New Delhi-1974, p. 153.

women. Further, the proportion of women in the organised sector has maintained an increasing trend and this could continue.

The matter causing concern is the change in the structure of employment between 1973 to 1994 for both men and women. The proportion of regular salary wage employment has declined significantly - for males in both the rural and urban areas and for females in the rural areas, while it has slightly increased in the urban areas. Self-employment has declined for both males and females in both urban and rural areas. Only casual wage employment has increased for both males and females in both urban and rural areas. Casual employment being associated with insecurity causes discomfort, particularly because it is more significant for women who are a larger proportion in the casual labour force. To some extent, the fears expressed about greater impoverishment driving women to paid work is founded on increasing casualisation and marginalisation of women workers. The changing structure is brought out in Table 5.[5]

Table - 5
Percentage Distribution of Employed (usual status, principal and subsidiary) by Sex and Category of Employment, All-India

Year	Percentage distribution of employed					
	Self-employment		Regular Salaried wage employees		Casual wage employment	
	Male	Female	Male	Female	Male	Female
			Rural			
1972	65.9	64.5	12.1	4.1	22.0	31.4
1977-78	62.8	62.1	10.6	2.8	26.6	35.1
1983	60.4	61.9	10.3	2.8	29.2	35.3
1987-88	58.6	60.9	10.0	3.6	31.4	35.5
1993-94	57.9	58.5	08.3	2.8	33.8	38.7
			Urban			
1972-73	39.2	48.4	50.7	27.8	10.1	23.7
1977-78	40.4	49.5	46.4	24.9	13.2	25.6
1983	40.9	45.8	43.7	25.8	15.4	28.4
1987-88	41.6	47.1	43.7	27.5	14.6	25.4
1993-94	41.7	45.4	42.1	28.6	16.2	26.0

With larger number of women trying to enter the labour force, unemployment of women and particularly educated women is increasing significantly and at a rate higher than that for men.

Shifts in Occupation

The 1991 Census captured shifts in the distribution of workers between different sectors/industrial categories. To quote the census, "while 69.4 per cent of the main workers in the country, excluding Assam and Jammu and Kashmir, were

[5]Source: Compiled by Socio Economic Research Centre, New Delhi, August, 1997.

working in the primary sector in 1981, their proportion has come down to 67.37 per cent in 1991 indicating a clear shift away from the primary sector. Within the primary sector, the proportion of workers in agricultural labour and those in mining and quarrying have increased. However, the proportion of workers in the secondary sector has remained more or less the same during the decade, being 12.96 per cent in 1981 and 12.13 per cent in 1991. Significant increase is noticed in the tertiary sector where the proportion of main workers has gone up from 17.63 per cent to 20.50 per cent. In the case of males, the proportion of workers in the primary sector has declined from 66.29 per cent in 1981 to 63.37 per cent in 1991; there is no significant change in the secondary sector; it has increased in the tertiary sector from 19.75 per cent to 23.32 per cent. In the case of females there is a decline in the secondary sector from 9.03 per cent to 8.07 per cent, increase in the tertiary sector from 9.35 per cent to 10.68 per cent with almost no change in the primary sector" as illustrated in Table-6.[6]

Table - 6
Main Workers by Industrial Sectors and Sex, 1981-1991, India*

Sector-wise/ Industrial Category	Persons (%)		Males (%)		Females (%)		%age of females to total in		Change in %age of females
	1981	1991	1981	1991	1981	1991	1981	1991	
Primary Sector	69.39	67.37	66.29	63.37	81.67	81.09	19.5	27.2	+7.7
Secondary Sector	12.96	12.13	13.96	13.31	9.03	8.07	14.1	15.0	+0.9
Tertiary Sector	17.63	20.5	19.75	23.32	9.35	10.68	10.8	11.7	+0.9
Total Main Workers (I-IX)	100	100	100	100	100	100	20.3	22.6	+2.3

* Excludes Assam and Jammu & Kashmir.

A similar shift is noticed in the areas. Surprisingly, in urban areas the proportion of workers in the primary sector has shown slight increase, that of workers in the secondary sector has shown a decline and those in tertiary sector have shown an increase. In other words, it appears that persons who are shifting out of the primary sector, mainly agriculture and allied services, appear to be getting absorbed in services rather than in the manufacturing sector.

The services sector includes workers in personal services and domestic services also.

A look at the proportion for 14 major States each with a population of 15 million and above indicates that there are three distinct patterns of shift, namely;

[6]Source: Census of India 1991, Series-1, India, Paper-2, Final Population Totals: Brief Analysis of Primary Census Abstract, Office of the Registrar - General and Census Commissioner, India, New Delhi, 1993.

(i) In all the major States except Bihar, the proportion of male main workers in the primary sector has declined and increased in the tertiary sector during the 1981-91 decade. In Bihar the proportion of male main workers in the primary sector has increased;

(ii) In most of the major States wherein the proportion of male main workers in the primary sector has declined, the proportion of male main workers in the secondary sector has also declined. Only in Gujarat and Maharashtra, this proportion has increased. Even in Maharashtra the increase is only marginal - 20.02 per cent in 1981 and 20.54 in 1991.

The proportion of male main workers engaged in the tertiary sector in all the 14 major States has increased and the increase varies between 5.68 percentage points in Haryana and 2.10 percentage points in Bihar. Bihar is closely followed by Gujarat where the proportion increased by 2.81 percentage points. In the remaining States the increase is between 3.01 and 4.00 percentage points; and

(iii) Among the female main workers, the proportion of workers in the primary sector has increased everywhere except in Kerala, Maharashtra, Tamil Nadu and West Bengal. The proportion of workers in the secondary sector has declined in most of the major States except Kerala and West Bengal. The proportion of workers in the tertiary sector has increased in most of the States, Rajasthan and West Bengal being exceptions.

To sum up, a shift away from the primary sector is taking place. But the increase is not taking place in the secondary (or manufacturing sector) but in the tertiary or services sectors. Among the females more and more proportion of workers is engaged in the primary sector, which is generally considered as a sector where wages are relatively low.

The NSSO quinquennial surveys brought out a clear shift from agriculture to non-agriculture for male workers but no such clear trend was noticeable for the female work force.

The National Sample Surveys have also indicated certain qualitative changes within the structure of employment of women as well as in relation to employment of men. Between 1977-78 (32nd round) and 1987-88 (43rd round) the proportion of men and women workers remain constant at 72 and 28 per cent respectively. Overall employment growth was faster in urban (4.12 per cent per annum) than in rural areas (1.33 per cent per annum). However, female employment in the rural areas grew faster than male employment, while it was slower than male employment in the urban areas. In the total employment, the share of rural areas had declined from 82 per cent to 77 per cent, but the share of rural female workers to total workers declined slightly from 24.9 per cent to 24.2. per cent. Women workers continue to be more predominantly rural than male workers.

The share of women workers in agriculture increased from 32 to 34 per cent and in construction from 14 to 24 per cent. Both these sectors employ substantial numbers of women. It has been analysed that the impact of differential rates of growth of women employment in different sectors has seen some structural changes of female employment. Agriculture accounted for 82 per cent of total women workers in 1977-78, its share declined to 76 per cent by 1987-88. All other major divisions of economic activities registered a higher share of 3.3 per cent in 1987-88 as against 0.93 per cent in 1977-78. The increase in other sectors was marginal. In the case of male workers, the share of agriculture declined more significantly from 67 per cent to 59 per cent. This explains the higher rate of increase of women's employment in the unorganised sector. Employment in the organised sector also grew faster at 3.09 per cent per annum for women against only 1.54 per cent per annum for men. The share of women in the organised sector workforce increased from 11.95 per cent in 1979 to 13.64 per cent in 1989. Public sector contributed significantly to the increase in the employment of women in the organised sector. Large part of this employment in the organised sector has gone to the educated. The proportion of educated persons in the female labour force increased from 47 per cent to 56 per cent.

The sectors of good promise for employment of women appeared to be livestock production and manufacturing. This has been significantly, owing to promotional activity of the Government through microcredit and training programmes of the Ministries of Women and Child Development and Rural Development.

One of the factors contributing to occupational shifts is migration of labour from rural to urban, rural to rural and urban to rural in different circumstances. The decline in the proportion of workers in agriculture is not yet very significant considering the very high proportion of reliance on this sector for employment.

The Concentration of Women's Employment

The census classification of the nine industrial and sectoral distribution (Table-3) clearly show the predominance of women workers in agriculture. Majority of women in agriculture are labourers working for a wage, and another significant proportion is cultivators. Consequantly, 58.43 per cent of women main workers are in agriculture. This is corroborated by the numbers that have been thrown out in the Survey (1987-88) of National Sample Survey Organisation (NSSO). The concentration ratio of women workers for two survey periods is given in Table 7.

Cereal crop production dominates; Production of oilseeds, cotton, fruits and coconut, sugarcane, spices, vegetables, flowers, plantations, other agricultural services have lesser numbers.

Another industry which has nearly 9 million workers in the primary sector is animal husbandry viz. cattle and goat breeding and production of milk.

In the secondary sector, manufacturing of beedi (1.7 million) and textiles and garments (1.07 million) weaving and finishing of cotton textiles in handloom, provide substantial employment (0.74 million); another significant industry is construction and maintenance of roads, buildings and waterways. All the other industry groups have less than half a million employment.

Table-7
Selected Indicators of Concentration of Women Workers by Industry Divisions (All-India)

NIC	Description	1987-88 P.C. workers M	1987-88 P.C. workers F	1987-88 Concentration ratio*	1993-94 P.C. workers M	1993-94 P.C. workers F	1993-94 Concentration ratio*
(1)	(2)	(3)	(4)	(5)	(6)	(7)	(8)
02	Raising of Stock	2.39	10.77	72.25	1.87	10.53	75.95
05	Forestry and logging	0.22	00.67	60.51	0.32	00.36	38.51
21	Manufacture of food	0.16	00.34	56.06	0.42	00.66	46.51
22	Manufacturing of beverages, tobacco and related products	0.47	01.55	65.43	0.11	00.08	28.79
25	Manufacture of jute and other vegetable fibre textiles (except cotton and coir)	0.05	00.06	42.80	0.08	00.19	58.33
96	Personal services	0.73	01.46	53.50	0.86	00.12	07.30
	All	-	-	36.58	-	-	35.97

* Concentration ratio=P.C. of women worker to total workers

In the tertiary sector, educational services (non-technical) and domestic services have a little over million workers each. Laundry and dyeing have 0.7 million workers, trade in grain and grocery has 0.67 millions. Another 12 industry groups have less than half a million workers but more than 100,000 workers each.

The NSSO has captured 384 industry groups. Among these, women workers accounting for more than 40 per cent in that industry group is only in 55 groups.

Women intensive industries that have more than 60 per cent of women workers are rearing of ducks and hens, cattle and goat rearing, manufacture of matches, manufacture of beedis, cashew processing, gathering of fodder, gathering of minor forest products, domestic services, cotton spinning, manufacture of coir, coir products, etc.

The women intensive industries are largely in the traditional sector. Most of these do not have a high skill requirement or programmed intensive training. The skills used in many of these are those required at the domestic level as household industry. In some of the traditional sectors like coir production, the Coir Board has been introducing improved technology and offering training to use the new technology. The Khadi and Village Industries Board has been involved in cotton spinning.

By far these traditional sectors offer low wages, and seasonal work. Organisation is also weak, leaving women with poor bargaining capacity. It must, however, be mentioned that these activities have geographical concentration in different parts of the country as is evident from the analysis of the selected states.

It is important to diversify employment of women into new areas. This calls for identification of areas of sustainable employment, supported by training, technology, access to markets and credit. It is important to intensify employment with upgraded skills even in the traditional areas, to enhance their economic contribution as well as their incomes.

Employment of women in the organised sector has still not ensured them support services like child care, health care, equal remuneration and most of all promotional avenues. Women predominate the lower hierarchies of employment and rarely move up to managerial and decision making positions. These are yet areas of concern.

Even for women employed in the organised sector, child care service is very conspicuous by its absence. Very scanty service is available in some urban areas. The reproductive role of women and the frequency of child bearing pushes them out of the labour market in a substantial part of their productive period. This hampers their economic contribution very significantly. The increasing awareness of family planning will be a measure of empowerment for women, releasing them for activities of their choice for a longer period of their lives.

Another major deterrent for women's employment is the lack of infrastructure for drinking water and fuel which occupies substantial part of their time for collection. Since water and fuel are essential for living, often they can consider employment only after their time is allotted for collection of water and fuel. These areas are slowly receiving attention. But we are far from any satisfactory solution.

New Perspective

Women have become aware. They advise us not to fritter away time and money on stereotyped training that does not lead to sustained employment and income generation. They have become prudent and want scientific analysis to be done and conclusions presented to them on what is feasible.

Poverty alleviation is among the most immediate objectives of economic development. The mainstreaming of women in economic development, starts with recognising what they are doing, but does not end there. They have to be acknowledged as a valuable human resource and true value given to their contribution. Secondly investments must be made in developing their potential in terms of education, skill development, technology transfers through technical training. Thirdly, special emphasis needs to be given for Research and Development (R&D) of appropriate scaled down technologies for occupations engaging women in large proportions. These are necessary for empowering women as equal partners in the economic development of the country. The illiteracy and cultural barriers need to be broken without any further delay. Work for women has now to be recognised as a indicator of empowerment rather than an indicator of impoverishment. Women have to move from being casual marginal workers to full time technically qualified persons who can contribute to the economy as much as to their families. This definitely will change the face of poverty that is currently of a woman.

14

Gender, Environment And Market Democracy

Vandana Shiva

1. The Re-birth of 'Free trade'

January 1st, 1995 heralded a new era in global trade. From this date, globalisation is legislated by the World Trade Organization (WTO). The WTO is armed with the power to make legal judgements in international trade relations and enforce the implementation of the Uruguay Round agreement. It has in fact replaced the General Agreement in Tariffs and Trade (GATT). Its primary objective is to ensure a free trade environment.

Globalisation is not new, even though its contemporary form is a new phenomenon. The colonisation of the entire world by European powers was the first wave of globalisation. The second wave began after the ex-colonies had gained political independence and was characterised by the universalisation of production and consumption pattern of Northern industrialised countries across the world. Better known as 'development', this universalisation was financed by bilateral aid agencies and multilateral development banks like the World Bank. However, since this universalisation is based on twenty per cent of the world's population, predominantly in the North, consuming eighty per cent of the world's resources, found mostly in the South, the globalisaiton of these production and consumption patterns would have needed the resources of five planets, not one. It therefore led to maldevelopment instead of development.

The third phase of globalisation is exemplified by trade treaties like the GATT, and the establishment of the WTO, which are imposing the interests of a handful of multinational corporations in all economic contexts—irrespective of their environmental and social impact.

The three phases of globalisation have also centered on different natural resources. The first phase of globalisation was clearly focused on the conquest of land. The second phase of globalisation was focused on oil and petrochemicals. The third and current phase of globalisation is focused on biodiversity and genetic resources.

2. Gender and Globalisation

The completion of the Uruguay Round of the GATT, and the establishment of the WTO, on January 1st, 1995 has drawn all domestic issues into the global economy. Furthermore, all matters related to life—ethics, values, ecology, food, culture, knowledge and democracy—have been brought into the global arena as matters of international trade. Needless to say, these have also brought the perspectives, and situations, of women in the remotest villages of the South into direct collision with the perspectives and power of men who control global patriarchal institutions.

Within this period of globalisation, gender analysis needs to make two major shifts.

Firstly, since globalisation is primarily a removal of national barriers to trade and investment, gender analysis needs to move beyond the exclusively 'domestic' model of analysis (which is either limited to the household or country) towards an understanding of gender relations between actors at the global level.

Secondly, gender analysis needs to move from the 'impact' and 'victimhood' model of thinking which focuses on 'the end result'. It needs to adopt a 'structural' and 'transformative' mode which address the underlying forces that form society in order to effect change. At present, most gender analysis is limited to how the global economy impacts on women. However, global financial, trade and corporated institutions impact on men and women, the rich and poor, and the different peoples, in different ways.

This is because they are 'gendered' institutions and structures. That is they are institutions created, dominated and controlled by men. And because of the predominance of men from the rich G-7 countries, these institutions and structures are therefore being shaped by a particular gender, class and race of humans. They are expressions and vehicles of the preferred visions, aspirations and assumptions of this particular group.

Gender analysis of globalisation therefore cannot limit itself to the impact on women. It needs to take into account the patriarchal basic of paradigms or models, processes, policies and projects of global economic structures. It needs to take into account how women's concerns, priorities and perceptions are excluded in defining the economy, and excluded from how economic problems and solutions are proposed and implemented.

Women, Ecology and Economic Value - 'Home' and 'Trade' as Metaphors

Ecology, economics and gender are all intimately connected to the construction of 'home' as a metaphor.

The household was originally the metaphor for the economy. The word 'economy' has its roots in the Greek word 'oikos', which originally referred to the family household, its operations and maintenance.

In 1988 Ernest Herschel, the leading German disciple of Darwin derived the new label 'oecologies' (from the same root word oilkos) to refer to the science of the relations of living organisms to the external world - their habitat, customs, energies etc.

Before the emergence of modern patriarchal models of 'economies', it was assumed that national economic affairs could be conceived as mere extensions of the housekeeper's budget. Similarly, 'oecologies' suggested that the living organisms of the earth formed a single economic unit resembling a household or family living intimately together.

With 'home' as the metaphor for both ecology and economics there was no hierarchical divide between domestic production and commodity production for exchange and trade. Neither was there a divide between nature's economy, the sustenance economy and the market economy.

Modern economic models however, reconstituted the metaphor of home—it was no longer the model for economic organisations. The home was effectively separated from the economy and made economically invisible. The home was also redefined as 'the absence of economy'.

As a result, the division of labour between the genders was also mapped out homologously—with females projected into the household, and males projected out into the economy. When the economy was an extension on the household, both areas had the participation of both genders. The removal of the economy from the household in reality led to the division or separation of the economy from the household on the basis of gender.

At the social level, this led to what Maria Mies[1] has called the 'housewifisation' of the domestic economy. According to patriarchal economic models, production in and for the home (and for need) is counted as 'non-production'. The transformation of value not disvalue, labour not non-labour, knowledge not non-knowledge, is achieved by two very powerful constructs—the production boundary and the creation boundary.

The Boundaries of Production

The production boundary is apolitical that, in its workings, excludes regenerative and renewable production cycles from the area of production. National accounting systems which are used for calculating growth, through Gross National Product (GNP), are based on the assumption that if producers consume what they produce, they do not in fact produce at all, because they fall outside the production boundary.[2]

Hence, all women who produce for their families, children and nature are treated as 'non-productive' and 'economically' inactive. When economies are confined to the market place, economic self sufficiency is perceived as economic deficiency. The devaluation of women's work, and of work done in

---

[1]Maria Mies, 'Feminist Research: Science, Violence and Responsibility', in Vandana Shiva and Maria Mies, 'Ecofeminism', (Kali for Women, New Delhi and Zed Books, London, 1993.)

[2]Ted Trainer, 'Developed to Death', Green Print, 1989, London.

subsistence economies of the South, is the natural outcome of a production boundary constructed by capitalist patriarchy.

By restricting itself to the values of the market economy, as defined by capitalist patriarchy, the production boundary ignores economic value in the two vital economies which are necessary to ecological and human survival. They are the areas of nature's economy, and economy value is a measure of how the earth's life and human life are protected. Its currency is life giving processes, not cash or the market price.

The Impact on Women and Nature

If we examine its impact on women, this market 'economic value' model has made women's work and all domestic production disappear in a blink of an eye. The exclusive focus on incomes and cash-flows (as measured in GNP) has meant that the web of life around women and the environment is excluded from central concern. The status of women and children, and the state of the environment, have never functioned as 'indicator's of development. This exclusion is achieved by rendering invisible two kinds of processes.

Firstly, nature's and women's contribution to the growth of the market economy is neglected and denied. Dominant economic theories assign no value to tasks carried out at subsistence, and domestic levels. These theories are unable to encompass the majority of the world's population—women and people of the South. As such, they are rendered statistically 'invisible'. Secondly the negative impact of economic development and growth on women, children and the environment goes largely unrecognised and unrecorded. Both these factors have lead to impoverishment.

The Facts Behind the Figures

Among the hidden costs incurred through destructive 'development' new burdens are being brought about by ecological devastation. These costs are invariably heavier for women, in both the North and South. It is hardly surprising, therefore, that rising GNP or rising global trade figures do not necessarily mean that either wealth or welfare increase proportionately. In fact, a very strong argument can be made to show that GNP and growth in international trade is increasingly becoming a measure of how real wealth—the wealth of nature and the sustaining wealth produced by women—is rapidly decreasing.

When trade in commodities is treated as the only economic activity, it destroys the potential of nature and women to enhance life, and produce goods and services for basic needs. More trade and more cash mean less life: in nature through ecological destruction, and in society through denial of basic needs.

And women are devalued. Firstly, because for many women in the rural and indigenous communities their work co-operates with nature's processes, and are often contradictory to the dominant market driven 'development' policies. And secondly, because work that satisfies needs and ensures sustenance is devalued in general. The deepening of the processes leading to maldevelopment has meant less nurturing of life and life support systems.

3. The Economies of Nature, People and the Market

As was mentioned before, the creation of 'growth' in the global economy has led to the destruction of nature's economy - through which environmental regeneration takes place. It has also destroyed the people's sustenance economy - within which women work to sustain society by what is perceived as 'invisible' unpaid work. This hard work is also often ironically called 'non-work'.

Of Other Economies and Sectors

But there are other economies and sectors that we should be aware of. Closely related to the concept of people's sustenance economy is what Hilka Pietila has termed the 'free' or informal economy in industrialised societies. This consists of the non-monetary core of the economy and society. The 'free' or informal economy includes: unpaid work for one's own and family needs; community activities, mutual help and co-operation within the neighbourhood and so on.[3]

In addition, there is the 'protected sector' which consists of production for domestic markets which is protected and guided by official means. This sector covers food, constructions, services, administration, health, schools, culture and so on.

Finally Pietila describes the familiar 'free-trade' economy, or what she called the 'fettered' economy which consists of large-scale production for export, and production to compete with imports. The terms in this economy are dictated by the world market, dependency, vulnerability, compulsive competitiveness and so forth.

Table A

	Time	**Money**
A. The free economy (informal economy)	54%	35%
B. Protected Sector	36%	46%
C. The fettered economy	10%	19%

In 1980, for example, the proportions of time and money that went into running each category of the Finnish economy is shown on in Table A.

In patriarchal economies, B and C (the 'protected sector; and 'fettered' economy) are perceived as the primary economy. And A, the 'free' or informal economy, is perceived as the secondary economy. In fact as Marilyn Waring[4]

[3]Hilka Pietila, 'Tomorrow Begins Today', ICDA/ISIS Workshop, Nairobi, 1985

[4]Marilyn Waring, 'If Women Counted', Harper & Row, San Francisco, 1988.

has documented, national accounts and GNP figures actually exclude that 'free' or 'informal' economy. These are seen as lying outside the 'production boundary'.

But what most economists and politicians call the 'free' or 'informal' economy is in reality for many women the 'fettered' economy. This is because, when the 'fettered' economy becomes 'poor'—that is, runs not deficit—it is the 'free' or informal' economy (which is predominantly made up of women's work) that pays to restore it to health. In times of structural adjustment and austerity programmes, cuts in public expenditure generally fall most heavily on the poor, and on women. In many cases, governments efforts to reduce the level of a country's fiscal deficit are implemented by making substantial cuts in social and economic development expenditure—hence real wages and consumption decreases considerably.

The Trade Metaphor Versus Nature's Economy

As the 'trade' metaphor has come to replace the metaphor of 'home' economic value itself has undergone a shift.

Value, which means 'worth', is redefined as 'exchange and trade'. So unless something is traded it has no economy value. And 'home' as the root, and metaphor, for the economy is substituted by the 'trade' metaphor, which is seen as the source of economic value.

The 'trade' metaphor, which is based on the assumption that something only has value if it is traded, has also rendered nature's economy as valueless. The marginalisation of both women's work and nature's work are linked to how 'home' is now perceived as a place where nothing of economic value is produced.

Nature's Resource Equals Life

This shift in economic value is central to the ecological crisis. It is reflected by the change in the meaning of the term 'resource'. 'Resource' originally implied life. Its root is the latin verb 'surgere', which evoked the image of a spring that continually rises from the ground. Like a spring, a resource rises again and again, even if it has been repeatedly used and consumed. The concept thus highlighted nature's power of self-regeneration and called attention to her prodigious creativity. Moreover, it implied an ancient idea about the relationship between humans and nature. The earth bestows gifts on human who, in turn, are well advised to show diligence in order not to suffocate her generosity. In early modern times, 'resources' therefore suggested 'give and take' along with regeneration.

But with the advent of industrialisation and colonialism, however, a conceptual break occurred. 'Natural resources' became those parts of nature which were required as inputs for industrial production and colonial trade. In 1870, John Yeates (in his Natural History of Commerce) offered the first definition of the new meaning: *in speaking of the natural resources of any country, we refer to the ore in the mine, the stone unquarried, the timber unfelled (etc.)*[5].

In this view, nature has been clearly stripped of her creative power, she has been turned into a container of raw materials waiting to be transformed into inputs for commodity production. Resources are now merely any material or conditions existing in nature which may be subject to 'economic exploitation[6]. With the capacity of regeneration gone, the attitude of 'give and take' has also lost its ground. It is now simply human inventiveness and industry which impact value to nature. Hence natural resources need to be 'developed'. It is only when capital and technology have been brought in that nature will find her destiny.

From now on it will become common sense that; 'natural resources cannot develop themselves; it is only through the application of human knowledge and skill that anything can be made of them, and most of the necessary work requires skill of a very high order[7]. Nature, and her regenerative and creative essence, has been transformed by this originally Northern worldview into dead and manipulatable matter. Her capacity to renew and grow has been denied.

Trading Water Rights—The Case of India

The trade metaphor is also guiding much of the work of environmental economics, making it indifferent to women's sustenance economy and nature's economy.

For example, the World Bank policy paper on trade liberalisation for India's agriculture sector recommends the creation of 'markets in tradable water rights'. It is argued that *if rights to the delivery of water can be freely bought and sold, farmers with new crops or in new areas will be able to obtain water provided they are willing to pay more than its value to existing users, and established users will take account of its sale value in deciding on what and how much to produce.*[8]

The institution of tradable water rights will guarantee the diversion of water from small farmers to large corporate 'super farms'. Tradable water rights will lead to water monopolies. In the logic of the market, tradable rights have a tendency to be sold to the highest bidder. Hence the wealthier you are the more power you will have over your access to water. It will also lead to over-exploitation and misuse of water—since those who deplete water resources do not have to suffer the consequences of water scarcity as they can always buy water rights from other farmers and other regions.

Besides aggravating the already severe ecological crisis in water resources, tradable water rights will destroy the social fabric of rural communities, creating

---

[5]Oxford English Dictionary, Second Edition.

[6]Joseph Meeker, 'Misused Resources', Resurgence No. 125, December 1987.

[7]Science and Technology for Development, 'Report on the United Nations Conference on the Application of Science and Technology for the Benefit of Less Developed Areas', Vol. II: Natural Resources, New York, United Nations, 1963, p. 18 Ref. 7.

[8]S. Pursell Gulati and A. Gulati, 'Liberalising Indian Agriculture', World Bank policy paper, No. 1172, 1993.

discord, and disintegration. The social breakdown in Somalia can be traced, in part, to the privatisation of water rights according to the World Bank policy. Tradable water rights are based on the assumption that no ecological or social limits should be placed on water use. Such limitless use will lead to abuse. The World Bank proposals on tradable water rights are in fact a prescription for social and ecological disaster.

The Peoples Struggle For Water and Land

The introduction of tradable land and water rights is often justified on environmental grounds. For example, a World Bank study by Pearce and Warford argues that;

In the absence of rights to sell or transfer land, the land owner may be unable to realize the value of any improvements and thus has little incentive to invest in long term measures such as soil conservation.[9]

This assumption is evidently false, since the best examples of soil conservation—the hill terraces of the Himalaya—are based on precisely the opposite reasons. Communities not threatened with the possibility of losing their resources and benefits have a long term interest in conserving resources.

The commodification and privatisation of land and water resources are based and promoted on the flawed belief that price equals value. However, all those working for justice in land and water rights, and working to prevent the ecological abuse of land and water, are asking for the opposite—the inalienable rights to resources. And where the resource is a common property resource, like water, the inalienability of common rights.

Experiments like the Pani Panchayat Movement and the Mukti Sangharsh Movement are leading the way for the ecological and equitable use of water. Pani Panchayats were formed to prevent the waste of scarce water resources through commercially remunerative cropping systems that have proven inequitable and ecologically destructive in the long run. To ensure equity, the Pani Panchayats treat water as a community resources, and not as private property. Furthermore, water rights are based on the number of family members not on the size of land holdings. The experiments of the Pani Panchayat have demonstrated that community management of a scare common resource is the only way to ensure both justice and sustainability.[10]

4. Freedom to Trade Versus Freedom from Hunger

With the completion of the Urugay Round of GATT, and the establishment of the WTO, the scope of the 'trade' metaphor has further increased. The two central impacts of the Uruguay Round are the removal of national boundaries

---

[9]Pearce David W., and Jeremy J. Warford, 'World Without End: Economics, Environment and Sustainable Development', Washington, DC: World Bank, 1993.

[10]Vandana Shiva, 'Ecology and the Politics of Survival', United Nations University Press and SAGE, London, 1991.

in trade flows, and the introduction of hitherto domestic concerns such as agriculture and intellectual property rights into the arena of international trade. The collapse of national borders in terms of trade, is linked to the treatment of entire domestic economies as 'non-value generating'. It is also linked to the introduction of the 'production boundary' at national borders.

The Liberalisation of Agriculture

Overall, agricultural exports have increased by about 71 per cent during the span of the last four year—from Rs. 21.98 billion in 1988-89 to Rs. 37.66 billion in 1992-93. On average, Indian prices of staple food grains are lower than world prices. For example, Indian rice prices are about 54 per cent lower than world prices. And prices of wheat in India are 17 per cent lower compared to world wheat prices. However, as more of these crops get exported, these domestic prices will rise, taking them beyond the reach of poor people.

As a result of the increasing domination of market forces in the Indian food sector, and reduced public policy intervention for food security, food prices increased by 63 per cent between 1989-90 and 1993-94. This has led to a decline in per capita food consumption in the last three years—from 510 gms per day in 1991 to 466 gms per day in 1993. In Rajasthan, the quota of wheat available under the Public Distribution Scheme has been reduced from 10 kg per unit to 3 kg; in Gujarat from 20 kg, to 10 kg; and in Madhya Pradesh from 12 kg to 3.5 kg.

This is in spite of the fact that the Essential Commodities Act has not been dismantled as yet. When, as demanded by trade liberalisation, food is available only at world market prices, starvation will most likely be the only certainty for the majority of the poor who were not even getting enough food prior to the 'reforms'. Tragically, famine seems the only inevitable future scenario for the country.

Why The Weavers Are Starving

The liberalisation of agricultural exports have also led to exports of cotton and yarn. The export of cotton has led to a doubling and tripling in the cost of yarn. It has also created massive unemployment in the decentralised handloom weaving sector which employs nine million workers, largely in home based production.

The main reason for the destitution of the weavers is that between 1991 and 1994 the prices of yarn had more than doubled from Rs. 226.30 to Rs. 415 per bundle for a count of 20, and from Rs. 174 to Rs. 491 per bundle for a count of 40[11]. The main reason for the rise in yarn prices is the liberalisation of exports. In 1994, cotton prices went up by 55 per cent, and yarn prices by 35 per cent. But there was hardly a 5 per cent increase in handloom cloth. In fact, hardly two per cent of the looms in Andhra Pradesh are working because of the crisis

[11]L.C. Jain, 'The Right Weave', Economic Times, February 3, 1995.

created by exports. Free trade exports thus translated into unemployment and starvation.[12]

How the People Pay

In the area of food and agriculture, this search for absolute advantage by capital can often be at the cost of local food security and farmer's survival. Applying this flawed logic of 'comparative advantage' to agriculture in poor countries like India can lead to policies that increase domestic food prices of cereals like rice and wheat because of exports.

It can also destroy the economic base of poor farmers in poor regions. For example, foreign imports of millets like sorghum, which are largely produced by Indian farmers, will put the millet produced by these local farmers in direct competition with the imported millet. Since these imported produce are usually much cheaper than locally produced grain or millet because of various hidden subsidies applied by exporting countries, local farmers will not be able to compete. Food security is therefore destroyed by 'liberalisation of both exports and imports'.

Ensuring Food Security

Ignoring this flawed comparative advantage logic, the National Council of Applied Economic Research (NCAER) study on "Export Competitiveness of Selected Agricultural Commodities" for India recommends the export of wheat and rice and the import of sorghum. It does not view coarse grains like sorghum as having export competitiveness. *'However, the less encouraging export competitiveness of maize and sorghum in itself is not a serious worry because these crops can be import substituted efficiently'.*

Food security in agriculture is based on a delicate balance between market forces and public policy, and the rights of consumers as well as producers. This balance would ensure that food prices are not too high to take food beyond the reach of already deprived consumers, and not too low so as to push out domestic farmers from production. Food is not merely an item of consumption. Food production is also the most significant source of livelihood for most Southern people. It is through their participation in food production that most people in India have an entitlement to food.

As Amartya Sen has so clearly articulated (in Poverty and Famines: An Essay on Entitlement and Deprivation), starvation and deprivation are linked more directly to declining entitlement than to decreased 'food supplies': *'In a market economy, a person can exchange what he owns for another collection of commodities. He can do this exchange of the two. The set of all the alternative bundles of commodities that he can acquire in exchange for what he owns may be called the exchange 'entitlement' of what he owns'.*

---

[12]Asha Krishna Kumar, 'Struggle to Survive', Frontline, March 10, 1995 p. 110-p. 112.

Cheap Food—A Prescription for Famine

Structural adjustment and trade liberalisation measures can create starvation and faminc by removing tariff barriers and allowing the flow of cheap food, which in turn displace peasants, and destroy their entitlements. The famines in Somalia, Rwanda and all of sub-Saharan Africa, can be linked to the removal of import barriers and the destruction of domestic production markets, imported food grains can be sold at much lower prices due to various hidden suicides applied by exporting countries. Hence the lowering of import barriers and flooding of local markets with imported food grains can actually contribute to hunger and starvation in societies which are agricultural based. While lower food prices might be good for societies with hardly any farmers, they are devastating for food security in peasant economies—where livelihoods depend on the sales of produce in domestic markets.

Therefore the impact of trade liberalisation on food security is different in different socio-economic contexts. For those items where domestic prices are lower than international prices, trade liberalisation leads to exports and thus a rise in domestic prices. Whereas for those items where domestic prices are higher than international prices, trade liberalisation leads to dumping, and a displacement of domestic producers from agriculture. In such a situation, cheap food can be a prescription for famine when it displaces domestic producers and destroys their entitlement.

The Unlevelled Playing Field

Furthermore, cheap food does not mean food produced at lower costs. High costs of production can go hand-in-hand with low food prices because agri-business corporations are simultaneously the sellers of inputs to farmers, the buyers of agricultural commodities from farmers, and the sellers of processed foods to consumers. So their profits are not only distributed across these different segments of the food production and distribution chain. But their profits are also spread space-wise across different countries, and timewise through futures trading. They can bring cheap food to consumers in spite of extremely high costs of production because of their monopoly control on the food chain.

Most national laws related to the production and distribution of food are laws aimed at curbing the monopoly control of trading interests. Trade-liberalisation is aimed at removing all restrictions for trade and trading interests. Trade-liberalisation therefore results in the removal of food security by removing the legal and policy instruments that protect the entitlements of the poor who have little or no purchasing power, and are therefore excluded from the market.

5. The Value of Knowledge: A Gender Analysis of the TRIPs Agreement of the GATT/WTO

The Trade Related Intellectual Property Rights (TRIPs) Agreement of the Uruguay Round of GATT, now institutionalised as the WTO, has for the first time brought into global trade the areas of ideas, knowledge and innovation. The clauses that refer to intellectual property rights (IPRs) in the areas of biodiversity and agriculture are of particular interest especially since this subject matter is closely related to women. Women are the original seed keepers.[13] Women still continue to be custodians of seed diversity[14]. Most women in our region are farmers. Women's rights and knowledge in agriculture and biodiversity are now being threatened by the TRIPs agreement of GATT/WTO. The TRIPs treaty is in effect setting up a 'creation boundary'.[15]

The agreements covering intellectual property rights, and the clauses supporting the patenting of life forms and processes, are the ultimate denial of nature's creativity and women's creativity. Furthermore, these stand to benefit only a certain sector of trade and society.

According to the TRIPs agreement of the WTO, the subject matter for patents has been expanded to cover both products and processes.

Art. 27.1 on 'Patentable subject matter' states:

> *Patents shall be available for any inventions, whether products or processes, in all fields of technology, provided that they are new, involve an inventive step and are capable of industrial application.*

The Indian Patent Act of 1970 does not provide for grant of product patents in the field of agricultural chemicals and pharmaceuticals. However, India's obligations under the WTO agreement made it necessary to have certain institutional arrangements in place before the January 1st, 1995.

According to Article 70.8(a) of the TRIPs agreements on 'Institutional Arrangements':

> *Where a Member does not make available as the date of entry into force of the WTO Agreement patent protection for pharmaceutical or agricultural chemical products, commensurate with its obligations under Article 27, that Member shall*
>
> *(a) not withstanding the provisions of Part VI, provide as from the date of entry into force of the WTO agreement a means by which applications for patents for which inventions can be filed.*

---

[13]Vandana Shiva, 'Staying Alive: Women, Ecology and Survival in India', Kali for Women, New Delhi, 1988.

———· 'Most Farmers in India are Women', FAO, June 1991.

[14]Vandana Shiva, 'Women and Biodiversity', Indigenous Visions, India International Centre, New Delhi, 1993.

[15]Vandana Shiva, 'The Seed and the Earth: Biotechnology and the Colonisation of Regeneration' in Vandana Shiva, 'Minding Our Lives', Kali for Women, New Delhi, 1993.

Further, Article 70.9 states that:

> *Where a product is the subject matter of a patent application in a Member [country] in accordance with paragraph 8 (a), exclusive marketing rights shall be granted notwithstanding the provision of Part VI, for a period of five years after obtaining marketing approval in that Member or until a product patent is granted or rejected in that Member, whichever period is shorter, provided that, subsequent to the entry into force of the a WTO Agreement, a patent application has been filed and a patent granted for that product in another Member and marketing approval obtained in such other Member.*

These obligations are heavily weighted in favour of international corporations and effectively undo the ten-year transitional period allowed under Article 65 of TRIPs—to change domestic patent regimes to align it with the requirements of the TRIPs agreement.

The economic rights a patent confers its owner is exclusive marketing rights. Article 28.1 on 'Rights Conferred' states:

A patent shall confer on its owner the following exclusive rights:

> *(a) where the subject matter is a product, to prevent third parties not having the owners's consent from the acts of making, using, offering for sale, selling or importing for these purposes that product.*
>
> *(b) where the subject matter of a patent is a process, to prevent third parties not having the owner's consent from the acts of: using, offering for sale, selling or importing for these purposes at least the product obtained directly by that process.*

Article 70.9 by obliging member countries to have an arrangement to give exclusive marketing rights for patent applications in subject matter currently excluded by our patent laws (in terms of economic impact) achieves the same results as if patent rights had been conferred for product patents in the area of pharmaceuticals and agriculture. As far as the economic impact of the ordinance is concerned, it will be the same as the impact would have been if the patent laws had been changed to cover product patents.

Further, the last phrase in Article 70.9 which relates the exclusive marketing rights to product patents applied for and granted in other member countries, biases an otherwise neutral sounding obligation against domestic innovators and companies of the South. In fact it favour transnational corporations.

This is because, firstly, it is transnational corporations that operate in many countries and can use this clause to their advantage. Secondly, because of global economic inequality and the devaluation of domestic currencies over a series of World Bank and IMF adjustments, the additional costs of transnational corporations filing applications in Southern countries are insignificant. Whereas the additional costs for an Indian scientist or company filing a patent application in the U.S. or Europe are exorbitant and will act as a barrier.

The obligation to give exclusive marketing rights on the basis of Article 70.9 is in effect loaded in favour of foreign corporations. Not only will this have serious economic consequences for Indian scientists and firms, it also undermines the fundamental rights of citizens granted under the Constitution.

6. Intellectual Property Rights and Human Rights

Article 47 Constitution of India.

> *The State shall regard the raising of the level of nutrition and the standard of living of its people and the improvement of public health as among its primary duties.*

This duty of the States is in fact a reflection of the fundamental right of citizens to have access to health nutrition.

The Rise of Monopoly Rights

The TRIPs agreement militates against people's basic human rights to food and health by conferring unrestricted monopoly rights to corporations in the vital sectors of health and agriculture. For example, the patent ordinance allows exclusive marketing rights in the area of agricultural chemicals. The Plant Varieties Act being drafted by the Government of India, to fulfill its obligation to include an IPR system to cover plant varieties and seeds under TRIPs, will give seed corporations 'breeders rights'. The combination of these two items will effectively undermine farmers rights and people's rights to food-as human rights.

The Patenting of Life

Article 27.5.3 (b) of TRIPs makes patents for micro-organisms obligatory. Further, recent judgements have allowed micro-organisms to be interpreted as genes, cell-lines, etc.

Article 27.5.3 (b) of TRIPs agreements states that:

> *Parties may exclude from patentability plants and animals other than micro-organisms, and essentially biological processes for the production of plants or animals other than non-biological and micro-biological processes. However, parties shall provide for the protection of plant varieties either by patents or by an effective sui generis system or by any combination thereof. This provision shall be reviewed four years after the entry into force of the Agreement.*

The problem with the TRIPs text of GATT is that while it appears to exclude living organisms from being patented, it will in fact put every country on that 'slippery slope; towards patenting life forms already evident in the U.S. Patent Office and U.S. Courts. It is in any case a tragedy that an issue that is directly related to the ecological and ethical fabric of our society, and to the economic options of survival available to people, should be left to a Ministry of Commerce.

New technologies for the control of global production are an essential aspect of the new WTO world order. Biotechnology is important for transnational corporations to increase their control over agricultural and food systems. But it is also important to them as a way to move out of their chemical based production systems, and its polluting effects, for which they have received heavy public criticism in recent years.

However, since biotechnology is based on biological organisms which reproduce and multiply on their own accord, these companies would have to find a way of having control of not only the organisms, but also their reproductive processes and 'offsprings' produced. This is why, for example, there was public outcry when Agracetus, a wholly owned subsidiary of the major transnational chemical company W.R. Grace, managed to obtain a patent on genetically transformed soyabean. Soyabean is a major world food crop and this 'species wide' patent means that the company will own all forms of genetically transformed soyabean for generations[16].

Hence monopoly control over production requires new systems of private property in life forms. This is where the 'intellectual property rights (IPRs) aspects of the GATT/WTO fit into the building of the 'free trade order'; which creates total protection for transnational corporations and denies protection to farmers as well as diverse life forms.

The GATT-TRIPs is not about trade. It is about the ethics of how we relate to other species, and what we hold as moral and cultural values of our civilisation. It is about how biodiversity is used and controlled—either by local communities who have protected it, or by corporations which have found new ways to exploit and own it.

In our culture, and according to our patent laws, life cannot be patented because it cannot be owned and it is not manufactured. The GATT/WTO will force us to give up our moral values, our economic priorities and our sovereignty. GATT-TRIPs pushed us into making all living organisms the property of a handful of corporations.

Behind the Fine Print

On first reading, it appears that the patent articles are about the exclusion of plants and animals from patentability. However, this phrase also exists in U.S. Patent Law. The existence of this phrase has however not prevented the U.S. from allowing patents for plants and animals. The problem is that the phrase

[16]Rural Advancement Foundation International (RAFI) Communique, 'Species Patent on Transgenic Soyabeans Granted to Transnational Chemical Giant—W.R. Grace', March/April 1994.

'plants and animals other than micro-organisms' does not cover parts of animals and plants. Nor does it include the cells of plants and animals that have been altered. It therefore allows the patenting of biological organisms.

Further, the words 'other than micro-ogranisms' removes the exclusion of micro-organisms from patentability, and makes the patenting of micro-organisms not only possible but an imperative, or in some cases compulsory. Since micro-organisms are living organisms, making it possible, an imperative or compulsory to patent them is the beginning of the 'slippery and dangerous' journey towards the patenting of all life.

Living organisms are central to production processes in biotechnology. The need for ownership rights to living organisms is essential for the next stage of capital accumulation by global corporations [and would make the patenting of micro-organisms an imperative, or even compulsory for these corporations]. At the core of the business are property rights and patents which guarantee profits, excluding others from rights and access to the means of survival[17].

The Impact on Women Farmers

Under the impact of the TRIPs agreement, women farmers of the South will stop being the custodians and owners of seed. Even the 'sui generis' option is pushing governments to give monopoly rights to the seed industry by the introduction of 'breeders rights' legislation.

The International Convention of the Union for the Protection of New Varieties of Plants (UPOV) had maintained farmers' rights to save seed, but this clause was removed in a March 1991 amendment. The new clause in UPOV (and TRIPs) can be used to enforce royalty payments on farmers if they save seeds of their own crops. With the stronger intellectual property rights regime being conceived under WTO, the transfer of extra funds (as royalty payments) from the poor to the rich countries would exacerbate the current debt crisis of South countries tenfold.

This is tremendously ironic, since most plant diversity actually originates in the South. And seeds and plant materials that are today under the control of the industrialised world, were originally taken freely from Southern farmers-to whom these seeds will now be sold back as patented material. As a result, seed companies will reap monopoly profits, while the genius of Southern farmers will go unrewarded and they will be banned from saving and using their own seeds.

IPRs in the area of seeds and plant material are in any case not easy to demarcate, since the genetic resources used by multinational corporations in claiming patents are the product of centuries of innovation and selection by Third World farmers - especially women. The UN Food and Agriculture Organisation (FAO) has recognized these contributions in the form of 'Farmer's Rights'. The Biodiversity Convention, signed at the 1992 Earth Summit also

[17]Vandana Shiva 'Monocultures of the Mind', Third World Network, Penang, 1993.

recognizes 'farmers rights' and accepts the need to make IPRs subservient to the objectives of biodiversity conservation.

Guilty Until You Prove Yourself Innocent

The TRIPs text, however, is biased since it only favours and acknowledges the innovation of global patriarchal institutions like Multinational Corporations (MNCs). It in fact gôes against the above mentioned agreements reached on other international platforms. The negative impact on farmers and other citizens of the South will increase due to the extended workings and terms of the patent, and the reversal of the burden of proof.

Article 34 of the text reverses the burden of proof in the area of process patents. In normal law, the accused is innocent unless proven guilty. Under this reversal of the burden of proof in the WTO regime, however, it is the accused who must demonstrate their innocence. If they cannot do so, then they are judged guilty of having infringed upon the right of the patent holder.

In the area of agriculture, this can have absurd and highly unjust consequences. MNCs are now taking out broad patents on plant varieties—covering ownership of 'traits' and 'characteristics'. With the reversal of the burden of proof clauses, it becomes legally possible for a corporation to accuse the farmers—who originally contributed to the particular trait within a seed—of patent infringement. There is no clause in TRIPs to offer protection to farmers in such cases.

When this situation is combined with potential cross-retaliation measures to be administered by the WTO, MNCs will have a very powerful tool to subsume all agriculture and all production under their monopoly control. This monopolization of the entire economy is arguably the main motive for setting up the WTO with a TRIPs council.

The Dawn of A New Age of Inequalities

The age of globalisation is deepening the categories of inequalities based on gender. These categories are the special project of a narrow group of men to exclude and deny the contributions of all other social groups in the production of intellectual and material wealth. This is happening even while they are using the intellectual and productive contributions of others in generating wealth, and ascribing value, for themselves.

The categories of economic values that are guiding globalisation are in reality violent and destructive to nature as 'producer', and to women as 'producers and knower's'. With the destruction of material and intellectual wealth of both nature and of Southern women, elements of 'non-holistic' or 'reductionist' science are becoming dialectically linked to 'non-holistic' or 'reductionist' elements in economics. These reductionist elements reduce all value to global market value, and register only those activities, and processes, that involve trade and cash transactions in dollars.

As the 'super state' system of the World Bank, IMF and WTO, and multinational corporations, reach for the resources and knowledge that Southern women have so far controlled and conserved, conflicts over economic value of nature and knowledge become reflections of globalised gender conflicts. Within the large spectrum, and the many levels, of conflicts effecting gender, race and class, it is the structures of Northern patriarchal power that stand in the most extreme opposition to the interests, values, visions and dreams of Southern women. Whether it is the women protecting seeds, and fighting IPRs in agriculture, through the Seed Satyagraha or it is the coastal communities resisting shrimp farming through their Satyagraha, globalisation has unleashed a new era of gender politics, with the poorest and most marginal women fighting to protect life in its freedom and its diversity.

7. All Things 'Trade-Related'

The most significant innovation of the Uruguay Round is the creation of the term 'trade-related'. By adding the prefix 'trade related' to any subject two magical moves become possible.

The first shift caused by the 'trade-related' prefix is the drawing of the areas of domestic decision-making into the global arena. Thus, ignoring cultural, socio-economic and political contexts in diverse societies. Intellectual property rights regimes, which have so far been only subject to national requirements, have been made global through the TRIPs Agreement of the GATT.

What the Environmentalists and Trade Unionists Saw

The second shift achieved by the term 'trade related' is the creation of areas where the 'darker', more visible, facets of free trade are transformed into reasons for its justification and expansion. When environmentalists and labour unions began to criticise GATT because it would destroy jobs and the environment, 'trade-related' social clauses and 'trade-related' environmental clauses were offered as a panacea.

Trade unionists and environmentalists who had been critical of GATT started to suddenly find a 'Blue GATT' with social clauses and a 'Green GATT' with environmental clauses. Each were apparently essential to the protection of worker's rights and environmental rights. What was forgotten was that, as, mere clauses in free trade-treaties, these fundamental rights would no longer exist as rights. They were metamorphosized into 'standards'. Standards are in the hand of global agencies, rights are in the hands of people.

Standards linked to international trade are inadequate instruments for protecting the rights of workers and the rights of nature for a number of reasons.

1. They are directed at the legislation of other countries, and not at strengthening domestic regulations in the area of labour and the environment. In fact, it is precisely because of the domestic deregulation of labour and environmental legislation that environmental and labour lobbies, especially in the North, turned in helplessness to the GATT in the hope of using environmental and social conditionalities against weaker trading partners.

2. They can only be used in areas dominated by international trade and exports and imports, leaving all other areas unprotected.

3. Because of their in-built selectivity and asymmetry, social and environmental clauses can often be a disguised form of trade protectionism practiced by the very countries which have pushed the free-trade treaties, and free-trade ideology, on the international community.

Why Movements and Governments Resist

Movements and governments of the South have each resisted social and environmental clauses, albeit for different reasons. Movements resisted these clauses within free-trade treaties because they perceive free trade as based on social and environment irresponsibility. They also feel that the globally mobile capital involved in free trade, that is always seeking out absolute advantage and profitability, conveniently externalises the social and ecological cost incurred. These movements are against free-trade, and they are for a protectionism that is people based, not super power based.

Movements resist 'trade' conditionalities because they want more local control, local autonomy and local decision-making in areas vital to life. Super power and 'super state' sanctioned trade retaliation measures are less democratic and more authoritarian than state regulation. This is especially in terms of centralisation, distance, unaccountability and inability of local communities to influence decisions that affect their lives.

Southern governments resist social and environmental clauses because they have fully absorbed the 'free trade' ideology of the deregulation of commerce in the 'blue' and 'green' clauses they see a hidden protectionism that violates the free trade logic. Since they represent, for the most part, the interests of dominant classes, they view free-trade as an opportunity to break free of social and environmental responsibility.

8. 'Trade Related Feminism' and the Need of an Ecological and Feminist Agenda on Trade

As feminist analysis begins to stress that free trade could be yet another patriarchal project which is based on gendered models, and impact, on gender on different levels, we will surely be offered a version of feminism which could be called 'trade-related feminism'.

Trade Liberalisation and the Marginalization of Women

In a seminar organised by the United Nations Fund for Women (UNIFEM) called 'Global Trading Practises and Poverty Alleviation in South Asia-A Gender perspective', a case study showed that trade-liberalisation has negative impacts on women as producers and consumers. Especially in the sectors related to essential needs like: food, water and clothing.

Most women in the South Asian region are engaged in the vital sectors of agriculture and food processing, textiles and garment production. These are also the major trade sectors for South Asia. Trends indicate that in these sectors, trade liberalisation has lead to women loosing out on both production options and consumption entitlements.

For example:

– In the Maldives, when exports in fisheries increased women's participation in the fisheries sector declined from 62 per cent in 1977 to 20 per cent in 1990.[18]

– In India, an ICSSR study has shown that growth in agro-processing, linked to foreign investment and exports, was creating more joblessness. Overall, employment in the agro-processing sector was actually decreasing.[19]

– The growth of aquaculture, linked to marine exports, has led to salination and the destruction of agricultural and fisheries livelihoods through the destruction of coastal ecosystems.[20]

– Exports of agricultural commodities have led to increased food prices and declining food entitlements. In India, food prices increased by 63 per cent between 1989-90 and 1993-94, leading to a decline in per capita food consumption over a three year span: from 510 gams per day in 1991 to 466 gms per day in 1993.[21]

– Inspite of the wide spread empirical data that reveals that trade liberalisation displaces women from production and consumption, there is a new discourse emerging on the 'integration of women in trade development'. In fact, the integration of women in trade development and promotion has become a priority concern of the International Trade Centre—the UN Conference on Trade And Development/GATT—which has designed a five year work programme to tackle it.

Women and the Development of Trade

If women's critique of maldevelopment created the discourses on 'Women in Development (WID), then women's critiques of 'free trade' are creating 'Women in Trade Development' (WITD) discourses in which women's development has been replaced by the development of trade. And instead of creating a shift in economic models on the basis of women's concerns, the dominant economic model aims to use women as their instruments.

As the International Trade Centre (ITC) documents states:

> *ITC is convinced that it is essential for women to enter society's mainstream to accelerate the trade development process in individual countries,*

[18] Maldives Country Paper presented at the UNIFEM Conference on 'Global Trading Practises and Poverty Alleviation in South Asia', held from 30th January to 1st February 1995.

[19] Devaki Jain, Keynote address at UNIFEM Conference, *Ibid.*

[20] Vandana Shiva, paper presented at UNIFEM Conference, *Ibid.*

[21] Vandana Shiva, paper presented at UNIFEM Conference, *Ibid.*

> *Trade promotion is not necessary the first priority among the roles women can play in development. Nevertheless, it is clearly acknowledged today that women are a major under-utilized resources in the search for increased export earnings.*[22]

Economic policy has not treated the empowerment of women as an objective, women are in fact reduced to being the means towards economic success. And instead of being a means to an end, trade has been elevated as the highest priority that people, societies and countries must strive for. A new cosmology is being written, with trade at its centre, and trade as the end to which every system must strive; and as the source of all meaning. A new 'trade related feminism' is being born, in which it is the freedom of trade and not the freedom of women that is the primary concern.

An Ecological and Feminist Agenda for Trade

The Uruguay Round of the GATT and the establishment of the World Trade Organisation has created two unprecedented shifts within global socio-economic development. Firstly, it has drawn issues that are not narrow economic issues into the domain of trade and economics. And secondly, it has drawn all economic and non-economic issues out of domestic decision-making and policy into the global arena—where ordinary citizens do not have access to avenues to democratically influence decisions, instruments and policies that effect them daily.

The Damage Done

International trade has been made the be-all and end-all of human existence in every society. And the dollar has been made the ultimate measure of value. Limitless destruction of ecosystems, and people's economies and livelihoods, has been legitimised in the pursuit of increased global trade and economic growth—as measured in foreign exchange. Large scale ecological disruption, the destruction of livelihoods and economic security for millions of people, and the wholesale destruction of biological and cultural diversity, is the inevitable consequence.

A New Agenda is Due

An ecological and feminist agenda for trade needs to be evolved based on the ecological limits, and social criteria, that economic activity needs to adhere to—if it is to respect the environmental principles of sustainability and the ethical principle of justice. This requires that the full ecological and social costs of economic activity, and trade, be made visible and taken into account. Globalisation that erases ecological and social costs is inconsistent with the need to minimise environmental destruction and human suffering.

---

[22]The Integration of Women in Trade Development: A proposal for an ITC programme for 1992-1997, ITC/TM (92/4).

Localisation-based on stronger democratic decision-making at local levels building up to national and global levels—is an imperative for conservation as well as democracy. Through the expanded decision-making roles of marginalised groups, including tribals, peasants and at local levels, certain criteria can be evolved to distinguish between economic activities that need to be locally controlled, and activities that can be globalised.

Globalisation has undermined the capacity of local communities and citizens of countries to influence policies that effect their lives. Localisation and decentralisation do not imply dictatorships or isolation. They are based on the principle of subsidiariety[23] and helps to discriminate between the different aspects of social and economic life. They establish the appropriate forms of governance for each activity to ensure the protection of people and the environment.

Reclaiming Ethics, Ecology and Equity

Aspects of human life necessary for survival need to be governed by a logical, deeper and wider than the logic of internal free trade. This involves reclaiming the areas of ethics, ecology and equity that have been subsumed under trade by the prefix 'trade related'. We need to redefine issues on the basis of ethical and ecological principles. Thus, while the Uruguay Round transformed patents on life from an ethical issue to that of a mere 'trade related' item of the GATT: the ecological and ethical movements against the patenting of life, its products and processes, are reclaiming the ethical dimension on the patents on life-forms[24].

Similarly, while food and agriculture were reduced to trade issue, social and environmental movements are reclaiming these as matters central to human rights, and cultural and ecological survival[25].

As we enter the next millenium, the values emerging from diverse social movements need to locate trade in its ecological and human context. Where necessary, limits need to be put on trade to protect the integrity of the earth and the integrity of society.

---

[23]This principle is used as a 'rule of reason' to draw a line between the respective competences of the centre and the component units of whatever style of governance applies, preference is to be given to action at a level as close as possible to the citizen.

[24]Vandana Shiva, 'Can Life be Made? Can Life be Owned?', Annual Environment Day Lecture, Pasirar, Pune, September 1994.

[25]'People's Charter on Food Security' based on the Policy Dialogue on 'Trade Liberalisation, Natural Resources and Food Security' held on 4th and 5th February 1995 in New Delhi, Third World Network (India).

15

Gender Justice and A Culture of Peace

Ingeborg Breines

Equal rights and opportunities for women and men, girls and boys are essential, if not a precondition for the full realization of UNESCO's vision of a culture of peace. The status of women and gender equality has had since the 80's a particularly prominent place in UNESCO's programmes and is presently one of the four priorities of the organisation. Despite previous and on-going efforts by the United Nations, Member States and civil society we are however, far from achieving gender equality on a global basis including within UNESCO's fields of competence: education, science, culture and communication. This article will not deal specifically and from a statistical point of view with the issue of gender injustice but will concentrate on and argue for the importance of gender equality and gender justice, *de jure* and *de facto*, in the realisation of the concept and vision of the UNESCO trans-disciplinary project: Towards a Culture of Peace.

The article will relate to the UNESCO Women and a Culture of Peace Programme that builds on relevant normative instruments at the United Nations and UNESCO, including the CEDAW (Convention on the Elimination of all forms of Discrimination Against Women), the Beijing Platform for Action, and UNESCO's Agenda for Gender Equality and the Statement on Women's Contribution to a Culture of Peace, both prepared for the Fourth World Conference on Women. The conclusion of the Agenda for Gender Equality reflects the point of departure of this article: "There can be no lasting peace without equality before the law and the full enjoyment of human rights by men and women"

A Culture of Peace

A culture of peace as defined by UNESCO encompasses not only peace as absence of war, but focuses on the content, the substance and the conditions of peace. In the words of the Director General of UNESCO, Federico Mayor: "The culture of peace is a transition from the logic of force and fear to the force of reason and love". In a Culture of Peace, dialogue and respect for human rights replaces violence; inter-cultural understanding and solidarity replaces enemy images; sharing and free flow of information replaces secrecy; and egalitarian partnership and full empowerment of women succeeds male domination.

Building the culture of peace entails unlearning the codes of the culture of war and violence that has pervaded our existence in a myriad of ways. It entails questioning the institutions, priorities and practices of this culture as well as the destructive production, trafficking and use of arms and drugs. It further entails challenging a series of concepts and notions such as the current notion of development based primarily on economic criteria; the narrow concept of security, often measured by the counting of arms and tanks, instead of measuring social and human security and the costs of war and violence; the notion of power as power over, rather than shared power; as well as different, other more sophisticated types of injustices, discrimination and exclusion.

The goals, ideals, and strategies that comprise the movement from a culture of war to a culture of peace are drawn from, and seek to revitalize major international, normative instruments which are basic to the United Nations' mission of helping secure peace in the world community, and protecting the human rights of all the world's citizens. It is in the spirit of these normative instruments that the UNESCO Culture of Peace Project insists on the prevention of violent conflicts; on acting in a timely manner with long-term preventive measures to radically attack the root-causes of violence: poverty, exclusion, ignorance, inequality and injustice, and to avoid the terrible waste of human lives and material resources occasioned by violent conflict and war.

It has been asserted that in this century more than a hundred million persons have died due to war and war-like activities. This decade alone has seen some hundred armed conflicts, and growing structural and physical violence in all parts of the world. The data also presents evidence of a growing tendency in modern warfare for civilian victims, mostly women and children, to largely out-number any other group as the casualties of war. According to the UNHCR, women and children account for approximately 70-80 per cent of the world's refugees.[1] In just one decade, the number of soldiers engaged in UN peace-keeping missions has risen from 10,000 to 85,000. The costs of these operations have also increased tenfold, shifting resources away from preventative peace-building initiatives. The vast amounts of resources used for peace-keeping and in-conflict and post-conflict humanitarian assistance depict our failure to meet basic human needs and concerns in an adequate and timely manner.

In a culture of peace, people would assume a more global identity, which does not necessarily replace, but rather builds upon other multiple identities such as sex, family, community, ethnicity, nationality profession and age. Building a sense of global, multiple identities, underlining the growing inter-dependence among all countries and peoples is likely to bring us closer to inter-cultural understanding which is vital for peaceful relations. Such an identity would also provide a sense of common humanity among all the peoples as citizens of the world. It is this universal human identity which could provide the

[1]United Nations High Commissioner for Refugees (UNHCR) 1997 Statistical Overview, July 1998.

strongest assurance for the protection of human rights. The universal human identity envisioned as the hallmark of a culture of peace would not tolerate disparities among any groups of human beings, including systematic discrimination of women.

Scenarios for the New Millennium

The process of transforming societies away from expressions of war and violence towards a culture of peace and non-violence, has become a system-wide challenge. UNESCO, with strong support from the civil society, has spear-headed the concept of a culture of peace that has been accepted by the wider UN system. The General Assembly resolutions 52/13 and 52/15 (November 1997) proclaimed the Year 2000 as the International Year for the Culture of Peace, designated UNESCO as the lead agency and requested the UN Secretary General in cooperation with the UNESCO Director General to prepare a draft UN Declaration and Programme of Action on a Culture of Peace for submission to the 53rd General Assembly (Autumn 1998). Nobel Peace Prize Laureates suggested to ECOSOC (July 1998), a Decade for a Culture of Peace and Non-Violence for the Children of the World to follow the International Year, and all Member States will be encouraged to develop their own respective National Programme of Action for a Culture of Peace.

As we approach a new millennium, the culture of peace concept provides us with a marvellous and new opportunity to reflect and to refine our visions for the future, confronting ourselves with such fundamental questions as: Why is the world seemingly more willing to pay for the costs of war and violence than the costs of peace? How can we reduce the enormous gaps between military and social expenditure? What are the main obstacles to a global culture of peace? Who benefits from the culture of war and violence? How do we learn to live together and how do we best celebrate human and creative diversity?[2] While these fundamental questions are not new to the human quest for peace, never before in history have they had the same urgency; and never before have they been considered from a gender perspective.

New and alternative approaches to development based on gender equality and equal partnership are essential to overcome pessimism and inertia, and to inspire new dynamism and hope in the future, for all the world's citizens. Women have distinct contributions to make to the traditionally male-dominated and defined power structures. Due to experiences gained from gender-specific roles, assigned throughout different life stages, and from the demands related to their 'mothering and caring functions', women might have different perspectives, alternative visions and methodological approaches. Largely excluded from formal decision-making, women share collective experiences from family and community work, despite their heterogeneity as a group. It is time that this

[2]Our Creative Diversity, Report of the Commission on Culture and Development, UNESCO 1996.

insight be used also in political policy making. With more men in caring functions and more women in political decision-making, old patterns will change and the potential of every human being will matter more than their sex.

Education: The Leading Modality for Change

"Since wars begin the minds of men, it is in the minds of men that the defences of peace must be constructed."[3] For UNESCO, education is the key to achieving equality, justice and democracy in every day life and a guarantee of a sufficiently broad basis for recruitment to decision-making positions. Education, both formal and non-formal, in schools, in the family, through mass media and social institutions, is the most important process by which people can gain the values, attitudes and behavioural patterns of a culture of peace. Education is the leading modality to promote a culture of peace, provided however, that the education include the excluded, is relevant to different socio-cultural contexts, is of high quality, is gender-sensitive, (i.e. recognizes the differences between women and men, honours their fundamental equality, seeks to overcome gender inequities) and encourages inter-personal, inter-cultural and inter-national dialogue.

Education for human rights, peace, democracy, non-violence and tolerance is particularly important for brining about a change towards a gender-sensitive culture of peace as defined by people themselves on the basis of their socio-political, economic and cultural conditions. The world's ministers of education meeting on the occasion of the International Conference on Education, Geneva, 1994, in adopting the *Integrated Framework for Action on Education for Peace, Human Rights and Democracy,* endorsed by UNESCO's General Conference, underlined their intention "to take suitable steps to establish in educational institutions an atmosphere contributing to the success of education for international understanding, so that they become ideal places for the exercise of tolerance, respect for human rights, the practice of democracy and learning about the diversity and wealth of cultural identities". They also pledged "to pay special attention to improving curricula, the content of textbooks, and other educational materials including new technologies, with a view to educating caring and responsible citizens, open to other cultures, able to appreciate the value of freedom, respectful of human dignity and differences, and able to prevent conflicts or resolve them by non-violent means".

In the report of the International Commission on Education for the Twenty-First Century[4] four pillars of education are outlined: learning to know, learning to do, learning to be and learning to live together, with the greatest emphasis placed on the challenge of learning to live together. Learning to live together is seen as a "second literacy", as indispensable to a culture of peace as literacy

[3]Constitution of the United Nations Educational, Scientific and Cultural Organisation, 16 November, 1945.

[4]Learning, the Treasure Within, UNESCO 1996.

itself. A sub-category of the "second literacy" might well be "gender literacy" - learning to interpret the nature of the gendered world which separates men and women in what some have called "gender apartheid", and to read the significance of the gender dis-aggregated data the UN now gathers as it "mainstreams" a gender perspective.

Girls and Women's Education

In most parts of the world, girls are under-represented at every school level. The gender gap widens the higher one advances in the educational system. Such factors as economic constraints, preference accorded to the boy-child, the distance to school, early marriage and teenage pregnancy constitute major obstacles and must be addressed.

Despite recent improvements, the present gender imbalance in educational opportunities is a challenge to concepts of justice and development. It is equally a challenge to peace. The world deserves literate women and men, critically and constructively participating in shaping our common future.

Equal access to education and training does not suffice. Renewed attention must be given to the relevance, quality and content of education. It should reflect the needs and aspirations of both girls and boys.

The lesser status assigned to women and girls in most societies and the resulting negative psychological effects hamper their pursuit of studies, work and social position. Specific measures such as the promotion of a broader implementation of relevant normative instruments and the development of appropriate gender sensitive teacher training, curricula and teaching material are required.

Given existing gender imbalances, it might be important to stimulate boys and girls differently, under the same curricula, to compensate for past biases in opportunities and expectations. Although basics of home economics, life skills education, preparation for parenting and values education based on gender equality are important for both girls and boys, these elements would, for compensatory reasons, be of particular benefit to boys, also as a vital means of reversing socialization processes that might lead to aggression and violence. Adolescence is a crucial period when important decisions are made regarding family-life and careers. There are some positive global trends towards longer schooling and delayed marriages. But there is also an increasing number of adolescent pregnancies and a growing exploitation of young women, both detrimental to their health and dignity. The aggregated impact of HIV and AIDS on education will likely affect the education of girls more than boys, thereby hindering the progress made in female education over the last decade.

Education, as an important factor for poverty alleviation, must also stimulate creativity and entrepreneurship, and be geared towards the world of work. In a world increasingly monetised, technical and vocational education and training, educational and vocational guidance and career counselling, as well as higher education need to target girls and women in order to break with practices confining women to low-skill, low-paid jobs, highlighting the relation between educational levels, occupational status, power and income.

Adult education facilitates skills training and retraining in a society in which the skills needed for survival are rapidly changing. Women still lag behind, despite the fact that women might be better prepared than men to confront uncertainties and instability, as they historically have had to cope with shifting life situations - imposed mainly by child bearing and rearing and economic trends which have made women move in and out of the labour market.

Adult education is crucial for women to keep up with new challenges and to compensate for past educational deprivation. Non-formal education, tailored to adult needs and interests, may contribute to financial autonomy and to strengthening participation in community life. For women in rural areas, or isolated communities, the combination of relevant technologies and innovative teaching methods may offer new hope.

The Culture of Peace radio programme in El Salvador is an example of women's empowerment at the grass-roots level. In the Buenos Tiempos Muher project, former factions work together on building a gender sensitive culture of peace, based on the development of self-esteem, dialogue, and the overcoming of violence both in the family and in society. A number of women correspondents ensure that the content of the radio programme is relevant to the population, especially to those living in deprived areas. They also ensure that a broad variety of women's voices are heard. The radio programme is broadcast on a regular basis on almost 50 radio stations, including former guerilla stations. Innovative educational material and popular games accompany the emissions.

Distance education has proved to be of particular value to women, who often are less geographically mobile than men, due to family obligations and cultural factors. Community radio, local-language newspapers, mobile teacher teams and libraries, solar powered transmitters, desktop publishing and satellites are all examples of distance education and learning across frontiers, effective means for reaching the unreached.

Higher education is a key component in the empowerment process, as it provides women with the necessary decision-making skills. Low female representation in the science, both in research and application, is largely a manifestation of gender biases in expectations and the quantity and quality of education that girls and women receive. Poor education and training hamper women's ability to articulate their needs and priorities and to make full use of existing opportunities. If women and men are to be partners in development, they must have equal access to knowledge.

Main-Streaming a Gender perspective

All four UN Conference on Women have had as their themes equality, development and peace. At the Beijing Conference in 1995 the need for action and the need to see the inter-relation between these themes were strongly underlined. This comprehensive and holistic approach to development which is only now finding its way into mainstream policies owes its strength and vitality to the productive and cooperative efforts of the UN, the women's movement and feminist research.

Since the 4th World Conference on Women in Beijing, the United Nations system has been committed to the main-streaming of a gender perspective in all its activities and policies. Mainstreaming a gender perspective requires compilation and analysis of statistical data showing life conditions of women and men, how women and men are involved in society at different levels, what they each contribute, their particular needs and interests, and how each gender benefits or suffers from policies and projects, including how resources and power are distributed and used.

UNESCO, as a member of that system, established the Women and a Culture of Peace Programme in 1996, *inter alia* with reference to the Beijing Platform for Action, which states that the "full participation of women in power structures are essential for the maintenance and promotion of peace". The main task of the Women and Culture of Peace Programme is main-streaming a gender perspective on the project Towards a Culture of Peace.

Besides analysing the gender related factors that hamper or inspire development towards a culture of peace, the Women and a Culture of Peace Programme works towards:

* Supporting women's initiatives for peace,
* Empowering women for democratic participation in political processes to increase their capacity and impact especially in economic and security issues, and
* Gender sensitive socialization and training for non-violence and egalitarian partnerships, with a special focus on boys and young men.

What do Women Bring to the Cause of Peace?

The prevailing gender disparities, the feminisations of poverty, and continued discrimination and violence against women have prompted a new search for effective strategies and concrete actions in order to remedy the situation and achieve the goals of equality, development and peace.

Women make up more than half of the world's population. Their physical resources are currently overtaxed and under-valued. Their intellectual and creative potential is largely ignored. As transmitters of cultural values, in particular to children and youth, and as agents for change, women are an under-utilized source of creative energy, experience and wisdom. Women's manifold contributions to society are, however, increasingly being made visible and acknowledged. The so-called "women's issues" are gradually being taken out of isolation and made societal issues of justice, human rights and human resource development, to be tackled by men as well as by women.

Women and men are in general socialized differently. In most societies women are educated for caring functions, not only for children, but also for the sick and the old, and even for able men. The world is desperately in need of this experience, which can be appropriately called women's "rationality of care". In general, women are also outside the present power structures and are therefore free to provide a substantial critique, much needed alternatives, as well as a rethinking of existing structures, institutions and practices.

Women have only to a limited degree participated in the description and analysis of political and economic reality and have therefore, on a general basis, hardly influenced policy-making. It is essential to involve women both in the description of reality and in policy-making. It is further necessary to listen carefully to how women define their visions of a culture of peace. Inspiration can be found from early twentieth century publications, and onwards, such as Robeya Sakhawat Hussain's remarkable utopia, *Sultana's Dream* (India 1905) where she describes a peaceful "Ladyland" with women in political decision-making positions; a society with a very high level of education, basing their energy consumption on solar power, without any violence, and in close contact with and respect for nature.

This type of vision or utopia is essential to inspire transformation and to strengthen the growing number of women who now want to influence decision-making, to solve problems at the root instead of utilizing "stop-gap" measures in emergency situations. The story about a fisher woman standing on the shore of a river unable to fish because she constantly had to rescue drowning persons in the river rapids is representative of an emerging attitude among women faced with the dilemma of short term emergency actions versus long term strategic planning. The fisher woman tried desperately to assist, but with no abatement in the flow of victims, decided finally to leave and go up-stream to see who was throwing those people who had not learnt to swim into the water.

A growing number of women want to change not only their realities but that of society at large and create a positive environment for future generations. To this end, several UN agencies assist in gathering, analysing and disseminating information on women's traditional and innovative methods and practices for peace building and conflict prevention and transformation.

Even though we do not as yet have irrefutable evidence that women in a critical mass would make a difference in political and economic decision-making positions, we cannot afford to continue to under-utilize half of humanity. All of the human talents that are evenly distributed between women and men are required and must be applied in solving the global problems that impede the realization of a culture of peace. Moreover, it is an acknowledged human right of both women and men to participate on equal terms in democratic processes at all levels of society. The exclusion of and discrimination against women cannot be tolerated, neither in the name of freedom of expression, market economy, cultural traditions and practices, nor through the interpretations of any religion.

There is some evidence that women politicians give priority to what is generally called "feminine values" like social security, education, ecological security, such as clean drinking water and food for the children, and that due to hardship they have developed strong survival skills and flexibility. In general women are also questioning the tremendous gap between military and social expenditure. This gives promise to the potential of women making a significant difference by encouraging policies that support gender equality and peace.

Other studies also describe foreign policy, and notably defence issues, as areas in which women and men are deeply divided in their attitudes and policy preferences. However it is imperative not to romanticize or over-emphasize (i.e. attribute to nature or female biology) by peacefulness of women in a way that under mines the overriding goal of an egalitarian partnership between women and men.

Enhancing Solidarity and Women's Participation in Democratic Processes

A growing number of countries are now moving towards democracy. None-the-less, the majority of existing democracies are still but "unfinished democracies". One third of the countries of the world have less than 5 per cent or no women in parliament. A very few countries have recently approached a critical mass of women in parliament, and only the Nordic countries for some years have had a critical mass of women (minimum 33.3 per cent) in both parliament and government. Throughout world history there have been less than 30 elected female Heads of State or Government. All of them held office during the last fifty years, most of them in the last ten years, with a maximum of ten women at the same time. At present only three countries have an elected woman head of state or government - Bangladesh, Ireland and Sri Lanka. An examination of the present situation reveals that there are only 1 per cent of women elected heads of state and government; 7 per cent of women ministers, and very few heading powerful ministries such as Foreign Affairs, the Interior or Finance; and 11 per cent of women parliamentarians. This implies that 99 per cent of the top political power is in the hands of men, as well as some estimated 99 per cent of the world's resources. Women have yet to take advantage of their majority position to influence political decision-making. It is equally important to develop and encourage networking among empowered women; parliamentarians, mayors and local leaders, to build solidarity and strengthen their roles as promoters of a culture of peace.

Women's solidarity is traditionally strongest in times of difficulties and distress, where women shoulder each others burdens, share survival strategies and actions, take care of children, aging, and sick, or support each other when men are absent. There is less proof of solidarity with women in positions of power and authority. The reason might be a lack of experience with women in powerful positions, lack of efficient networks and support groups, and also the tough competition to get through the series of obstacles often referred to as the "glass-ceiling". Recruitment to higher positions often has been from women of a better-situated class. The few women who have risen to positions of power usually have had to adapt to existing patterns in order not to be marginalised by the rest of the power structure, thereby risking alienation from other women.

Conditions have not always encouraged solidarity among women in power, nor between them and other women.

The preparations for the Beijing Conference brought to the forefront a new solidarity among women. At the same time the call for working partnerships between women and men at different levels of society grew stronger. While there is not yet enough evidence to draw conclusions as to how this new women-men solidarity is developing, it is seen as a necessary complement to women-women solidarity, and an essential condition for a gender-sensitive culture of peace.

In order to encourage the process leading toward gender equality in political decision-making, it is important to strengthen this new type of solidarity, both through broad women's support for women in decision-making positions and through the accountability of "empowered" women towards their female constituencies. The formation of women's caucuses in representative bodies, and international associations are significant developments in this process.

Only Because He is a Man - The Question of Quotas

While there seems to be broad agreement at an inter-governmental level of the need for practical measures in order to ensure gender equality, the question of quotas, (i.e. calling for specific percentages or numbers of women in various political and economic bodies and other public institutions), remains politically delicate.

There is a clear reluctance to institute concrete, practical, measurable steps to undo the injustices that are strongly imbedded. Is change slow in coming because the full picture of gender inequality is not widely known, or is there the assumption that much more has been achieved than is actually the case? Is it that the majority of men and some women are still not gender-sensitive and therefore opt for keeping things the way they are? Or is it that some men are afraid of partnership and real equality with women and are not ready to give up their privileges? Could it be that some women because of privileged circumstances and others because they have not been socialized to ask for anything for themselves or their sisters have not sought change? Or is it that in periods when jobs are scarce, women are not encouraged to seek work or positions? Could it be that quotas for women are not always practised satisfactorily? Or that some women find quota systems to be demeaning when there should be fair distribution and human rights?

Masculinities

The first broad attempt by the UN to put male roles and masculinities in relation to peace issues on the world agenda, was made by UNESCO, when organizing an Expert Group Meeting on Male Roles and Masculinities in the Perspective of a Culture of Peace in Oslo, Norway, September 1997. The concept of the meeting, that brought together an equal number of women and men, gender researchers, peace researchers, and activists, stems from the realization that a culture of peace can only be achieved through more egalitarian, partnership-oriented male roles that replaces stereotypical views of masculinity based on dominance, force, and aggressiveness. It also reflects the understanding that rigid and stereotyped gender roles prevent individuals from realizing their full potential and run counter to the principle of participatory democracy. The participants acknowledged that whilst women's roles and status have been broadly debated over the last decades, men have been seen as the standard human being - the norm - and men's roles and positions have hardly been discussed, and much less questioned.

It was argued that most men through their upbringing, feel entitled to dominant positions in the family, work and political life, and react negatively when this entitlement is not fulfilled. These reactions might lead to domestic violence, violence in schools or in the street, adherence to extremist gangs and sects, or wanting to join legitimate structures which use force, such as the police an the military. It might also lead to reinforced structural violence like exclusion, or the refusal to vote on concrete measures towards gender equality in the workplace or in different levels of society.

The Oslo Meeting explored the social, cultural and economic conditions producing violence among men, political and practical strategies for reducing men's violence, and the possibilities for raising boys in ways that emphasize qualities such as emotional response, caring and communication skills that are vital to a culture of peace. There is a clear link between masculinity and violence. Statistics, however insufficient, show that men (often young men) are responsible for almost 90 per cent of all physical violence, though it must be emphasized that most men are not violent, nor naturally violent. There seems to be a general "masculinization" of societies, including the emergence of militarized masculinities in communities under threat. The masculinization has in some societies even reached young girls who have started using violent methods in their search for equality and recognition.

The meeting also undertook the task of formulating recommendations for practical measures that enhance the development of a gender-sensitive culture of peace, in relation to society and its major institutions. Since some groups of men are becoming a risk factor, not only to themselves, but to society at large, notably the poorly educated, the unemployed, the demobilized soldiers, and groups rigidly linked to power structures, special emphasis should be given to developing insight and training to address the uncertainties, conflicts, frustration and feelings of "dis-empowerment" to prevent recourse to violent behaviour.

State supported parental leave for fathers, establishment and or strengthening of networks of young men against violence, training in non-violent conflict-resolution and conflict transformation on different levels of the school-system were among the recommendations for a post-patriarchal society for the next millennium.

Commitments

Among the main obstacles to a gender-sensitive culture of peace are the myths that nothing can be changed because (i) violence is inherent in human nature, and (ii) violence is effective. Women who subscribe less readily than men to the myth of the efficacy of violence, have shown themselves as strong supporters of a culture of peace. Many women - and some men - have committed themselves to the principles of the UNESCO Statement on Women's Contribution to a Culture of Peace, notably to:

* support national and international efforts to ensure equal access to all forms of learning opportunities, with a view to women's empowerment and access to decision-making;

* promote relevant quality education that imparts knowledge of the human rights of men and women, skills of non-violent conflict resolution, respect for the natural environment, inter-cultural understanding and awareness of global inter-dependence, which are essential constituents of a culture of peace;

* encourage new approaches to development that take account of women's priorities and perspectives;

* oppose the misuse of religion, cultural and traditional practices for discriminatory purposes;

* seek to reduce the direct and indirect impact the culture of war on women - in the form of physical and sexual violence or the neglect of social services for excessive military expenditure;

* increase women's freedom of expression and involvement in the media as well as the use of gender-sensitive language and images;

* promote knowledge and respect for international normative instruments concerning the human rights of girls and women and ensure widespread dissemination in order to further the well-being of all, men and women, including the most vulnerable groups of societies;

* support governmental and inter-governmental structures as well as women's associations and NGOs committed to the development of a culture of peace based on equality between men and women.

16

Political Empowerment and Gender Justice

Susheela Kaushik

What is Political Empowerment

Of late there is a lot of reference to the concept of political empowerment of women. The word 'empowerment' has been variously used to convey many meanings. To some it is a way of endowing women, who otherwise are powerless, with the necessary dosage of capacity to act, influence and decide. To others it is a further step in reinforcing and strengthening the constitutional provisions of equality and rights, democratic processes and secular polity in India so as to increase women's equality and rights. It is also viewed as another strategy for women's development, as the earlier concepts and approaches like welfare and development have been inadequate to resolve women's question. The welfarist measures like infrastructural support and protective legislations, or the developmental programmes like education, employment and income generation, while being necessary, do not seem to bring about, by themselves, gender justice or guarantee women's human rights. The absence of enough women in decision-making and implementing levels have been viewed as being responsible for the lack of proper understanding of women's issues and energetic articulation of their interests at suitably high levels, the myopic approach and aspects in women oriented policies and the failure to reach out to the targetted group. The absence of women at the politically powerful and socially visible leadership positions have also been responsible for the increasing devaluation and the consequent atrocities against women. To get more and more women to the political positions so as to enable them to collectively influence and direct the laws, policies and programmes in their favour, there is a need to have some additional measures, besides what is already available by way of the constitutional provisions for political rights. Political empowerment hence is a process of equipping women with more fuel and power to emerge in positions of decision-making. Paradoxically speaking, the very constitutional rights as a free citizen of a democratic country, need to be utilised to further the same constitutional provisions which seem to stand in need of a reinforcement to facilitate the fulfilling of the constitutional guarantees. It thus looks like an external attempt which seeks to help a marginalised group, by adding on to the existing potential, through an induced mechanism. Often, however, it is the strengthening of self-confidence and self-image through knowledge, capacity building and support systems that leads to the empowerment of women. Thus the external inputs act more as catalysts.

The political empowerment of a citizen thus appears to be a contradiction theoretically but a felt necessity practically, particularly in view of the hierarchical structure of the society based on feudalism, class antagonism, casteism, religious fundamentalism and patriarchy. In the case of women all the negative forces combine at times to make them politically the most powerless section. It is then that an external set of measures like affirmative or protective action and "positive discrimination" is evolved. Reservation or quota in the political bodies is one such affirmative action that is being suggested for making the constitutional gender equality a reality. Others could be training and capacity building.

Indian Constitution and Women Political Rights

India achieved Independence in August 1947, and adopted its democratic Constitution in January 1950. It granted political rights to women on equal standing with men, under the universal adult suffrage, irrespective of caste, class, religion, place of birth, educational or property qualification. It thus recognised the need for free and active political participation of women in an equal measure and anticipated their political empowerment so as to enable them to contribute to the building of the new nation and vice versa. The women, though many of them illiterate and bogged down by the feudal -patriarchal order did not disappoint.

The women of India thus started their march to their new freedom in Independent India. Five decades later, in 1997, we pause to look back only to find that the march that started on the basis of gender equality, social, economic and political justice under Gandhi, Nehru and Ambedkar, had halted somewhere at the very early phase itself.

The political processes in India are confirming that much of the deterioration taking place in the context of women's status and rights, can be arrested only if more women come forward to sort it out. The developmental strategies and processes are unleashing a torrent of negative and harmful forces that are leading to social catastrophies and atrocities; in this women are emerging as the major victims. Whether it is the caste/communal riots, peasant or workers' struggles, poverty and indebtedness, or dowry/sexual assaults, women are becoming more and more direct victims. Fundamentalism, rightist extremism, casteist vindictiveness and feudal/patriarchal domination are expressing themselves most forcefully by attacking the women first.

A participatory democracy would be essential to preserve women's rights, and in a way democracy itself, from being made a pawn in the hands of a few lumpen, scheming, unethical and patriarchal vested interests.

Such participation by empowered women as well as the empowering of many more women are needed also to fulfil the hopes and aspirations of many women who have an overwhelming faith in the leadership of women. As many studies have pointed out, women particularly view that women leaders would worry about women's problems and hence would prefer them any day to men.

Why is the number of women in politics so low? There are various reasons for the low participation as contestants. The political parties are, by and large, reluctant to choose women as candidates, as they are viewed as depriving men of their chances. Even the small number of women who contest gain their candidature by their relationship with already established party leaders. The subordinated position of the 'ordinary' women in the families, their routine and normal duties of looking after the family, bringing up children, performing the unpaid work, do not allow them much scope to participate freely in the public-political activities. Elections in India as in all other modern democracies, have become very complicated, violent and dirty. They are enormously expensive, inviting thereby very many legitimate and not so legitimate ways of funding and managing them. Women cannot obviously fit into this matrix of elections. Political participation of women, is thus lower than even men of weaker sections.

Reservation or Quota

As a tool for empowerment the method of reservation had emerged as early as 1974 during the discussions of the Committee on the Status of Women in India. At the local level the Committee recommended the establishment of village-level statutory women's councils to ensure greater participation by women in the political process. The Commission also recommended the inclusion of women in all important committees, commissions or delegations that are appointed to examine socio-economic problems.

The National Perspective Plan for Women was drawn up by the Government of India under Rajiv Gandhi's leadership in 1988. It believed that since a broad participation of women was limited due to nexus of factors, there was a need to adopt special measures for empowering women. It hence recommended that 30 per cent of women must be represented in all committees and commissions of the Government. It further recommended that reservation should be made for 30 per cent seats at panchayat to zilla parishad level and local municipal bodies for women. It also urged that political parties must ensure at least 30 per cent of the candidates fielded for elections are women till such time as women can stake their claim to nomination as equals.

Reservation as a Tool to Empowerment

This had finally led to the introduction of reservation to not less than one third of the seats in the Panchayats and municipalities. The 73rd and 74th amendments to the Constitution provided for this reservation as well as the reservation for the chairpersons for not less than one third of these bodies in local government.

This was a landmark in women's empowerment and an achievement for women's movement towards social justice.

In the past few years, after the enactment of these Amendments, the issue of adequate political representation in the parliament and state assemblies has emerged as the single most important demand of the women's movement in India.

The Beijing Conference too gave priority to the political empowerment of women.

Despite all this, the 1996 elections witnessed only 4.3 per cent of women candidates; out of them more than two-thirds were independents. Less than 10 per cent of total candidates put up by parties, were women. Women had constituted only 7.1 per cent of total Lok Sabha members.

The 1998 elections to Lok Sabha was not much better. The proportion of women contestants had gone up marginally to 5.7 per cent while the women MPs were now 43. This worked out to only 7.1 per cent of the total membership in Lok Sabha (Table 1, 2 & 3 at the end). Thus with all the nation wide debates over the introduction of the 81st Amendment Bill, for reservation and more women in politics, the impact on the parties was near absent.

Reservation for Legislative Representation

This had convinced the women that they can never come up under the existing process of nominations and that they needed some compulsion like quota and reservation. The President's Address to the Parliament in May 1996 as well as in March 1998, the subsequent UF Government's Common Minimum Programme as also the BJP's National Agenda of Governance promised such a reservation for women in Parliament and state legislatures. The women's movement outside and the women M.Ps within the Parliament had been pressurising persistently the U.F. and BJP led Governments to introduce the amendment bills to grant such reservation. Finally on 12 September 1996 the 81st Constitution Amendment Bill was introduced. The Bill sought to reserve one third of constituencies, by rotation for women, for a period of 15 years.

The Bill had been reformulated as the 84th Amendment Bill in the Twelfth Lok Sabha by the BJP led coalition government and had even been approved by the cabinet. But it is yet to be introduced. Not merely all the demands and campaigns of the women from the grassroots to national level had fallen on deaf ears but even all the manifestoes of all the national parties had bitten dust. The united efforts of all the female politicians, both elected and defeated to Lok Sabha and Rajya Sabha were torn to pieces when the patriarchal male politicians, overtly and covertly gunned for it and finally shredded it to pieces in front of the speaker, thereby thwarting any attempt to introduce it.

In the process the male politicians of the day emerged as alienated from their own constituents, who voted for increasing the number of women in politics mainly to take the politics away from these male politicians. Even while the people had progressed, the political parties and its functionaries remained stagnant. Reservation for women by jolting the system, would have moved it back to years of fifties and sixties when India under its able, enlightened, farsighted and constructive leadership, had sought to found a progressive, equitable and just social order.

It is somewhat amusing to see the arguments against reservation for women in the national and state legislatures as they are full of inner contradictions:

– It is alright to give reservation for women in local government. There the 72nd and 73rd Constitutional Amendment Bills were passed unanimously (with just one vote against in Lok Sabha) and that too within a few hours, without anything like a debate. What was just and fair and would strengthen democracy at the grassroots, becomes anti-constitutional and unfair when it comes to higher levels of decision-making.

– Is it then empowerment of women or condescension for the women, who by majority belong to the rural areas? Or is it that women can be tolerated at decision-making levels only at the local government level? Apart from other things, it also shows the lopsided priorities of a political system in which the self-government at the grassroots level is treated with contempt and low priority.

– No one opposed reservation *per se* as no one would now like to be seen as being on the other side of SC, OBC and ST. So no one raised the issues of equality vs. privileges or merit vs. birth etc. These are now settled issues in a way.

– In fact, the resistance to reservation was based on exactly opposite arguments. All those who opposed Mandal Commission Report and the reservation for OBCs as dividing India, and promoting the interests of only the elites among the OBC, were now in support of women's reservation without any class/caste divide. All those who supported the OBC reservation without class and gender concerns, are today raising the issue of class and caste. Obviously politician's memory is short. The fact that such caste/community concerns are not raised in the context of Panchayati Raj and municipalities even today is indeed surprising. Such political parties and their male leaders have not cared to know how the elected women are faring in the panchayats and municipalities - not even the women of the castes/communities they profess to support.

– All those political parties/leaders who were never anxious about the female half of the communities/castes they profess to fight for, are today shedding tears for justice, fairness and rights for their women.

– All the political parties, which stood for the reservation for their own caste/community women, did not put up adequate number in the 1998 Lok Sabha elections or any woman candidate in the bye-elections to Lok Sabha/State Assemblies or Rajya Sabha held in 1998. The only exception was the Congress (I) Party. What type of a commitment was it then, when they tore the bill apart, in a (violent) gesture of professed justice for the women of select caste and community.

– Even while they are against reservation for women, they are not against women *per se*. After all they are happy to see their wives, daughters, daughters-in-law or widows (after their own death), and other close female relatives to get into politics, and protect and promote their interests. They are only against other capable women from entering the male preserved and male protected *sanctum sanctorum* of legislatures. The 'competent' and independent women from higher castes and class of urban India would 'pollute' this place, a reverse form of brahmanical order. Women's movement in India has all along opposed this brahmanical despotism and domination of religion as being gender unjust; it would equally oppose casteism and group rights of minority religion/tribes as being violent and oppressive. What it demands is justice, equity and equality, rather than excessive patriarchal protection and benevolence.

Thus while the women of all castes, communities, rural-urban and political parties stand united on the issue of political empowerment and reservation in politics, the male politicians would like to divide them on the basis of religion and caste as the latter categorisation would benefit the religion and caste based parties. Their tactics of "divide and rule the women" is definitely against any canon of gender justice and gender equality.

Empowerment in Local Government and Gender Justice

However, the question which needs to be raised here is, would political empowerment lead automatically to justice for women? Is it a means to achieve gender justice both to those who get politically empowered as well as to other women in the community? A glance at the experience of the women in the panchayats and municipalities particularly in the past four to five years subsequent to the 73rd and 74th Constitutional Amendments came into operation, would be relevant. Many studies have come out on the experience of elected women to the panchayats all over India. To what extent do the women feel that with their empowerment and emergence in politics, they have been able to achieve equality, rights and justice?

Despite the wide campaigning and popular support for the political empowerment and participation of women, the attitudes of males to the emerging role of women is somewhat ambivalent. While agreeing theoretically, they find it difficult to get rid of the patriarchal thinking process and mindset. Often this emerges in the anxiety to preserve male domination by claiming male superiority in experimental knowledge, physical strength and wide information on things mundane and public.

In the course of our studies we had come across much display of this in the form of derisive attitude towards women, devaluation of their views, indifference to their self dignity and self image, and domination over them by physical threats and sexist behaviour. Violence and use of bad language were often witnessed in the panchayat. Any idea put forth by them were defeated by men. The anti-female bias of officials thus came out strongly. The husbands often do not reconcile to their wives' position and do not allow them to move out independently. Instead they themselves performed the functions. Many people criticise their functioning because they are women. The chairpersons, particularly, seem to be subjected to this.

Harassment and Violence: Quite a few occurrences of violence during the election campaigning as well as in their functioning have come to light. Some women candidates were not allowed to file their nomination by males, on the ground that women should do only household chores. The villagers had in some cases accused them of having relations with men and tried to prevent them from contesting or winning.

Subjecting the women to all types of rumours and character assassination and harassing them is quite common. Many women belonging to SC were humiliated and discriminated; their capacity to chair the panchayats were particularly questioned and undermined. Even after being elected some women faced violence. Even the officials seem to tease the illiterate women members when the latter seek to get their work done. The officials in particular, often are not comfortable with elected women and try to dissuade them. In collusion with them the male members from opposition bring frequent no-confidence motions against the women chairpersons and threaten them. Many women pradhans have said that the men cannot tolerate a woman as their chief. There are threats by political parties and also instances of members being sexually abused by close relatives and even officials. The election, thus, seemed to have created more problems for the women than before when they were a mere housewife.

At the same time there were many positive developments like the women discarding their purdah/goonghat, sitting with men, getting to be mobile, demanding their right to speak and protesting against injustices to them. Women's reservation has also been wholeheartedly supported not merely by women but also by many males. They believe that reservation had helped women to come out of the four walls of the houses, raised the awareness of women in the community and brought about changes in the social attitude. Being women, in many places they are also respected and heard in the meetings. Some men even appreciate women's functioning as they sensed some sincerity and meaning when the women speak.

Can political empowerment of women help as a tool to promoting justice for women in the community as a whole? Many elected women speak about their prioritising developmental needs and activities for women, helping the women to fight for their rights against property disputes, dowry extortions, domestic violence and alcoholism. There are many who, however, could not do much due to the absence of adequate political and financial powers, family responsibilities and roles, patriarchal social norms and family controls.

Political empowerment, particularly at the local and rural level, thus need to be further reinforced with support mechanisms such as information, capacity realisation programmes etc. if such an empowerment process is to be taken to its logical end so as to lead to more of justice for women.

In the absence of such a gender justice and gender equality, the concept and rights of citizenship will remain denied to more than half of the Indian nation. The Constitution, the rights it grants to the citizens irrespective of caste, class and sex will remain falsified. Above all the commitment and the pledge in the form of its Preamble which solemnly pledges to justice - Economic, Political and Social, will be proved as false, at least in the context of women and children.

Table - 1: Women's Participation in Lok Sabha 1952-98

Year	Total Number	Total Contestants	Total Women Contested	Number of Women Members	% of the Total Seats
1952	499	864	51	22	4.4%
1957	500	1951	70	27	5.4%
1962	503	1985	68	34	6.7%
1967	523	2396	66	31	5.9%
1971	521	2784	86	22	4.2%
1977	544	2439	70	19	3.4%
1980	544	4520	142	28	7.9%
1984	544	5481	159	44	8.1%
1989	517	6160	189	27	5.3%
1991	544	8699	325	39	7.16%
1996	543	14274	599 (4.3)	39	7.18%
1998	543	4693	252 (5.7)	41	7.1%

Table - 2: Women Members in Rajya Sabha (1952-96)

Year	Total No. of Seats	Total No. of Women Members	Percentage
1952	219	16	7.3
1957	237	18	7.5
1962	238	18	7.6
1967	240	20	8.3
1971	243	17	7.0
1977	244	25	10.2
1980	244	24	9.8
1985	244	28	11.4
1990	245	24	9.7
1991	245	38	15.5
1994	245	20	8.16
1996	220	19	8.63

Table - 3: Number of Candidates Contested and Elected to the State Legislative Assemblies by Sex - 1984-85 to 1993-94

Sl. No.	States/UTs	1984-85				1987-88				1989-90				1991-92				1993-94			
		Contested		Elected		Contested		Elected		Contested		Elected		Contested		Elected		Contested		Elected	
		Men	Women	Men	Women	Men	Women	Men	Women	Men	Women	Men	Women	Men	Women	Men	Women	Men	Women	Men	Women
(1)	(2)	(3)	(4)	(5)	(6)	(7)	(8)	(9)	(10)	(11)	(12)	(13)	(14)	(15)	(16)	(17)	(18)	(19)	(20)	(21)	(22)
	States																				
1.	Andhra Pradesh	1895	77	284	10	-	-	-	-	1634	70	277	17	-	-	-	-	3104	127	287	7
2.	Arunachal Pradesh	110	5	30	-	-	-	-	-	168	02	58	02	-	-	-	-	-	-	-	-
3.	Assam	1104	29	121	05	-	-	-	-	-	-	-	-	1607	50	131	05	-	-	-	-
4.	Bihar	4134	104	309	15	-	-	-	-	6482	147	316	08	-	-	-	-	-	-	-	-
5.	Goa	232	10	29	01	-	-	-	-	243	09	38	02	-	-	-	-	301	10	36	4
6.	Gujarat	1095	42	166	16	-	-	-	-	1836	53	178	04	-	-	-	-	-	-	-	-
7.	Haryana	-	-	-	-	1287	35	85	5	-	-	-	-	1844	41	84	06	-	-	-	-
8.	Himachal Pradesh	284	10	216	08	-	-	-	-	436	18	64	04	-	-	-	-	399	17	65	3
9.	Jammu & Kashmir	-	-	-	-	515	13	75	1	-	-	-	-	-	-	-	-	-	-	-	-
10.	Karnataka	-	-	-	-	-	-	-	-	1964	79	214	10	-	-	-	-	2380	118	117	7
11.	Kerala	-	-	-	-	1220	34	132	8	-	-	-	-	783	26	132	08	-	-	-	-
12.	Madhya Pradesh	2374	76	272	16	-	-	-	-	4062	154	309	11	-	-	-	-	3562	167	308	12
13.	Maharashtra	2147	83	60	-	-	-	-	-	3616	148	282	06	-	-	-	-	-	-	-	-
14.	Manipur	359	5	139	08	-	-	-	-	282	06	59.	01	-	-	-	-	-	-	-	-
15.	Meghalaya	-	-	-	-	268	3	58	02	-	-	-	-	-	-	-	-	283	7	59	1
16.	Mizoram	-	-	-	-	141	4	39	1	158	4	40	-	-	-	-	-	118	3	40	-
17.	Nagaland	-	-	-	-	211	3	59	1	140	-	60	-	-	-	-	-	177	1	60	-
18.	Orissa	775	25	113	04	-	-	-	-	871	42	140	07	-	-	-		-	-	-	-
19.	Punjab	824	33	184	16	-	-	-	-	-	-	-	557	22	111	06		-	-	-	-
20.	Rajasthan	1458	46	32	-	-	-	-	-	2995	93	189	11	-	-	-	-	2341	96	190	9
21.	Sikkim	184	11	226	08	-	-	-	-	113	05	30	2	-	-	-	-	175	9	31	1
22.	Tamil Nadu	1453	46	394	31	-	-	-	-	2968	78	224	10	2741	102	202	32	-	-	-	-
23.	Tripura	-	-	-	-	213	7	58	02	-	-	-	-	-	-	-	392	15	59	1	
24.	Uttar Pradesh	5850	169	28	02	-	-	-	-	5896	206	407	18	7622	229	409	10	9456	260	408	14
25.	West Bengal	-	-	-	-	1461	36	281	13	-	-	-	-	1829	74	273	21	-	-	-	-
	Union Territories																				
1.	Delhi	-	-	-	-	-	-	-	-	-	-	-	-	-	-	-	-	1257	59	67	3
2.	Pondicherry	115	4	29	01	-	-	-	-	206	06	30	-	202	06	29	01	-	-	-	-
	Total	24393	775	2632	141	5316	135	787	33	34070	1120	2915	113	17185	550	1371	89	23945	889	1727	62

Source: Election Commission, New Delhi.

17

UNIFEM'S Work on Gender Justice

Chandni Joshi

Working towards gender justice necessarily entails a women's empowerment framework, a framework within which the United Nations Development Fund for Women (UNIFEM) functions. It was established as the Voluntary Fund for the UN Decade for Women in 1976, in response to the demand for a Fund for women within the UN system to work towards gender equality and gender justice. Empowerment, as UNIFEM sees it, is about changing or transforming power relations in favour of those who previously exercised little power over their own lives. If power means access and control, then empowerment is the process of gaining access to and control over resources, knowledge, belief systems, values and the self. Power also means to enable or to facilitate. In this sense, empowerment entails creating enabling conditions for human well being the building of human capacity and the process of inner transformation of the self. It is a framework that can tap powerful reservoirs of hope and enthusiasm among people who have been subjected to viewing themselves and their worlds in negative, fragmented or broken terms.

In an effort to achieve the goals of empowerment, I would briefly like to outline the setting of UNIFEM's activities. Working strategically for gender justice and equality of women and men, UNIFEM is a learning and advocacy organization.

By building on the women's economic empowerment framework, UNIFEM considers interventions that really contribute towards systemic change, piloting new approaches for women's empowerment that can be replicated on a wider scale, and that also test new policy options and tools for gender equity. UNIFEM's world view looks at three areas of concern: strengthening women's economic capacity, engendering governance, and promoting women's rights to eliminate all forms of violence against women.

UNIFEM strengthens its role as a catalyst and provider of strategic and technical know-how to the UN system in the area of women's empowerment and gender equality, especially in the context of the recent UN reforms. It forges new synergies and effective partnerships between women's organizations, governments, the UN system and the private sector, so as to leverage political and financial support for women from a range of stakeholders in the development process. Its great successes have been the fostering of networks and linkages that really contribute to women's empowerment and gender justice. By building a learning and knowledge based organization, UNIFEM is a vehicle for catalyzing systemic change to eradicate feminized poverty.

UNIFEM's mission, policy framework and strategies were strongly endorsed by the Fourth World Conference on Women held in September 1995 in Beijing, which was a milestone in the history of UN work for women. A call to commitment and action, it was the culmination of a chain of global conferences, embracing all the issues covered by them and more. In its wide canvas were included all development and human rights issues within the control of our socialization process, relationships and mindsets, which empower some and disempower others, which build barriers and create demeaning stereotypes, and negate everything that development stands for. The goals of Beijing were:

- sharing power equally
- obtaining full access to the means of development
- overcoming poverty
- promoting peace and defending women's rights
- inspiring a new generation of women to work together for equality and equity.

UNIFEM is an aid to and advocate for women in the developing world, striving to give women voice and visibility in their search for gender justice. Recognizing that women are critical actors in families, communities, and economic systems, and that they need access to resources as well as to social services, UNIFEM believes that the best way to help women in developing countries is to strengthen the organizations they create and control, while fostering links and partnerships at every level. The Platform for Action can only become a reality when the partnership between government and civil society extends into the implementation stage. This partnership has to be mobilized at all levels: the family, the local community, and the State. One of the ways of doing this is to help ensure the participation of women in all levels of development planning and practice, and to recognize their contribution.

Though the status of women and their situation has improved in the last two decades, much as yet remains to be done. This is very tellingly captured by the United Nations 1995 Human Development Report, which notes:

'Women still constitute 70 per cent of the world's poor and two-thirds of the world's illiterates. They occupy only 14 per cent of managerial and administrative jobs, 10 per cent of parliamentary seats and 6 per cent of cabinet posts .... In many legal systems, they are still unequal. They often work longer hours than men, but much of their work remains undervalued, unrecognized and unappreciated. And the threat of violence stalks their lives from cradle to grave."

We are presently at the beginning of the United Nations proclaimed International Decade of Poverty Eradication (1997-2006). This was declared by the United Nations in late 1995 to urge governments and organizations to pursue the implementation of the outcomes of major UN conferences relating to the eradication of poverty. Spreading like a cancer, the South Asia region is home to the largest number of poor in the world wearing an increasingly feminine face. The close alliance of Poverty and Gender is a disturbing commentary on our times, and a disadvantage compounded. Though Poverty has always been there, it is unfortunately scaling new heights as we approach the 21st Century. The following statistics reveal that:

* Women constitute nearly 70 per cent of the world's one billion poor. Rural women living in absolute poverty, rose by 50 per cent over the last two decades.

* In countries with economies in transition, women have become the major victims of unemployment with a 14 per cent unemployment rate as compared to 9 per cent among men.

* The growth of single-parent homes headed by women has contributed to the feminization of poverty, which is a growing phenomenon.

The structures that keep women in poverty are many. They are found in the home, the marketplace, the workplace, and in the political institutions where decisions are made. There is recognition today that poor women have the least access to basic needs, both within the family and outside it. In difficult times, such as periods of economic stagnation, recession or even some structural adjustment processes, women living in poverty pay a disproportionately high price. It is no longer a matter of debate that there exists a crucial inter-linkage between gender and equity in poverty alleviation and sustainable development.

In South Asia, women constitute a major workforce for the region, which derives most of its income and resources from labour-intensive industrial production and household industries, primarily within the textile, garment and agricultural sectors. These are key export sectors for South Asia and of particular importance for the region's access to foreign currency and international markets. They are also major employers of women, either in wage employment or as unorganized labour in the informal sector. The latter remain unreflected in national accounts. Their work is neither recognized nor documented. According to the Worldwide Facts and Statistics about the Status of Women, $11 trillion is missing from the global economy each year because of unpaid housework, childcare, agricultural and other labour performed by women. Furthermore, wages for women lag behind men for similar work in all countries, with women performing an estimated 60 per cent of the world's work, but owning only 1 per cent of the world's land and earning just 10 per cent of the world's income.

In order to change this present scheme of things, a new development ethics and morality need to be placed at the core of development thinking and practice, based on the perspectives and realities of women's lives. A world is envisioned, where women and men have a parity in living conditions, opportunities, options and incomes, and where gender equality is an intrinsic dimension of true people-centred development.

Towards this end, there is a move now toward a new dynamic paradigm that identifies the well-being of people rather than the current level of per capita national income as the essence of development. Concepts such as sustainability, human development, social development, gender-responsive development, women's rights as human rights, equity and social justice are increasingly central to the development debate. The present approach of 'gender and development', recognizes the fact that women and men have different life courses and that development policies affect them differently. Today there is a search to address these differences by mainstreaming gender into development planning at all levels and all sectors, in order to ensure equal outcomes. There is a recognition of the fact that improving the status of women cannot be understood as a separate isolated issue and can only be achieved by taking into account the status of both women and men. There is a recognition that alternate models of masculinity need to be explored, encouraging gender sensitive men to raise the awareness of other men about women in untraditional fields like, the socio-economic and political fields, and their cultural and legal status. There is equally a need to acknowledge that women's empowerment does not mean the disempowerment of men but the enrichment and the inclusion of each and every member of the human family. The goal of gender justice is enabled by adopting a holistic approach, which blends women's empowerment and gender planning perspectives, decentralized approaches, and treats women not just as objects of policy and programmes but as part of a process of transformation of social attitudes.

In order to assist this, UNIFEM supports innovative and catalytic initiatives which demonstrate effective development alternatives, facilitating a more gender responsive enabling policy environment. It has sought over the years to create a platform, lobby and facilitate the equal partnership of women and men in the policy making process. There is today a consensus among national governments, NGOs and the donor communities that sustainable development is only possible through actual people's, women's and men's, participation, and that planning should be participatory with a bottom-up approach. In order to achieve this, UNIFEM has developed the Alternate Development Module, which it has successfully used in the Peasant Women's Summits, Mainstreaming Gender Consideration in the National Development Plan in Nepal, in the Preparatory process to Beijing and in making the Ninth Development Plan of India more gender responsive. These have been a response to preserve the continuum of all the UN conferences and meetings that have taken place, leading the process to its logical conclusion - for women to be part of the planning process itself.

In this article, I would like to share with you some of UNIFEM's mainstreaming efforts in the South Asia region. To go back to the earlier part of this decade, the Fund has been investing effort in different regions to bring together people engaged on the development of new concepts and approaches, and needs of various users such as the government, women's groups, academia, and media.

In the early 1990s, in a pioneering initiative, UNIFEM supported a series of Peasant Women's Summits in four countries of South Asia - Nepal, India, Pakistan and Bangladesh. They were the first of their kind in the world because the peasant women had the opportunity to share the same platform with the policy-makers and to express their views on the management of the natural environment. By creating these channels of communication between the micro and the macro-levels, gender concerns were mainstreamed in agricultural policy, thereby enabling the creation of a gender perspective in a key area affecting the lives of women living in poverty. UNIFEM followed these summits up with a four country meet with official delegations from the four governments in Lahore, 1992, and four of the peasant women went to attend the Earth Summit in Rio in the same year. This initial effort to influence policy makers and the scientific establishment to listen to the voices of peasant women has been followed up further in India by UNIFEM and the Centre of Women's Development Studies, which held regional conferences of peasant women for a dialogue with the government and the agricultural universities, leading to their voices being incorporated in the Ninth Development Plan of India. In Pakistan it led to the UNIFEM supported radio programme; in Bangladesh it led to the formulation of the national conservation strategy; and in Nepal the peasant women were linked with the agricultural universities.

Engendering national development plans is a key strategy in mainstreaming gender concerns. In Nepal, to make the national development planning gender responsive, UNIFEM undertook an intervention to mainstream gender considerations in the national development plan, seeking to sensitize the Eighth Plan of Nepal. This it did by strengthening the capacity of the National Planning Commission, through the examination of structural obstacles to women's full participation in the development process, and by identifying a set of appropriate corrective measures in policy, institutional responsibilities and legal framework, that could be legislated in the Eighth Five-year Development Plan.

In the early 1990s, UNIFEM supported Maldives to conduct a national survey leading to the preparation of a secondary data report which used existing statistical data. This report reflected the importance of planning for the involvement of women in mainstream development. The initiative culminated in a National Seminar on Women in Development in August 1992, jointly organized by UNIFEM, the Department of Women's Affairs, the Ministry of Planning and Environment and UNDP. For the first time women and men from the Atolls came together, in this effort to sensitize policy makers and senior level officials of the government, leading to increased awareness on the gender dimensions in development. It further sought to help identify the development needs of women, and awaken a commitment to increase the participation of women in development efforts.

India witnessed a most dramatic mobilization of women from all walks of life on the eve of the Beijing conference, something that owed its origins to the richness of the women's movement and to the abiding democratic spirit in which the government and the movement continuously listened and interacted with each other. UNIFEM played a key role in bringing partners together, and in carrying the voices of grassroots women to Beijing. In India, the activities culminated in the Regional Lobby Workshops followed by the National Preparatory Meet, bringing together women from the grassroot, representatives of the government, about 400 NGO delegates, prominent activists, and representatives of the international agencies. A forum was thus provided where different voices, different concerns, different levels, all turned together towards the common goals of equality, peace and development.

UNIFEM undertook a unique exercise to include women's voices in the Ninth National Development Plan of India, which has lead to the empowerment of women as one of the Plan's objectives. It facilitated a process in which some of the most distinguished and representative leaders of the women's movement came together as a think tank. The think tank helped to raise the voices of hundreds of women mobilized from different walks of life to influence the national planning process. This was accomplished at various stages of the planning process through research and study, including a review and evaluation of past plans. This was followed by hosting five regional meetings and a national consultation where the outcome of the regional meetings was presented to the policy makers and planners. The objective was to set in motion a participatory planning process by the women themselves. This resulted in women sharing their concerns with policy planners, at different stages, with the official planning process. By these efforts UNIFEM created space for women at every stage, assisted and built their capacity to understand the macro-planning process and demonstrated a new model of gender mainstreaming of the plan through the agency of women themselves. UNIFEM has discussed and held negotiations with other South Asian governments and representatives of the women's movement, on trying this methodology and process in their particular countries. Within India itself, the participatory process of engendering the national development plan is now being replicated at the state level. A process such as this, additionally, lends itself to yielding both gender-sensitive public policy as well as data and statistics.

In the South Asia region, as a follow-up to the Beijing Conference and to mainstream women in development planning, UNIFEM has provided technical assistance to various governments of the region. It is a fact that this region is one of the richest in terms of experimentation with successful alternative development responses and innovative strategies, which instead of marginalizing women, have in fact, built on women's empowerment. Whether it is SEWA or the Grameen Bank or Mahila Samakhya or the Production Credit for Rural Women, the lesson that comes out loud and clear is that, if gender equality is to be achieved, women's concerns and perspectives need to become central to the whole process. There is a consensus that incorporating a gender perspective in macro policies and in the allocation of resources, holds the key to sustainable development. And this can happen only when women are in a position to question the relationship of subordination and inequality, which define the social, economic, cultural and political organization of societies.

A key element for gender mainstreaming is the establishment of sex disaggregated data for gender responsive policies and plans. A paucity of this data, as well as prevalent misconceptions and prejudices about women's actual input to economic development greatly hamper this process. Since women are not perceived as economic entities, their work and contribution to the economy remains undervalued and under-recorded, contributing to their invisibility to policy-makers and development planners. Highlighted by the Platform for Action, and in order to facilitate a more integrated approach to gender-responsive development planning, UNIFEM has been, and is working to improve statistics on gender, thus removing the cloak from women's productivity. It is true that as long as women remain statistically invisible, their work their lives, and their disadvantages will remain invisible to policy makers and leaders. Words do need numbers to influence development interventions.

In order to put women squarely on the books, UNIFEM is working to ensure that the productivity of half the workforce does not remain in the shadows. By improving statistics on gender issues, it is providing a strategic entry point for a more integrated approach to gender responsive development planning, which has the participation of women in all levels of development planning and practice. Therefore, by engendering the development process that leads to a growth in resources and services earmarked for women, UNIFEM hopes to lead to the overall empowerment of women.

As early as 1991 UNIFEM assisted in the Census Exercise in both India and Pakistan, and initiated dialogues with the Census Bureau of Statistics in Nepal. With its comparative advantage of a historical commitment to improve the visibility of women in national accounting, UNIFEM has been providing technical support to a number of countries in the South Asia region. In collaboration with other UN organizations, UNIFEM worked to make the 1998 census of Pakistan more gender responsive, and is working with them to engender the 2001 censuses of India and Nepal. Sri Lanka too, is working towards the development of a satellite accounting system to reflect the true worth of women's contributions.

In the area of Women's Human Rights, UNIFEM works in partnership with women's groups, governments and the UN system to promote the realization of women's rights (civil, cultural, economic, political and social), and to support efforts to eliminate all forms of violence against women. UNIFEM also supports innovative actions at the community level to ensure that human rights are enjoyed by women everywhere. The Women's Human Rights Programme works in three main areas: mainstreaming women's human rights into the policy and practice of the UN human rights machinery; combating and eliminating violence against women; and strengthening women's knowledge of their rights and use of existing instruments to promote and protect them, with a particular focus on the Convention on the Elimination of All Forms of Discrimination Against Women (CEDAW).

UNIFEM's mainstreaming activities on human rights have been a logical follow-up to the extraordinary impact women made at the World Conference on Human Rights in Vienna, where they emerged as one of the most dynamic forces demanding the inclusion of issues related to the human rights of women, particularly in the area of violence against women. In India, UNIFEM has provided technical support to the Government of India to finalize the first periodic report required after the ratification of CEDAW through a consultative process. In Asia, UNIFEM's office collaborated with UNICEF to produce and launch the joint publication, widely known as the 'CEDAW Kit', an advocacy tool for both advocates and government representatives, which examines the role of CEDAW as the Bill of Rights for Women.

In 1997, the Trust Fund for Action to Eliminate Violence Against Women was established within UNIFEM. It supports innovative initiatives in the areas of awareness-raising and advocacy, capacity building, legal literacy training, prevention and deterrence of violence and action-related research. For example, UNIFEM is pioneering an intervention to train Afghan women-led NGOs based in Pakistan; and in collaboration with a Lahore based NGO, is working on a novel pilot programme with three Lahore schools to introduce a human rights education curriculum. And in India, in collaboration with a specialized NGO, and through the agency of high level judges, an exercise is being undertaken to identify bottlenecks and obstacles in the justice system, advocating for the institutionalization of gender training of all female and male judges in the region.

Additionally, UNIFEM has supported the publication and dissemination of a Gender Resource Directory, listing services in the metropolitan Calcutta area for women fleeing from violent home situations. Within the region, UNIFEM and other UN agencies, are collaborating on the issue of violence against women and girls. These initiatives include looking at the effectiveness of the legal system in India, Sri Lanka, Pakistan, Nepal and Bangladesh, identifying critical areas requiring reform; at the elimination of trafficking of women and girls; and at building a regional alliance of women and men drawn from different spheres and professions to share their experiences in countering violence against women. This has lead to the formation of a regional network which would act as a pressure group within and across countries, working towards a gender-based violence free society, advocating and disseminating alternate role models of masculinity and feminity.

In order to address the issue of 'Peace' in the region, a process has been initiated whereby women from the SAARC region have come together around it. This UNIFEM initiative provides support to national and regional women's networking on Peace in India, Pakistan, Nepal, Bangladesh and Sri Lanka. Working to test out community-based strategies, a UNIFEM intervention is piloting a model in three North Indian states which are prone to gender based violence. This involves setting up neighbourhood communities of women and men, sensitization of police, advocacy, and counseling.

As this year is the 50th Anniversary for the Universal Declaration of Human Rights, 16 Days of Activism Against Gender Violence Campaign, from November 25 - December 10, 1998, is being celebrated globally. Many UN agencies including UNIFEM have already taken up the initiative to celebrate this cause. In its continued efforts to work in the area of women's human rights, UNIFEM, South Asia Regional office has chosen to focus its energies for this cause, leading up to, and on the official dates of the campaign from November 25, 1998 (International Day on Violence Against Women), to December 10, 1998 (50th Anniversary of the Universal Declaration of Human Rights). Its prime activities in this campaign, which has now become a UN system initiative, will be a Silent March, which will have slogans and placards decrying violence against women; an Information Sheet on women's human rights to be disseminated strategically at police stations - duly informing both women and the law enforcement personnel of their rights and responsibilities respectively. Other activities include artistic performances, an essay and poster competition, launch of a stamp and coin, all geared towards raising awareness, and breaking the culture of silence, which dominates the issue of gender based violence.

In order to mainstreaming gender within the UN system, UNIFEM has strengthened its support to the UN Resident Coordinators and provides technical advice to the UN system in the coordination and formulation of gender policies and programmes. Furthermore, there is an UN inter-agency working group on gender, with three sub-groups, looking at the issues of poverty alleviation and economic empowerment, violence against women and data collection.

The ultimate goal of all UNIFEM intervention is the attainment of gender justice, albeit in different areas of women's lives - each as important as the other. Both gender justice and gender equity are at the core of Women's Development Agenda for the 21st Century as the central principle of a new development process that would benefit women and men equally. Based on a principle of social justice, the Agenda addresses women's livelihood needs in terms of their entitlements to and control over resources. Furthermore, it aims to empower women to reorient and reshape policies and decisions through their active and full participation in the entire development process, seeking to empower women in claiming their basic right to sustainable livelihoods and secure lives. UNIFEM thus, continues to move upstream on the micro-macro continuum taking experience gained at the micro level and using it to affect change at the macro level.

A vehicle for change, UNIFEM facilitates the challenge for leadership and mainstreaming, through articulating a women's development agenda, exemplified in the interventions mentioned in this paper, that cross divisions between issues. There exists a close inter-relationship between development, democracy, human rights, human security, and sustainable livelihoods, and there is a need for all to be addressed, for the creation of a healthy and sustainable planet for the 21st century.

Bibliography

1. UNIFEM Annual Report 1996
2. UNIFEM in-house material
3. Platform for Action and the Beijing Declaration
4. Link in to Gender and Development - Gender and Youth Affairs Division, Commonwealth Secretariat, London
5. Women in Development - Issues, Challenges and Strategies in Asia, ADB, Manila
6. ESCAP Jakarta Declaration for the advancement of women in Asia and Pacific

18

Health and Gender Justice

Mira Shiva

The Human Development Index for India was 135 in 1996 and it has further deteriorated to 139. The Gender Development Index for India according to the Human Development Report is 103. It hides in its midst the neglect and denial of millions of women, where food, health education are concerned. The deep rooted discrimination against women continues to grow. To the discriminatory and biased social attitude towards women, certain castes etc is added the distortions emerging out of increasing consumerism and market economy where monetary gain and purchasing power take priority over other values of health, survival, nurturing, sustenance of life, peace, harmony, compassion, and curing. Women with little or no economic and social rights find themselves more and more marginalized while others find themselves more and "more commodified" with a minority who have joined as entrepreneurs, business women, managers and in administrative services etc. having improved their lot.

What have 50 years of independence done to women and their health? It is in fact life expectancy of women has increased, infant mortality rate, maternal mortality rates have come down.

Women continue to shoulder the responsibility of the family. The double and the triple burden is a reality as they take on more and more work for augmenting the family. In the case of nuclear home, with less and less support from the joint family system, they find themselves caring not just for husbands, children but also in-laws. If there are household animals eg. goats, cows and poultry etc., its the women who obtain fodder and give them fodder, food and water.

While it is women who feed the family and feed the world, the fact remains that 80 per cent of our pregnant women are anaemic, 20 per cent are stunted, making them high risk mothers, vulnerable to obstructed labour due to small pelvic bones. Large number of women put on a mere 2-3 kg. of weight during pregnancy - when they should be putting on 8-10 kg weight. It is therefore not surprising that 1/3 of the babies born are low birth weight babies and these children can never quite make up and when UNICEF reports show 52 per cent of our children under five as being undeveloped and malnourished i.e. worse than sub-Sahara Africa. It comes with a sense of shock, shame and disbelief!

Our maternal mortality rate (MMR) of 460/100,000 is almost 4 times that of Vietnam 110/100,000 - a much poor country which has seen war. For every woman who dies during labour, 30 other survive to suffer the consequences of complications.

Table 1

PERCENTAGE DISTRIBUTION OF DEATHS BY CAUSES RELATED TO CHILDBIRTH AND PREGNANCY (1981-87)

Specific Cause	1981	1982	1983	1984	1985	1986	1987
Abortion	13.7	10.1	10.7	10.8	11.5	8.0	7.6
Toxemia	8.0	12.5	12.1	10.8	6.7	11.9	6.6
Anaemia	17.7	24.4	18.9	23.3	23.3	17.0	17.8
Bleeding of Pregnancy and Puerperium	23.4	26.2	23.5	18.8	15.9	21.6	21.9
Malposition of Child Leading to Death of Mother	9.2	7.2	8.3	6.2	7.7	6.2	10.1
Puerperium Sepsis	13.1	8.3	1.6	10.8	13.9	13.1	16.7
Not Classifiable	14.9	11.3	14.6	19.3	21.2	22.2	19.3
Total	100	100	100	100	100	100	100

Source: Survey, Causes of Death (Rural) - 1984 and 1987, 1995, Radical Journal of Health, Vol. 1.2.

In India, 125,000 women die due to pregnancy and childbirth related causes. The MMR in Orissa is the highest, followed by Madhya Pradesh (see Figure 4). Kerala has the lowest MMR - 87/100,000 live births and the lowest infant mortality rate - 17/1000 live births. Major causes of maternal mortality in India are anaemia-related and due to lack of rational management of high risk mothers and of those needing emergency obstetic care (see Figure 3). Due to inadequate access to health care services, partially due to their non-availability near by or due to non-affordability or non-availability of transport on the resources required to purchase private services.

For every women who dies during childbirth, around 18-20 women survive with complications, for example, cervical lacerations pelvic inflammatory diseases, anaemia, uterine or bladder prolapse, vesico vaginal or recto vaginal fistula (*leaking of urine or stools*), infertility etc. Since it is not a matter of demographic concern, reliable figures regarding these complications are not easily available.

It is often forgotten that besides problems related to the reproductive tract, women also suffer from communicable and other diseases during pregnancy.

Women in malaria endemic areas are prone to the disease, which itself can lead to abortions, still births and low birth weight babies. Viral hepatitis in pregnant women has a higher mortality as compared to men or non-pregnant women. Tuberculosis, rheumatic heart disease, diabetes, etc. are known to worsen during pregnancy. There is a need to address the above communicable diseases in order to bring down maternal mortality and maternal morbidity.

In the absence of trained personnel accessible and affordable maternal health services, 84 per cent to rural women and 42 per cent of urban women are being assisted at childbirth by untrained personnel. In the light of this, it is not surprising that maternal mortality figures continue to be unacceptably high. In the obsession with meeting family planning targets, training and skill development in clinical diagnosis and rational management of women's health problems have suffered.

The proliferation of profit oriented junk food, junk drinks, the increasing difficulty in getting simple, essential basic food at affordable prices has become an additional factor. It is recognised that the initiative and efforts taken to address women's issues have been inadequate, distorted, vertical, top-down and have rarely emerged out of women's priority concerns. Rarely have women's experiences, views, concerns and local health practices received the priority they deserve. For example, the universal package of iron folic acid and tetanus toxoid' has been presented as the main solution for improved maternal nutritional health. Women's access to adequate food or caloric deficit, due to her continued hard physical labour till the end of pregnancy, the need for equitable distribution of food, and work within and outside home remains a non issue. Even when it is women in the reproductive child-bearing age that have received attention, the focus has been the fertility control. The problems of girls, specially adolescents, women who are unmarried, childless, older, disabled, deserted etc., have been neglected.

The marginalisation of women is worsened when it is associated with poverty, illiteracy, rural background, lower caste, widowhood, desertion, disability, single marital status or childlessness. Probably in no other country are women spoken of as 'devise' and denied their rights to personhood and discriminated against because of their gender. This phenomenon is worst in the northern states of India, where low female literacy, combined with low social status of women, has resulted in keeping them oppressed in the name of community, culture, tradition, family honour and religion. In areas where women and girls are neglected, their health status is obviously negatively affected.

The failure to address the socio-economic, political roots of the continued poor health of our women has been one of our biggest tragedies. The other, of course, has been the 'misdiagnosis' of women's health problems, the 'misprioritisation' and propagation of demographically driven technological fixes, as the ultimate solution to women's health problems.

Parameters for Women's Health

Usually the parameters being used to assess women's health status mainly reflect demographic concerns. Gender desegregated data is often not collected. Review of research papers and documents reflects' the proliferation of material on demographic-related studies; but less on women's morbidity, suffering and pain. There are tremendous differences in the health status of our people in different states, within different parts of the same state, between the genders and between different caste and class groups in the same place. Desegregated data is essential for realistic planning, decentralised decision-making and ensuring that policies and programmes are need-based. Some of the parameters for assessing women's health could be as follows.

Mortality of Women

Even though a large number of women die needlessly during childbirth No. 1 cause of death in the reproductive age group is *Tuberculosis* and has been so since 1980's. The second commonest cause of death in reproductive age group is *suicide* and the 4th commonest is *burns (RGI-1995)*

Many of the cases of suicide are actually homicide for dowry related causes. So are the burns. Gender aggregated data on *poisoning* and *burns* do not exist. Violence against women is not included as a specific category in medical categorization and record keeping, resulting in constant under extraction of a worsening reality.

TOP 10 CAUSES OF MORTALITY OF WOMEN IN REPRODUCTIVE AGE GROUP 15-44 YEARS

1981	1991	1994
1. TB of Lungs	1. TB of Lungs	1. TB of Lungs
2. Bronchitis / Asthma	2. Burns	2. Suicides
3. Typhoid	3. Suicides	3. Heart Attack
4. Non-Preg Anaemia	4. Heart Attack	4. Burns
5. Congestive Heart	5. Cancer	5. Cancer
6. Gastroenteritis	6. Congestive Heart	6. Non Preg Anaemia
7. Burns	7. Acute Abdomen	7. Bronchitis Asthama
8. Bleeding of Preg	8. Non Preg Anaemia	8. Acute Abdomen
9. Drowning	9. Bronchitis/Asthama	9. Malaria
10. Cancer	10. Non Class/Fever	10.Snakebite

Sex Ratio

The sex ratio i.e. number of females per 1,000 males, which should be more favourable to women due to their biological advantage, is inverse in India. As can be seen from Figure 1, it has been getting worse with each census.

Figure 1

SEX RATIO

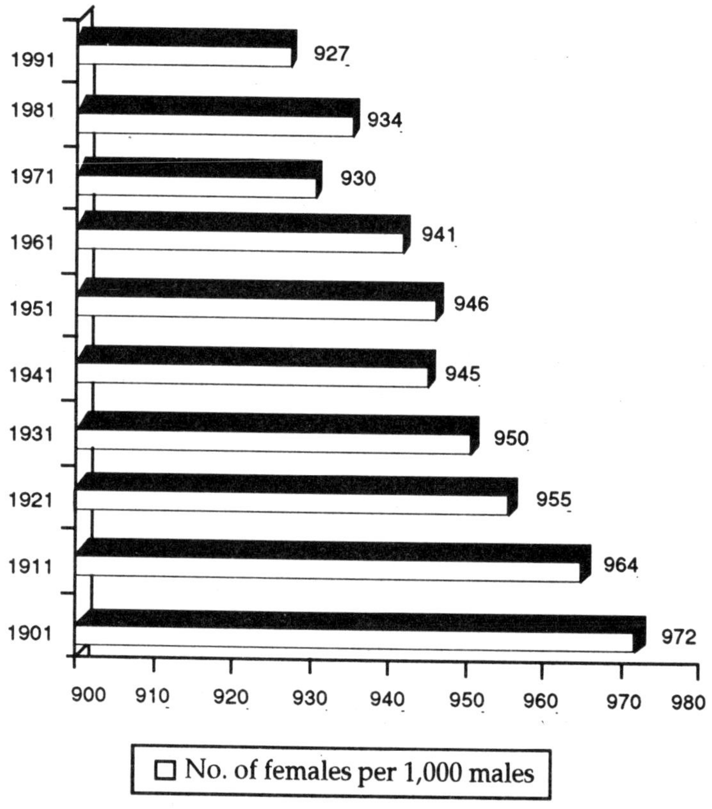

Source: India Country Report prepared for the World Congress for Women - Beijing, 1995, New Delhi, Department of Women and Child Development.

Figure 2 provides a list of the ten districts in the country with the worst child sex ratio. The irony of it all is that Punjab and Haryana are not economically backward; the extremely patriarchal nature of agriculture-based economies is the influencing factor. Tamil Nadu is considered a success story as far as female literacy and decrease in birth rates are concerned. Yet, female infanticide continues to be practised in some districts of Tamil Nadu. Here, as in Bihar, poverty seems to the driving force.

Figure 2

TEN DISTRICTS WITH THE WORST CHILD SEX RATIO, 1991

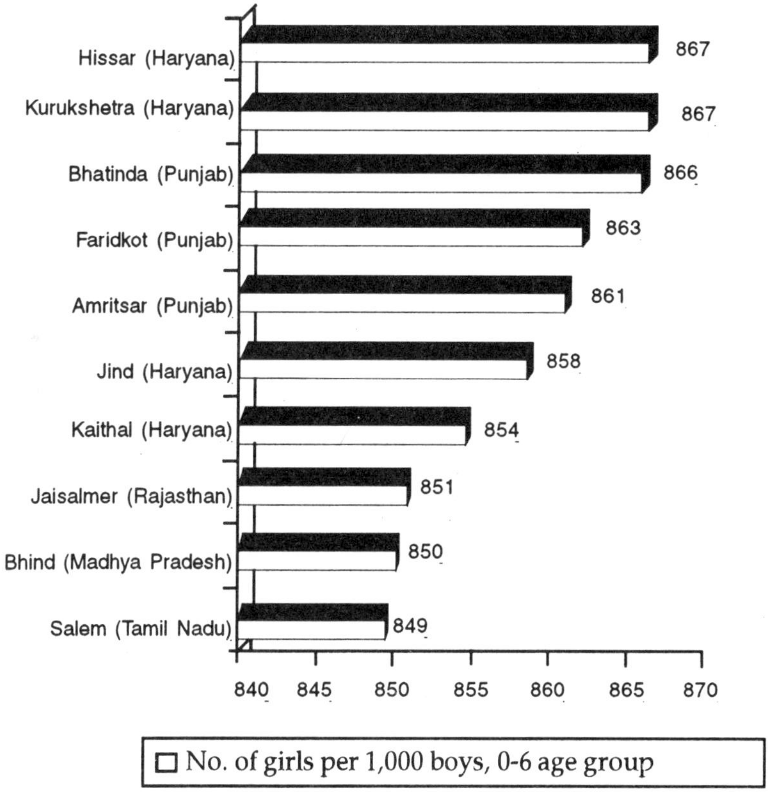

Source: Census of India, 1991, New Delhi, Office of the Registrar General of India.

Maternal Mortality

In India, maternal mortality and the complications related to pregnancy are very high, as compared to some of our Asian neighbours; the maternal mortality rate (*number of maternal deaths per 100,000 live births*) is much lower in East Asian countries (Figure 3). Even African countries like Tunisia and Kenya have succeeded in lowering their maternal mortality rate *(310, and 190/100,000 live births respectively)*. The maternal mortality rate in the U.K. USA and Sweden is 11, 10 and 100,000 live births respectively.

Female Literacy

Areas with low levels of female literacy have high rates of maternal mortality, infant mortality, birth and cases of female foeticide and dowry deaths. The sex ratio is also the worst in these places. The low female literacy, specially in the

Figure 3

MATERNAL MORTALITY RATE IN SOME ASIAN COUNTRIES

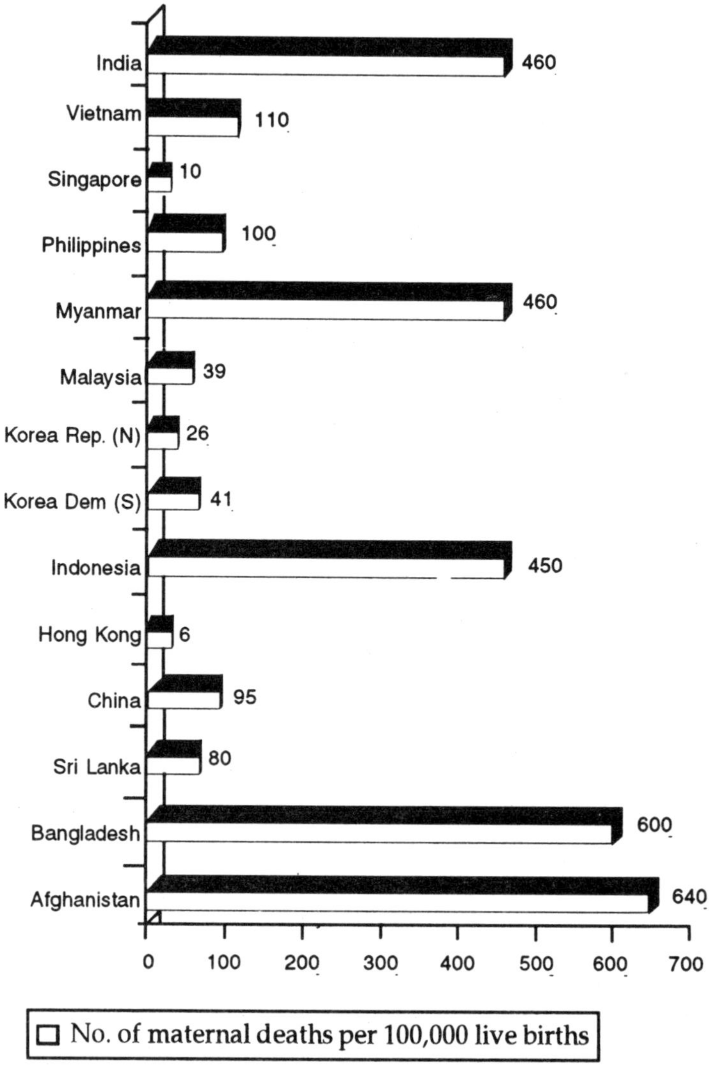

Source: The Progress of Nations, 1995, UNICEF.

BIMARU states, is a matter of concern. A comparison of literacy rates with the infant mortality rate and birth rate in the four best and the four worst states, as far as health parameters are concerned is given in Table 2.

We need to seriously address the various reasons for girls not being sent to school. Even though governmental decision has been taken to provide free primary education, it means little to those families that have to keep their girls

Figure 4

MATERNAL MORTALITY RATE IN INDIA

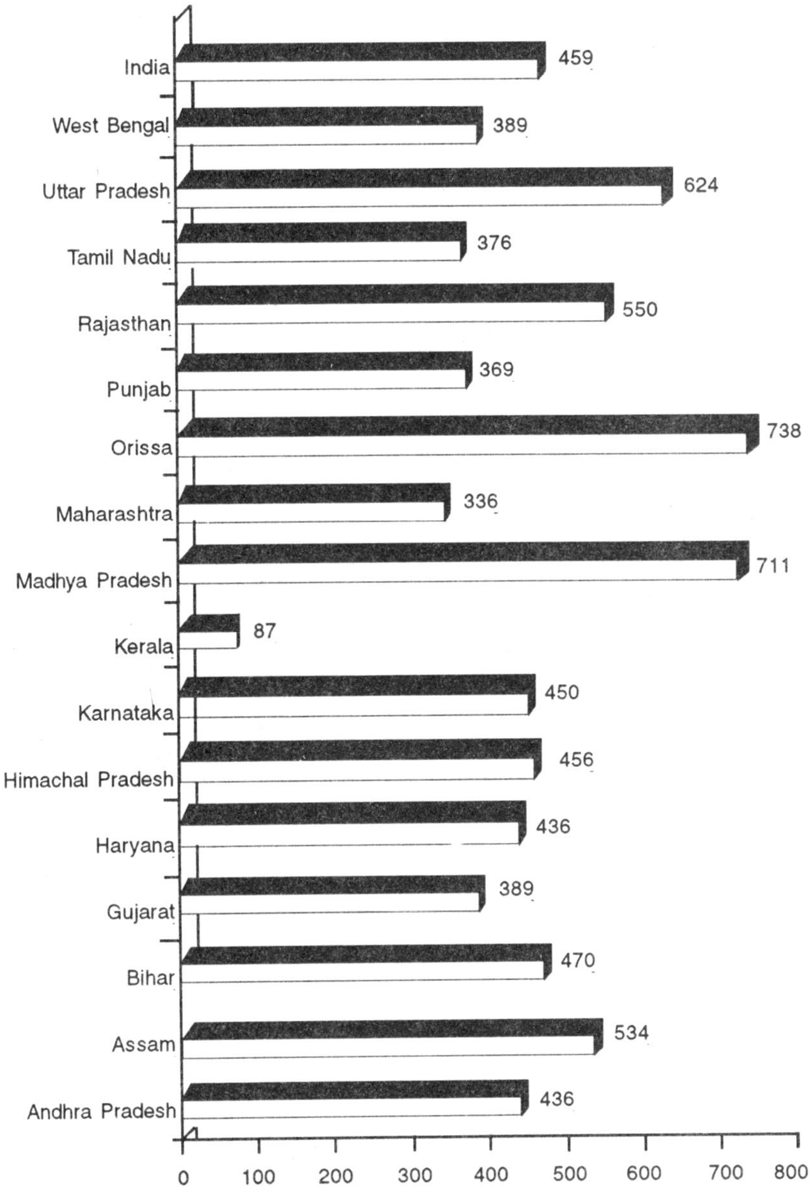

☐ No. of maternal deaths per 100,000 live births

Source: Progress of Indian States, 1995, New Delhi, UNICEF.

Table 2
COMPARISON OF SOCIAL AND HEALTH PARAMETERS IN SELECTED STATES, 1992-93

	Literacy Rate (per cent)	Infant Mortality Rate (per 1,000 live births)	Birth Rate (per 1,000 population)	Death Rate (per 1,000 population)	Natural Growth Rate (per thousand)	Total Fertility Rate
India	52.2	74	28.7	9.3	19.4	3.4
Madhya Pradesh	44.2	98	32.8	12.6	21.3	4.4
Uttar Pradesh	41.6	88	35.4	11.6	24.4	5.1
Rajasthan	38.6	84	33.7	9.1	24.8	4.6
Bihar	38.5	66	32.5	10.6	22.1	4.4
Kerala	89.8	16	17.3	6.0	11.3	1.8
Tamil Nadu	62.7	59	19.00	8.2	11.1	2.2
Karnataka	56	65	24.9	8.0	16.8	3.0
Andhra Pradesh	44.1	63	23.7	8.6		

Source: A. Bose, Changing Paradigm, National Family Health Survey 1992-93 India, IIPS, 1993, Natarajan K.S., Population Projections for India.

at home to care for younger siblings, perform housework, etc., for economic reasons. Fear of sexual harassment and sexual violence prevents many girls from attending schools that have male teachers, and are located far from their homes or even outside the village, or with an overwhelming number of male students. There is also the added fear of not being able to get a groom with a higher educational qualification than the daughter.

Gender Discrimination

When gender discrimination has been socialised and internalised, it is no longer visible to the gender insensitive. Unfortunately, religion, health care, education, the legal system, employment and the media, reflect and promote gender discrimination.

Efforts at building a gender perspective and gender sensitisation in health care and development has repeatedly met with resistance from patriarchal structures. Men continue to control decision-making, limited family resources, women's sexuality, freedom of movement, access to the world outside the home, etc. Under these circumstances, women remain totally dependent and powerless, unless they find strength within, or support from the outside. Women need a supportive environment to ensure that they are fed adequately, are educated and can make decisions regarding their life and their children.

Access to Health Care Services

In India, 80 per cent of health care is in private hands. With a move towards further privatisation, the present trend of poor utilisation of health services by women can only worsen. We must learn from the experiences of Africa and Latin America.

> In 1985, when user fees were introduced for services at the Ahmadu Bello Hospital in Zaria Hyeria, the number of obstetric admissions came down in 1988, when additional charges were levied, admissions came down further and maternal mortality increased. After user fees were imposed, the number of women attending STD clinics plummeted by 65 per cent; male attendance decreased by 40 per cent. (Moses et. al 1992)

It is unlikely that health services will be made more accessible and affordable to women. According to the World Bank's own report, states having the maximum need for health services have significant gaps in health care infrastructure, health personnel (Figure 5) and health services.

In a country where around 40 per cent of the people live below the poverty line, either health care has to be made accessible and affordable or non-allopathic alternatives given a much greater priority.

Access to Food and Nutrition

As food prices have increased access to basic uncontaminated food became more difficult. The proliferates of costly processed food with lesser nutritive value flood the market. Polished rice, fine flour milled at high speed and high lump coarse grains with higher nutritive value disappear. Discrimination in breast feeding and feeding of our own girl child is probably the saddest reality.

In early adolescence, because of growth spurt associated with puberty and onset of menstruation, the nutritional needs of girls increase, especially of iron, vitamin A, calcium and iodine. Denial of adequate food to girls, partly due to non-availability and partly due to discrimination, continues to be a major problem. As inadequate diet has life-long consequences for girls, their growth and development is jeopardised. Early marriage and early pregnancy further deplete their inadequate reserves.

In India, 2-10 per cent of maternal deaths are due to Eclampsia; 50 per cent of women suffering from Eclampsia, which can be fatal if untreated, is mainly among the poorly nourished. Poorer women experience more still births, neonatal deaths and marked malformations of the foetus at birth, as well as higher pre-natal mortality. Rising food prices, limitations of the public distribution system and shift to non-edible cash crops, will undoubtedly worsen the existing nutritional status of women.

Figure 5

PRIMARY STAFFING GAP

All India

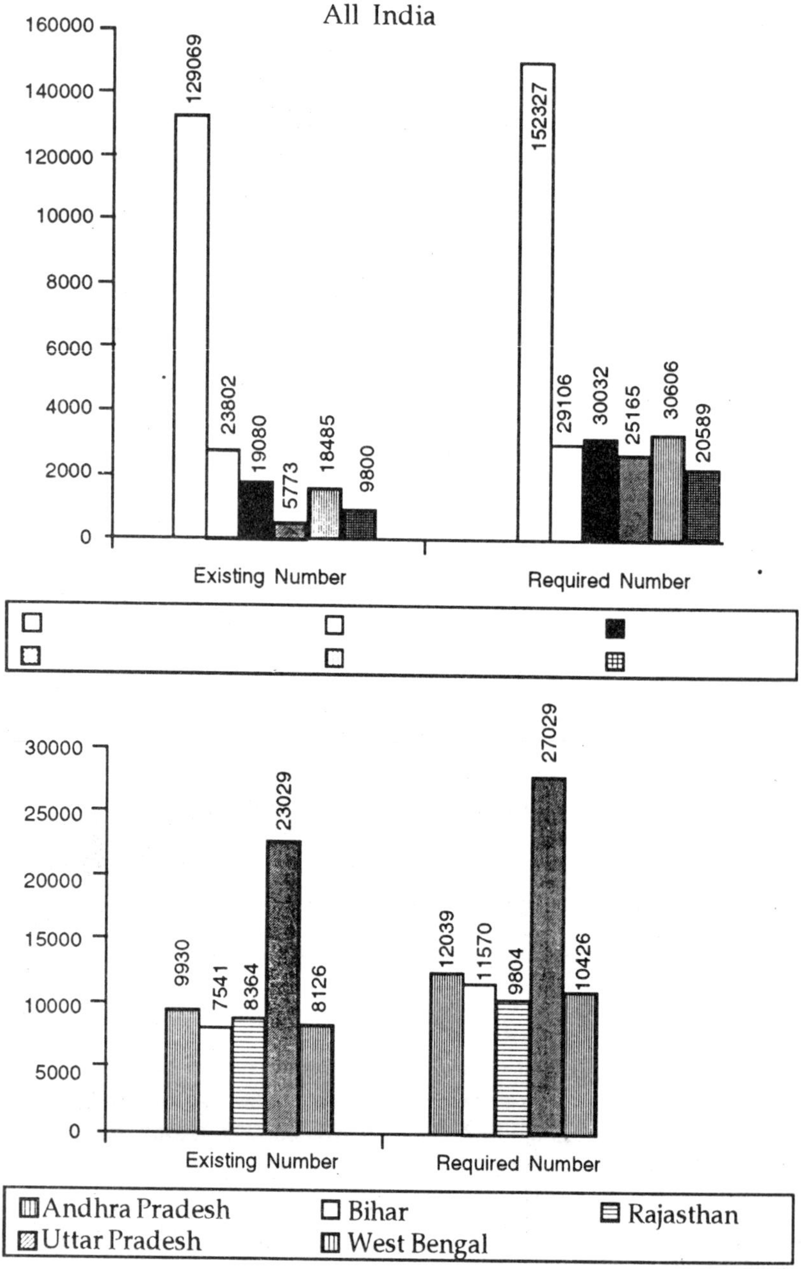

Intensity of Nutritional Disorders
Due to Lack of major micronutrients

Low birth weight of new borns due to anaemia (below normal weight of 2.5 kg)

28.2% of all cases

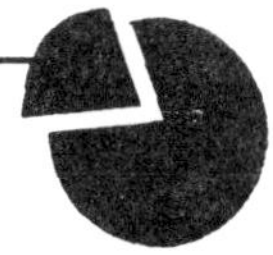

Maternal deaths due to anaemia

20% of all deaths

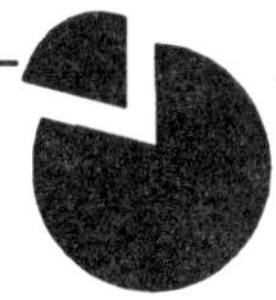

Iron deficiency anaemia

50% of population

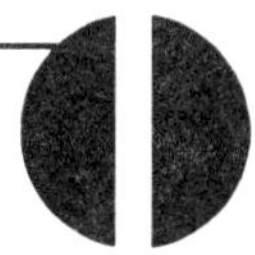

Area of the country not covered by ICDS

20%

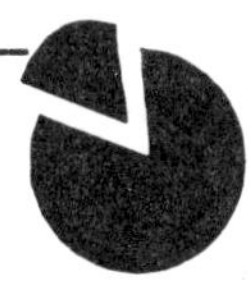

Source: Towards better nutrition for women and children, Problems and programmes (Dr. Sarla Gopalan, Secretary, Ministry of HRD, Department of Women and Child Development).

Communicable Diseases, Malaria

Development programme involving massive construction, result in creation of mosquitogenic and malariogenic conditions.

The water logging due to the Indira Gandhi Canal in Rajasthan which resulted in deaths of over 4000 people in 4 districts - Bikaner, Barmer, Jaisalmer and Jodhpur alone in 1994.

The construction of roads and railway tracts in Haryana without keeping the natural drainage pattern of the monsoon water to nalas and river tributaries feeding into the Jamuna resulted in inundation of several thousand hectares of agriculture field which, following rains in 1996 resulted not merely in deaths of over 1500 people in Districts of Nuh with Falciparum Malaria etc. but loss of two consecutive agricultural crops financially crippling thousands of farmers. Large number of the victims in both these cases were women and children and that amongst the poorest who could not have access to medical care.

1998 saw unprecedented floods in Eastern UP and Bihar, causing an increased epidemic of malaria and other communicable diseases. Once again, women and children were among those with less access to medical care.

Each episode of Falciparum Malaria results in fall of Haemoglobin by 1 or 2 gms. Women, most of whom are already anaemic, can hardly afford such repeated malaria attacks. Pregnant women are more vulnerable as they are known to have an abortion, premature delivery, still birth, or low birth weight babies. Deaths due to complication occur due to the effect of the malarial parasite on the kidney, liver, cerebral malaria, fall in blood sugar (Hypoglycemea specially in pregnant women and patients on Primaquin or algical malaria where patients go into shock.) Non-availability of diagnostic and treatment facilities makes the situation worse. Since treatment for women when sick is usually delayed - even those lives that could be saved are lost due to discrimination and neglect.

Tuberculosis

Incidence of TB started falling in the west following improvement of the socio-economic status of people, better working, living and eating conditions and when added incomes from colonies made European colonizing countries richer.

In India we have 14 million TB patients with 2.5 million infections, 5 lakh deaths annually. It was only following association of TB fund with AIDS victims in New York and increasing incidence of TB due to disease carried by immigrants that TB was identified as a "global emergency" and DOTS (Directly Observe Treatment Short Course) was launched by WHO - World Bank etc. and the vertical program based on the World Bank loans launched last year, initially as a pilot project now to cover 112 districts in the country with the plan to increase it to 400 districts.

TB affects women the hardest. Due to their poor nutritional and health status, work overload, mental stress and anxiety they are vulnerable.

On being infected - they are rarely taken to medical facilities for early diagnosis in time resulting in the infection worsening. The starting of treatment is delayed and even when started due to high cost of anti-TB drugs. They are not treated properly adequate drugs not bought or — by health care services as well as by family members, wives are asked to go to their maternal homes and return after treatment. Since Ginitourinary TB results in infertility women on being childless are deserted. Worse so is the fate of women who inspite of illness have to continue struggling for the family till they drop dead as they are too sick to contribute.

Remarriage for a child in many cases is known. TB being a sickness associated with stigma, marriage of girls with TB can be jeopardized hence their illness from potential in-laws is hidden and timely and adequate treatment suffers. Women with TB are unable to pursue work and husbands affected with TB-if they are the only wage earners are unable to bring home money to feed the family. Pulmonary TB is No. 1 killer of women in the Reproductive Age Group in India and has remained in No. 1 position since 1981. Yet ironically in addressing women's health concerns - it is contraception and motherhood that usually get priority.

Due to the high costs of TB care and the irrational and irresponsible medical management of TB, the emergence of multidrug resistance has added the problem and made TB Public Health Enemy No. 1 as well as personal and a family tragedy and a big economic drain for the family and the nation.

The anti-TB drug costs have spiralled and the production of cheaper anti-TB drugs pharmaceutical decreased. Indebtedness incurred for TB treatment is one of the major causes of indebtedness for the family.

ANTI-TB DRUG PRICES

	Pack	Pre DPCO-95	Post DPCO	%
Etambutal	10s	5.92	13.00	120
Pyrazinamide	10s	17.01	31.10	83
Rifampicin	10s	24.00	63.96	167
Rifampicin Isoniazid	10s	25.57	60.50	137

DRUGS PHARMACEUTICALS (Monitored Drugs)
Estimated Demand & Production Achievement
(Organized Sector)

Name of Drug	A/c Unit	94-95 Actual Prodn.	95-96 Estimated Demand	95-96 Actual Production
INH	T	1.00	487.30	0.00
Thiaceta Zone	T	40.55	98.70	25.53
Ethambutal	T	669.66	584.10	670.38
PAS	T	5.55	60.00	5.0
Pyrazina Mide	T	47.02	97.00	49.40

Source: Annual Report 96-97, Chemical Ministry Drug Utilization Patterns GOI/Prescription Audits Issue of Medical Ethics / CPA.

The Revised TB strategy is based on DOTS (Directly Observed Treatment Short Course) is also based on World Bank loans which will have to be returned with the interest however low. It is planned for 116 districts in this loan period.

The key concerns related to TB however remain:

1. Increasing creation of Tetra Genic socio-economic living and working conditions.

2. Collapse of the public health services.
3. Increasing privatisation of medical care i.e. about 80 per cent of medical care with private sector unwilling to follow the guidelines of rational TB care.
4. Non-availability of anti-TB drugs.
5. Decreasing production of cheaper standard anti-TB drugs eg. INH and Theacelazone.
6. Spiralling costs of anti-TB drugs.
7. Inadequate diagnostic facilities for sputum testing for T.B. - i.e. inadequate microscopes, inadequate trained microscopists (with 60 per cent technicians posts lying vacant).
8. Poor public awareness and behavioural patterns about spread of TB through droplet infection i.e. through coughing without covering mouth and spitting around and recognition of cardinal signs of TB i.e.

chronic cough > 3 weeks
fever > 3 weeks
chest pain
sputum with blood
Haemoptysis

Pharmaceutical Policy

The unregulated growth of the pill jungle in terms of proliferation of drugs that are non-essential irrational and hazardous and their aggressive marketing and irresponsible prescription and unquestioned consumption continues to be a major public health problem.

The spiralling costs of drugs has made much needed essential life saving drugs unaffordable on the one hand and cause of increasing indebtedness on the other. In 1986 and 1994 the Drug Policy was modified—each time the Drug price control basket was decreased and the drug prices increased. With over 20,000 drug manufacturers and inadequate drug control machinery the quality control has suffered. Neither the good manufacturing practices are stringently enforced nor is the quality control of the drugs in the market ensured.

Inadequate number of drug testing labs, with facilities to test biological as well as chemical contamination has continued. The JJ Hospital Tragedy in Bombay due to glycerol adulterated with toxic diethylglycal resulted in Lentin Commission Report. The I.V. Fluid contamination Tragedy in Delhi where 30,000 I.V. fluid bottle contaminated by fungus manufactured by Osler's Pharma were being sold—having been given quality clearance from Delhi Drug Control authorities. (the testing sample obviously having been swapped with an uncontaminated one). Some years ago HIV+ive anti-drug was given to several Rh-ive pregnant women in Delhi, Bangalore and Pune. Even when found HIV+ive patients could not be traced since there is no such mechanism, even when warning about Batch No. was given. Since most people do not read newspapers nor read English on the batch No. Anti D continued to be used.

Women many of whom are anaemic requiring caesarean section, hysterectomies or have pregnancy related bleeding APH, PPH, and bleeding after abortion suffering from very severe menorrohajia. Functional uterine haemorage suffering from Cancer of the Cervic the commonest cancer amongst women require blood transfusion. Infusion of blood obtained from professional donors which is inadequate in Haemoglobin, in amino acids does very little good, use of contaminated blood untested for Hepatitis B&C for HIV, AIDS, or Malaria, syphelis is a major health hazard. With the change in the blood bank, policies are allowing sale of blood and blood products only from licensed registered district level blood banks fulfilling all the various requirements. There is a fear that women anyway denied medical care specially costly medical care by their own families—may not be given the blood in time.

Encouragement of donation of blood by family members must be welcomed. Unarticulated fears and deeply internalised myths that 100 drops of blood is equal to 1 drop of semon and therefore donation of 1 bottle of blood will cause loss or decrease of potency and libido must be sensitively tackled. Great care regarding blood and blood products is required while policy changes requiring HIV testing for blood products has been brought about. The major concern continues to be the use of contaminated unsterilized syringes when facilities for sterilization do not exist for equipment eg. speculums and unchanged gloves.

With increased importance being given to RTIs as part of reproductive health and more institutionalized deliveries their will be increased use of medical intervention examinations, injections etc. with non-availability of continuous water supply, electricity supply increased in idtiogenic problems is possible.

At the global level the pressure being put on WHO by the drug industry not to raise concern about the impact of WTO on pharmaceuticals is a matter needs serious questioning. More than a decade ago when WHO under Dr. Halfden Mahler who called the pharmaceutical issue as new colonialism in the World Health Assembly in 1981 raised the issue of strong resolutions for rational use of drugs - US threatened to withdraw the contribution it is supposed to make to WHO. Since availability of essential drugs, having an essential drug list to guide purchase, drug prices, drug imports etc will be guided by "Trade" priorities and no "Health" priorities—for women's health and health of the poorer majority it is crucial that national and global policies do not jeopardise public health, specially of the most vulnerable.

Hazardous Drugs

While women are denied medical care when needed, specially essential and life saving drugs, giving of many of these drugs without adequate information, without exclusion of pregnancy and breast feeding—even essential drugs can inadvertently cause health hazards to the new born foetus. TERATOGENIC EFFECT OF DRUGS—Congenital malformation of foetus with hormones taken during pregnancy is known. Information about (1) graded essential drug list (2) list of drugs known to cause Teratogenic effect. Teratogenic effects of

Thalidomide, Diethy/Stilbaestrol and high dose estrogen progestone have been a warning.

The use of irrational and potentially hazardous drugs which are prescribed without providing any significant therapeutic gain must be restricted—

eg. misuse of steroids for conditions where they have NO ROLE irrational patent with antibiotic combination in high dosages for long duration. Unbiased information about commonly used drugs must be made widely available.

eg. aspirin is the best pain killer but it should not be taken on an empty stomach, never when dengu fever is suspected or there is a bleeding problem

radical treatment of malaria requires complete treatment with primaquin

to prevent relapse in case of Plasmoclum Viva x by acting on the parasites in the liver.

by acting

Contraceptive Care, Family Planning and Population Control

India has a population of 930 million people in spite of spending Rs. 60 billion on demographically driven population control programmes, since 1951. Neither have contraceptive needs been met, nor has the birth rate come down significantly. The states in which it has, for example, in Kerala, it has not been because of population control programmes. It has been because of land reforms, assurance of minimum wages, high female literacy, access to health care services, free education for children, adequate transport and communication facilities, the presence of a left state government, and of large Christian community that puts emphasis on education, health care and community service. The above have met the needs of the people and they have voluntarily chosen to have smaller families. Tamil Nadu's midday meal scheme resulted in higher female literacy, increased economic participation of women and influenced the demographic pattern.

Genderisation of Family Planning

The genderisation' of family planning responsibilities can be gauged from the fact that while in the sixties, 11 per cent of sterilisations were tubectomies, in 1993, 96 per cent of sterilisations were tubectomies. Every contraceptive, whether old-oral contraceptives, IUCD, laproscopy; new-Depoprovera, Net En; and even those being researched—Quainacrine, RU 486, Norplant, anti-fertility vaccine, are all targeted at women.

The concerns regarding anti-fertility vaccine trials are genuine and so is the concern about safety and reliability effect on baby reversibility need to the seriously assessed.

Contraceptive Technologies

In India, thousands have died due to inadequate facilities for conducting a simple blood test to diagnose malaria, and failure to provide timely basic anti-malarial drugs. In such a country, the rational use of contraceptives is not going to be easy. It is only possible when we can ensure quality care, rational drug use and rational health care, with adequate follow-up. As an example, take the case of Norplant, an imported, long-acting hormonal contraceptive, effective for five years, targeted at women. It consists of six matchstick-like silastic capsules with hormones, inserted subcutaneously, i.e. under the skin, after an incision in the upper part of the arm. Both the insertion and removal require training and equipment. Economically, socially and medically, its rationality is seriously doubted. Amongst several other side effects, menstrual disorders are a prime cause for concern. Ensuring rational drug use of simple painkillers, anti-malarial drugs, etc., has been extremely difficult. In such a situation, can we ensure rational use of hormonal preparations that require the exclusion of pregnancy, diabetes, hypertension, thromboembolic phenomenon, hepatitis, etc, and are to be given for several year (*for spacing purposes*), month after month *(Net En)*, or at three months intervals *(Depoprovera)*?

The failure to take responsibility for post-marketing surveillance of contraceptives, as is usually done in the West by manufacturers, is a matter of concern. The failure to acknowledge the adverse effects of such products is for a variety of reasons—manufacturers would like to make their profits and demographers would like to see a change in demographic patterns. In the past, every contraceptive technology was launched as 'God's gift to womankind' and as the magic solution to the world's greatest problem, namely, population growth. Global solutions based on technological fixes did not work in the past, nor will they now. Responsible use of contraceptives which are pharmaceutical-based require adequate health infrastructure, adequate training of health personnel, gender sensitivity and an integrated approach which addresses the various health problems of women. The trials of anti-fertility vaccine also need to be seriously questioned.

Even though very clear guidelines exist for chemical trial and there is a full chapter on contraceptive technology in the ICPD document, yet chemical trials of quinacrine did take place inspite of WHO's non clearance, ICMR's and DCIP's refusal.

Lack of Power-Lack of Choice

An unequal power relationship exists between the genders. Women continue to lack the freedom to make their own choices, whether it is in the matter of remaining single, getting married or selecting the person they want to marry. After marriage, the pressure to produce a male child within nine months of marriage has forced the reproductive role on many young women. This has had a number of far-reaching, negative, physical and psychological consequences. When the question of an 'unwanted marriage' cannot be challenged, it is unlikely that its consequences, an 'unwanted pregnancy', can be meaningfully challenged.

The women's health movement, within and outside the country, has highlighted the fact that when women are not allowed to make choices about their life, they are hardly in a position to make choices about contraceptive methods, 'negotiate' with their partners to use condoms or to respect their reproductive rights, their feelings and their emotional needs.

Male Responsibility

One of the main reasons of the failure of the family planning programme has been the lack of male involvement and male responsibility. The issue of male responsibility in matters of contraception, STD, AIDS, sexual violence, growth of red light areas, trafficking of women, spread of pornographic literature and blue films, growing market for aphrodisiacs and male potency drugs, need to be addressed. The role of male sexual behaviour, gender relations, sexual and gender responsibility, role of the 'Y' chromosome from the male partner in determining the gender of the child etc., have been overlooked in the obsession with costly, imported, contraceptive technologies. Since no 'technology seller' stood to gain, fertility awareness was never considered important enough. Years of protests by the women's health movement has met with indifference and even hostility.

It is little wonder that over the decades, even the existing male responsibility in matters of conception and contraception has been systematically eroded. In the name of empowerment, contraceptive responsibilities have been transferred to the women. In health programmes and policy planning, it should be ensured that pregnancy is made a matter of male concern and responsibility.

Prostitution

* Over 1 lakh.
* *30%<20 years old.*
* 60% sold or tricked into the profession.
* Selling of their Last Resource i.e. THEMSELVES for SURVIVAL of themselves and their children.
* Selling *Feminization of Poverty.*
* 1/3 *Households in India Women Headed*
* WOMEN FORCED TO BEGET CHILDREN AND THEN REAR THEM
* Selling *Male Irresponsibility in Sexual Behaviour*

  Selling SEXUAL VIOLENCE

  Selling Trafficking of Women

  Selling Pornographic films magazines photos

  Selling *Degradation* of *Women as Human beings*

  Selling Potency drugs

  Selling entertainment industry

  Selling usage of YOUNGER AND YOUNG GIRLS.

Reproductive and Child Health

A new National Health program, reproductive child health has been launched with idea of setting up model agencies and NGO's to channelise funds to monitor Reproductive Health Care (RHC) work.

The revised strategy of family planning is supposed to be a target free approach (TFA), with revision of training manuals and greater budget allocation for schemes on family planning for voluntary organisations. The family planning programme has been known by many names namely, the Family Welfare programme, Maternal and Child Health programme (MCH), the Child Survival and Safe Motherhood programme. There is now an attempt to broaden the concept of family planning to include 'reproductive health care' and it has now been renamed 'Reproductive and Child Health'. The essential Reproductive and Child Health package focusses on

- Prevention of unwanted pregnancy.
- Safe pregnancy, labour, and delivery.
- Early diagnosis and management of RTIs, STD and prevention of AIDS.
- Child care, immunisation, food supplement.

Table 3

CENTRAL PLAN OUTLAY BY MINISTRIES / DEPARTMENT

	94-95		95-96		96-97
	B.E.*	**Actual**	**B.E.**	**R.E****	**B.E**
Health	578	599	647	626	792
Indian Systems of Medicine and Homeopathy			23	23	23
Family Welfare***	1430	1672	1581	1506	1535
Women and Child Development			730	821	847

Source: Economic Survey - 1995-96, Government of India, p. 168.
Note: * B.E. - Budget Estimate
** R.E. - Budget
*** 92-93 Family Welfare 1000 cr.

Other aspects like infertility, sexual violence, prolapse of uterus are not adequately addressed in the Reproductive and Child Health (RCH) package. It is definitely an improvement on the earlier family planning programme and meet demographic goals since the monitory allocation and evaluation is based on demographic parameter. However, reproductive health cannot be a substitute for a women's health programme, it can only be a component of it. The budget allocations detailed in Figure 6 and Table 3, reflect global priorities and that of the Indian government i.e. in RCH, it is the Family Planning component that is being given the highest priority.

Figure 6

PROPOSED EXPENDITURE ON FAMILY PLANNING AND REPRODUCTIVE HEALTH BY UNITED NATIONS AGENCIES

(In Billions of US$)

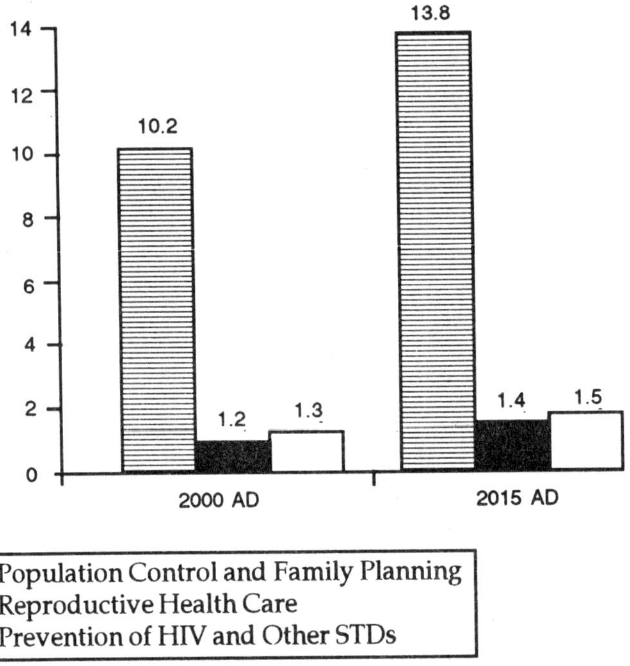

Source: International Conference on Population and Development, Programme for Action, January 1994, A United Nations Conference 171/PC/524 p. 72.

Reproductive Health Problems

Reproductive Tract Infection

Reproductive Tract Infections (RTIs) need to be diagnosed early and both partners treated. However, to prevent RTIs, it is equally important to ensure responsible behaviour by male partners, access to adequate water, privacy while bathing, toilet facilities, etc. There are three types of RTIs and each needs to be addressed appropriately.

• Sexually transmitted diseases, for example, Gonorrhea, Syphilis, Trichomonas Chlamydia, HIV, AIDS.

• Endogenous, due to overgrowth of existing bacteria, for example, Candidacies during pregnancy.

• Infections caused by instrumentation, for example, following a pelvic examination, septic abortion, etc.

Dr. Rani and Abhay Bang's community based study in Ghadcharoli, Maharashtra, revealed that 92 per cent of the women suffered from some form of gynaecological infection. On an average, 3.5 gynaecological problems per person was noted. Infections ranged from vaginal infection to dysmenorrhea *(painful periods),* etc. A large percentage of women were unaware of the presence of any infection and were asymptomatic (R.A. Bang, A.T. Bang et. al 1989).

RTIs can cause pain, discharge, infertility, ectopic pregnancy following pelvic inflammatory diseases, etc. It is well known that women are more prone to infections than men because of a larger mucosal surface and fluid dynamics. Young girls are more vulnerable to RTIs, specially STD, as compared to older women. Women infected by partners with HIV pass it on to their unborn child. Addressing AIDs will be far more difficult in a country like India, where leucorrhea and gonorrhea, which can be prevented and treated, have not yet been successfully addressed with the aim of 100 per cent—delivery under the RCH program, with inadequate sterilization of equipment possibilities due to problem of running water and electricity the fear of spreading STD and HIV and Hepatitis B are real.

Abortions

Twenty per cent of maternal mortality is due to abortion-related causes. Medical Termination of Pregnancy (MTP) has been legalised under the MTP Act of 1971, under certain conditions, i.e. only prior to 12 weeks; it is not allowed after 20 weeks, unless it is a life-saving measure and is performed after consulting two doctors.

The spiralling number of abortions and abortion deaths reflect the increase in the number of inflicted, unwanted pregnancies which women have to bear. Women also have to bear the consequences of the abortion, be it death due to bleeding and sepsis following abortion, or a sense of shame and guilt, specially when it involves young unmarried mothers. The majority of abortions are almost a substitute for family planning, as they are sought by married women, some being multigravida (Chabra and Nuna 1995).

Infertility

Since infertility is a medical as well as a major social problem it has to be addressed at both levels. There is a need to change public opinion and attitudes towards childlessness of women. Even if the problem is structurally or functionally in the male partner, it is the woman who is labelled a 'banjih' or 'barren' and not treated in society with empathy and acceptance.

Uterine Prolapse

Heavy work at construction sites involving carrying bricks and *taslas,* climbing heights, or digging hard ground, predispose women to uterine prolapse. Daily womanly chores of walking long distances on steep hills in search of water or fuel, or climbing 2-3 storeys up a narrow staircase with buckets of water, have a similar effect. Uterine prolapse is a major problem amongst hill women. Certain childbirth practices, such as pressing the abdomen during labour to hasten delivery without opening of the mouth of the uterus also leads to prolapse of the uterus, especially if this is associated with a poor perennial muscular tone due to frequent pregnancies and malnutrition.

Cancer of the Cervix

Cancer of the cervix is the commonest cancer in Indian women. Several factors are implicated and include an early marriage, repeated childbirth, poor hygiene of male partners, multiple partners and repeated infections. While the above are primarily reproductive health problems, it is clear that they cannot be addressed through gynaecological interventions alone.

Women and Work

Girls start working earlier than boys, work longer and harder throughout their lives. The poorer the family, the harder the women and girls have to work. The energy consumption in mere survival tasks of - fetching fuel, water, fodder, care of animals; washing; cleaning - which are exclusively women's responsibility, results in negative nutritional balance and caloric deficit. The situation worsens when women also have to perform hard labour for wages; when women have to walk long distances to fetch water and fuel in environmentally degraded regions, especially in hilly areas; take care of large extended families, in which the caring of children, elderly, sick husband and animals is done by women alone - with little or no help. A study by ASTRA (1981) had shown that the energy consumption of women was much higher than of males due to the double burden of work.

All the above domestic work is unpaid work and is considered unproductive work. Even when women work outside the home, they do not get equal wages for equal work and are made to perform unskilled jobs which are poorly paid, more hazardous and demanding. Women involved in specific occupations face various occupational health hazards. Rural women cooking in poorly ventilated huts using wood and cow dung cakes as fuel, are exposed to 100 times the acceptable level of smoke particles. This is equivalent to smoking 20 packs of cigarettes a day and can cause Chronic Obstructive Pulmonary disease (lung disease). Bidi rollers inhale tobacco dust. Women using sewing machines, bend over in dim light and suffer from back and eye problems. Electronic assembly line workers report loss of vision (visual acuity). Fodder choppers report loss of limbs. Women in health care and nursing, ward aids, sweepers, etc., are exposed to tuberculosis, HIV, hepatitis and other hospital infections. Textile workers complain of pulmonary tuberculosis. Women working in stone quarries with stone crushers, etc., suffer from pneumoconiosis, silicosis, etc., and restricted lung capacity. Handling of toxic chemicals can cause cancer, dermatitis, miscarriage and birth defects. Women involved in farming are exposed to overwork, long hours with no rest, heavy work right through pregnancy, exposure to pesticides, injuries caused by handling agricultural implements, etc. Women forced to earn their living as commercial sex workers are prone to contracting STDs, HIV etc., from their male clients. Thirty per cent of commercial sex workers in Mumbai were found to be HIV+.

Violence Against Women

Violence against women has been recognised as a major women's health issue. It is a worsening public health problem and an occupational health hazard. While men are victims of violence in incidents of street violence, crime, etc., violence against women is perpetuated by their partners and people known to them.

Crimes against women in the form of sexual violence, sexual harassment, etc., are definitely increasing. Epidemiological studies need to be undertaken to identify the cause, extent, nature, spectrum and forms of this pathology and its pathogenisis. Measures needed to deal with this phenomenon should also be identified. Health personnel are not training adequately and sensitively to recognise and address this problem medically, legally and psychologically. They are ill-informed and ill-equipped to give legal advice and counselling. Setting up of crisis centres offering counselling, early medical check-ups for trauma, signs of violence, STDs, HIV, are part of health measures which women need, but which are almost exclusively provided by women's organisations. Lack of awareness and inaccessibility of educational material on healthy and responsible sex and sex life, prevents young minds from developing positive attitudes and behaviour patterns, gender sensitivity and gender responsibility.

Table 4

INCIDENCE OF CRIMES COMMITTED AGAINST WOMEN DURING 1992-1994

Crimes	1990	1991	1992	1993	1994
Rape	9,518	9,793	11,112	11,242	12,351
Kidnapping and Abduction	11,699	12,300	12,077	11,837	12,998
Dowry Deaths	4,836	5,157	4,962	5,817	4,935
Torture	13,450	15,949	19,750	22,064	25,946
Molestation	20,194	20,611	20,385	20,985	24,117
Sexual Harrassment	8,620	10,283	10,751	12,009	10,496
Importation of Girls	-	-	-	-	167
Sati Prevention Act	-	-	-	-	2
Immoral Traffic (Prevention) Act	-	-	-	-	7547
Indecent Representation of Women	-	-	-	-	389
Total	68,317	74,093	79,037	83,954	98,948

Source: Crime in India - 1994, National Crime Reporting Bureau (M.H.A), p. 212.

Domestic violence, rape and sexual abuse are more widespread than acknowledged (See Table 4). Marital rape-forced prostitution; abuse of children (see Table 5), neglect of widows and elderly women, are some known forms of violence. Twenty to 60 per cent of women are reportedly beaten by their partners. Studies show that women in developed countries, because of domestic violence and rape, lose one out of five healthy days of their life. Gender based violence can lead to an unwanted pregnancy, forced abortion, miscarriage of a wanted baby, STDs/HIV/AIDS, gynaccological problems, head injury, broken bones, depression, suicidal tendency, etc. The situation becomes worse when women do not have access to friends, family and health care.

Eighty per cent of rapes are perpetuated by relatives or men known to the women; 24 per cent of rapes involve young girls, less than 16 years of age (India Country Report, World Congress for Women, Beijing 1995). Increasing use of rape to take revenge on the menfold during communal violence and for trade and blackmail have been reported.

Table 5

VICTIMS OF CHILD RAPE, 1990-1994

Year	Age Group		% Share of Child Rape Victims of Total Rape Victims
	Below 10 Years	10-16 Years	
1990	394	2105	24.8%
1991	1099	2630	35.8%
1992	532	2581	26.5%
1993	634	2759	27.8%
1994	727	3259	30.2%
% Change in 1994 over 1993	14.8%	18.1%	
% Change in 1994 over 1990	84%	84.8%	

Sex Determination and Female Foeticide

In 1982, the women's movement highlighted the increasing incidence of female foeticide following the use of sex determination. However, authorities grudgingly acknowledged the problem only when Census data and numerous studies pointed to the worsening of the sex ratio at the national and state level.

Even though the Bill on Pre-Natal Diagnosis was passed in 1991 and became a law in January 1996, it is unlikely that women will stop going in for sex determination testing of their foetus. Family and societal pressures to have a male child have not decreased. Repeated abortions to avoid giving birth to a female child take their toll on the woman's health.

Even though it is well known fact that the 'Y' chromosome responsible for the male sex of the baby is contributed by the father, wives or daughters-in-law failing to produce a son are discarded. Efforts by the Peoples Science Movement and women's organisations to disseminate information regarding the role of the 'Y' chromosome from the father in sex determination, has been very creditable. Such information should be imparted as part of formal school education, non-formal education and literacy campaigns.

There have been reports of increasing female infanticide from Salem district in Tamil Nadu. This is a post-independence phenomena that started with the introduction of the dowry practice in the community. Similar reports have been received from Bihar and Rajasthan. It is clear that with the pressure for smaller families, the demand for the birth of a 'male child' will become more compulsive. As dowry demands grow, girls will increasingly be seen as a 'curse' and boys as potential 'investment', who will bring brides with dowries.

Violence of Denial and Neglect

Differences in nutrition, educational opportunities, freedom of movement etc., between children of different genders within the same family, are not seen in societies in which women are treated with dignity and accepted as equal partners.

A high rate of female infant mortality, fertility, maternal mortality and low female literacy, female nutritional status, age of marriage, have been noted in places where women have a low social status.

Opportunities for education, skill development, play, recreation, rest, adequate food, freedom of movement, speech and choice, etc., are denied to women. Studies show that female children are breast-fed for a shorter period (*five months less*) than a male child. Girls are given 'less' and poorer quality of food, as compared to boys. This situation worsens in the case of second and third daughters. They may not be given milk, eggs and protective food like pulses, vegetables, fruits, even if they are available at home.

Even in economically well-off families and so-called prosperous states like Punjab, this selective discrimination has been noted. The relative risk of a girl dying:

* between the age of 0-4 years, is 11 per cent higher than in boys.
* between the ages of 5-14 years, the risk increases to 22 per cent.
* between 15-34 years, the risk increases to 31 per cent.

Even if a girl is allowed to be born, her chances of dying continue to be significantly higher. Girls are denied medical care; studies show that the utilisation of hospitals/services by girls and women is much less as compared to boys and men.

Mental Health

According to the World Development Report, 1993, depressive disorders and self-inflicted injuries, rank 5th and 6th amongst diseases and injuries affecting women between the ages of 15-44. Some of the known causes of depression are childlessness, physical, sexual and mental abuse; widowhood, desertion; conflicting demands of domestic and income-generating roles; a combination of work pressures and harassment at work, etc.

Efforts at exploring the extent and nature of women's mental health problems have shown that psychiatry, with its Western roots, is incapable of understanding the social cultural reality of India - the second class social status of Indian women, the nature of discrimination faced by girls and women, etc. As such, psychiatrists are unable to offer meaningful, non-pharmaceutical solutions to successfully deal with mental health issues. Unscrupulous men wanting to get rid of their sisters or wives and thus secure their property or one more round of dowry, seek false certificates from unethical psychiatrists. On the basis of such certificates, hundreds of innocent women are flung into mental asylums or jails. Patriarchal laws permit only a husband, brother or father to have her discharged; mothers and sisters do not have the right.

Serious efforts have not been made to improve the physical, mental, social and economic health of women. In spite of overwhelming constraints, women have struggled to survive, raise children, build homes, provide health care and nurture their family. It has neither been recognised nor appreciated that it is the labour, the perservance and the caring provided by its women that sustains the world.

Women's Health is dependent on the *Socio Economic Realities*

Basis - Caste, Class, Gender, Rural
- *Environmental* Degradation
- Water, Fuel Fodder, Food, Medicinal Plant

Triple Burden - Work at home
- Wage work - occupational
- Reproductive - responsibilities
(conception contraception, child rearing, child care)

Inequity Inequitable Distribution ↕	*Intra household*	• family responsibilites • share of work • share of food • decision-making

Health Parameters	*Social status*	• inverse sex ratio • dowry deaths, rapes
	Health status	• IMR, MMR, Life Expectancy • suicides, 1-4 yr. Mortality, • sex determination
	Nutritional status Food: Work	• Height - stunting • weight - under weight • Anaemia
Discrimination & Neglect		Nutritional deficiency e.g. IDD
Maternal Health		• Age of marriage • Age of pregnancy • Abortions - foetal wastage

Maternal mortality 1.1% of all reported deaths
15% of deaths amongst women in reproductive
age 15-45 years
Maternal morbidity for 1 death 13-100 face
severe complications

Discrimination and Violence Against Girls and Women: Role of Health Personnel and the Health Sector

In the past, medical and health practitioners have chosen not to recognise and address the deep-rooted, which has a negative impact on the physical, mental and social health of girls, women and society itself. Violence against women, concerns millions of women; this collective pain and suffering is enough reason to warrant an end to the epidemic of violence and discrimination against women. Medical education has to be socially relevant. Teaching of Obstitics and Gynaecology is not teaching of women's health, the gender, and social roots of ill health the women's status in a society reflects the time development at that society. Fifty years after independence we see diseases of industrialization, hypertension, diabetes, heart disease, alcoholism in one section and diseases of poverty in another section added to which are reproductive health problems, the mental health problems - many of which require not more drugs, doctors and dispensaries but healthier social environment which lets the women live and develop optimally, physically, mentally, socially, economically with all 'her' contributions acknowledged and appreciated at home, at work and in national policies and programmes.

19

The Girl Child in India

Kusum

Introduction

Our children are our greatest national resource and there is a growing sensitivity of the need to provide special measures for protecting their rights and interests. The various international covenants, human rights instruments and national policy programmes are a pointer to this. The Geneva Declaration of the Rights of the Child, 1924, the Universal Declaration of Human Rights 1948, the U.N. Convention on the Rights of the Child, 1989 and many other international declarations and world conferences have emphasised the need for special care of the child. The Indian Constitution, with its "paediatric" conscience also makes provisions for the welfare of children pursuant to which many laws have been made. Article 23 prohibits traffic in human beings and forced labour and article 24 prohibits employment of children below the age of 14 to work in any factory or mine or other hazardous employment. Article 39(e) directs the state to secure conditions in favour of children so that their tender age is not abused and they are not compelled by economic necessity to take up jobs unsuited to their age and strength, while under article 39(f) the state is directed to ensure that "the children are given opportunities and facilities to develop in a healthy manner and in conditions of freedom and dignity and that childhood and youth are protected against exploitation and against moral and material abandonment". Article 45 provides for free and compulsory education for all children upto the age of 14. Apart from these constitutional provisions, there are various national policies and programmes for the welfare of children. The National Policy for Children, 1974 lays down that, "it shall be the policy of the state to provide adequate service to children, both before and after birth and through the period of growth to ensure their full physical, mental and social development." Pursuant to all this, various plans of action and schemes have been adopted providing measures for the welfare of children.

The Girl Child

Despite all this, a girl child in India is in a doubly vulnerable position because of her age and her gender. Discrimination against her begins right from conception and birth and continues through childhood, adolescence and womanhood. The reasons for this gender bias are socio-legal and cultural. Our society suffers from a son-syndrome. A son is required to continue the family name, to look after family business and property and to provide economic and emotional security to parents in their old age. Besides, he alone can perform the last rites and obsequies of the father and "deliver him from hell". A girl on the other hand is a responsibility as her chastity is to be protected and also a financial burden because of the customary dowry. Since after marriage a girl leaves her parents house to stay with her husband and in-laws in most Indian societies spending on her education and health is viewed as a futile investment and is like watering another person's garden. Though times are gradually changing discrimination and bias on these accounts is still very vivid and persists.

Sex-Selection

The discrimination against the female child began until a few years back, with her birth. But new medical technologies and procedures, have facilitated pre-birth, nay, even pre-conception bias against the female gender.

The advancements in medical procedures which enable sex detection has led to the practice of sex selection by aborting female foetus. Though India is not the only country where a male child is preferred to a female, it has the dubious distinction of being the only country where medical technology is so blatantly misused through a network of clinics and centres to do away with the unwanted female babies. People are lured to undergo the popularly known "boy-girl" tests by advertisements through hoardings, handbills etc. There have been appalling reports of various clinics/centres performing the tests followed by abortion of female foetuses. Agitations and efforts by a group of activists who organised themselves to fight this reprehensible practice led to the enactment of the Maharashtra Regulation of Pre-Natal Diagnostic Techniques Act, 1988. Since the Act was confined to that state only, it led to an influx of such cases to bordering states which had no law against the tests. Testing services were made available through couriers and mobile vans fitted with necessary infrastructure to draw the amniotic fluid and testing techniques. In 1994 the central government enacted the Pre-Natal Diagnostic Techniques (Regulation and Prevention of Misuse) Act which is applicable throughout the country. Despite the Act, however, which puts a complete ban on sex detection, the practice is still widely known. The Medical Termination of Pregnancy Act, 1971 suffers from various loopholes which enable and facilitate the misuse of the provisions purely for selective elimination of the female foetus.

It may be pointed out here that medical technologies and procedures have enabled not only sex selective abortions but also sex selective conceptions. A very recent report[1] in a popular daily is a pointer to the role played by medical

[1]Nirupama Dutt, "Girls not wanted" *Indian Express* June 3, 1998.

science in catering to the desires of the people who crave for a male child. A farmer couple, both over 60, wanted a male child as an heir. The wife's menstrual cycle was reinduced and fertilisation of a mature egg and a 'Y' sperm obtained by chromosomal separation to ensure a male child. This was done *in vitro* and after fertilisation the embryo was transferred into the woman. After a few weeks an ultra sound was done which confirmed not only the pregnancy but also a male foetus. The doctors and the couple are delighted and proud of their success. A reference may here be made of the Delhi Artificial Insemination (Human) Act of 1995. Though the Act clearly prohibits the segregation of 'XX' and 'XY' chromosomes so that couples do not resort to pre-conception sex selection there can be no mechanism to monitor the same. In Punjab, reportedly, one comes across several advertisements saying "plan your family by 'X' - 'Y' separation of sperms".

Female Infanticide

Female infanticide is another horrendous practice which is indicative of the bias against a girl child.[2] Female infanticide is banned by legislation since 1870. Even so, there are reports from various parts of the country about female babies being killed within a few hours of birth "as a measure of compassion". According to a study conducted by the Indian Council of Child Welfare, an unwanted infant girl is killed within the first three days by giving poisoned milk, stuffing husk in the nostril, choking her by a wet pillow, abandoning her in the cold or by other cruel means. In a shocking case of infanticide reported a few days ago from Faridabad, a mother strangled her newly born girl-child to death after her husband got angry and humiliated her over the birth of the third female baby.[3]

Health

Gender bias in health-care also is indicated in several micro level studies of hospital records apart from documented evidence showing that female child has to struggle for survival because of poor nutrition. Starting from the feed of the mother's breast, there is a discrimination between the boys and girls. A recent analysis of data related to 19 states from the 1992-93 National Family Health Survey of India reported that girls are breast feed for shorter periods than boys, they are less likely to be vaccinated than boys and are consistently less likely to receive treatment for diarrhoea, fever and acute respiratory infection.[4]

---

[2]Elisabeth Burmiller, *May you be the mother of a hundred sons* (Penguin Books) 1991; Usha Rai, "Female Infanticide Thrives in South" *Indian Express* (8.8.92); Pushpa Iyengar, "Girls in Salem are born to die" *Times of India* (30.8.92); "Female Infanticide on rise in Salem" *Hindustan Times* (6.9.94).

[3]News report, "Mother kills new-born daughter in hospital" *Hindustan Times* October 15, 1998.

[4]Sharmila Joshi, "A precarious childhood: Health of the Girl Child", *Times of India* 26.5.98.

The quantity and quality of food the girls receive is inferior to what their brothers get. In many families it is a common practice for mothers to keep apart the best food especially for the sons. It is said that "while diseases kill the girls slowly, deprivation of food kills them quickly". Girls are reportedly taken to hospital only in emergency. Even in the most basic health care requirement of immunization, the girl child is sought to be neglected. According to one study,[5] more percentage of girls than boys die upto 14 years suffering from fever, infection, and various kinds of other disorders. Likewise a 1994 UNICEF publication says that of the 12 million girls born in India every year, three million do not survive beyond the age of 15. Just diarrohea alone claims close to 1.5 millions infants each year in India-that is one in every three months.[6]

Education

The constitutional directive under Article 45 provides for free and compulsory education upto the age of 14 for both boys and girls. Apart from that, free education upto the age of 14 has been held to be a fundamental right by the Supreme Court in *Mohini Jain v. State of Karnataka*[7] and *Unni Krishnan v. State of Andhra Pradesh.*[8] Expanding the scope of article 21 of the Constitution, the court recognised that the right to life and personal liberty guaranteed under this article means right to live with human dignity and that education is a key to that. However, notwithstanding the constitutional provision and judicial pronouncements, the literacy rate is very low. In case of girls the enrolment rate is lower still and withdrawal rate around puberty is high. In all the census years, "the female literacy rate is inordinately low compared to boys."[9] According to a UNICEF Report[10] in 1991, 60.8 per cent of India's girls in the seven + age group were illiterate. This is because of lack of access to educational opportunities and facilities, apprehensions of sexual exploitation and early assumption of domestic responsibilities. Besides, the socio-cultural attitudes also contribute to lower literacy rate amongst girls. It is believed that the ultimate goal of a girl is to produce children and look after the home. Higher the education of a girl, more difficult it is to find a suitable match for her. There is also a feeling that educated girls are less likely to adjust in the family than uneducated girls.

Labour

India has a very high rate of child labour. Census reports indicate an increasing trend in employment of girls. The girl child is made to work not only in her own

[5]S. Barsa "Girl Child: A Statistical portraiture of Discrimination", in J.A. William (ed.), An Anatomy of the Girl Child, Madras: Asian Youth Centre, at 55-57 (1991).

[6]See Sharmila Joshi, Op. cit. n. 4.

[7]1992 SCALE (2) 90.

[8]1993 SCALE (2) 290.

[9]See Damodar Suar, "Discrimination against the Girl Child in India", 44 *Social Action* July-Sept 1994, 14-26 at p. 16.

[10]See Sharmila Joshi "Free and Compulsory Education is imperative" *Times of India* 25.5.98.

household but also as a domestic servant elsewhere. With both husband and wife working these days, a girl child is preferred as servant because she is docile, hard working and safe. Minor girls are also employed in other unorganised sectors and industries which are beyond the purview of the protective labour legislations. There are periodic reports of such girls being employed in some hazardous occupations because of a superstitious belief that employment of pre-pubertal girls would bring luck and prosperity.

It needs no saying that a girl child labourer is especially in a more vulnerable position because she is a child, she is a girl and she is a labourer. She is exploited and discriminated on all these counts.[11]

Prostitution

Child prostitution is yet another issue in the context of the girl child which needs serious thought. The inhuman and barbarous conditions under which these girls live in the brothels have been exposed through the public interest litigations before the Supreme Court.[12] Various directives have been issued to the state governments to take preventive and remedial steps for their rescue and rehabilitation. It is estimated that there are about 2.5 million sex workers in the country and out of these slightly less than half a million are child sex workers. According to a survey conducted by the Peoples Union of Civil Liberties, about 50 per cent of the cases were of those who started working as prostitutes at the age of 14 to 15; 42 per cent started at age 11-13 and rest when they were less than 10. With the increase in tourism, flesh trade has increased too, leading to high incidence of AIDS.[13]

Child Marriage

In the context of the girl child, serious thought needs to be given to the problem of minor brides. Child marriage has very harmful effect on the mind, body and health of the girl. Prior to the Indian Penal Code, 1860, there was no provision prohibiting the cohabitation of a man and his wife—whatever her age. The Law Commissioners who drafted the Code in 1846 mooted the idea of penalising consummation of marriage below a certain age. The Code of 1860 fixed the age at 10 and the husband who consummated the marriage with his wife who was below 10 was to be held guilty of rape and the punishment prescribed could extend to transportation for life. For 30 years this continued to be the legal position until the decision of the Calcutta High Court in *Queen Empress v. Hurree Mohan Muthee (where the death of a girl* of eleven years caused by haemorrhage from rupture in the course of cohabitation)[14] led to the introduction of a Bill raising the age from 10 to 12. In 1924 Dr. Hari Singh Gour introduced

---

[11]Neeti Mohanti, "Gender Perspectives in Child Labour", *Social Welfare*, April 1997, vol. 44, no. 1 at p. 9.

[12]*Vishaljeet v. Union of India* AIR 1990 S.C. 1412.

[13]See *Child's Right Bulletin*, vol. 1, no. 3 March 1998 at p.6.

[14]*Queen Empress v. Hurree Mohun Mythee* (1891) 18 Cal 49.

a Bill to further amend the rape provision in section 375 of the Indian Penal Code, 1860 raising the age to 14 years in both marital and extra-marital cases. The Bill was referred to the select committee which reduced the age from 14 to 13 in the case of marital rape. Opinion on the Bill being sharply divided it could not get through. However, public opinion was very strong on the need to raise the age for marriage consummation. In 1925 the age for legal consummation of marriage was raised to 13. The Child Marriage Restraint Act 1929 raised the age for marriage to 18 to 14 respectively for boys and girls. In 1949 the age was raised to 15 for girls and by an amendment in 1978 the age of marriage has been fixed at 18 for girls and 21 for boys. Marriage in contravention of this requirement is punishable with fine and/or imprisonment. Never-the-less the law, child marriages are very much in vogue. In Rajasthan alone, thousands of children reportedly get married on "Akha Teej" day each year. Marriages of infants are reported from other parts of the country too. Sometimes the brides—and grooms too—are so young that they have to be carried by their mothers. The National Women's Council had drafted a Bill which sought to make it compulsory for all marriages to be recorded and registered. The move was, however, rejected on the plea that it has the potential to hurt the sentiments of the minority.[15] One really wonders whether it is an honest and genuine concern for the sentiments of the community or political expediency. Kingsley David, a world renowned demographer aptly observed, "the actual age at marriage is determine not by law but by social and economic conditions". To this, I would add "strong political considerations" too. It is heartening to note that in a bid to check the practice of child marriage, the National Human Rights Commission has recommended introduction of a system on priority basis, for compulsory registration of marriages. It has also, reportedly[16], issued notice to the Chief Secretary of Rajasthan calling for detailed report on news item alleging inaction on the part of administration in preventing child marriage.

In this context it would be pertinent to note that our marital rape law is very anomalous. Under section 375 of the Penal Code "sexual intercourse by a man with his own wife not being under 15 years of age is not rape". Thus if a wife is 15 or above then whether she consents or not, the husband cannot be guilty of rape. If she is below 15 then the husband would be guilty but here also the law makes a distinction between a wife below 12 and a wife above 12.

Under section 376 where the wife is below 12, the penalty is the same as provided for the offence of rape generally, but if the wife is not below 12 i.e. she is 12 or above but below 15 (after 15 there is no offence at all) then it constitutes a lesser offence and the punishment is milder. It is anachronistic that despite the amendment of 1978 raising the age for marriage to 18 for girls, the age for marital consummation remains at 15 under the Penal Code. This

---

[15]Radhakrishna Rao, "Child Marriages: Not in Rajasthan Alone" The Child's Rights Bulletin, March 1998, vol. I, No. 3 p. 19.

[16]"NHRC steps to curb child marriages" *The Hindu*, 19.8.98.

inconsistency needs serious thought if the practice of child marriage with its concomitant baneful effects on the girl child, is to be controlled.

Conclusion

Besides the above, there are various other spheres and modes of discrimination and exploitation of the girl child like rape, sexual abuse, maintaining and thrashing about which one often reads in newspapers and other studies. Several action plans, schemes and programs have been adopted to improve the status of the girl child. For instance under a scheme in Haryana, known as "Apni Beti Apni Dhan" (One's daughter one's valuable source) the state undertakes to provide sustenance and upbringing of a girl child. Many other states have similar schemes. SAARC has declared 1991-2000 as the "Decade of the Girl Child" and a National Plan of Action for the Girl Child for 1991-2000 has been drawn up by the government which recognises the rights of the girl child to equal opportunity, to be free from hunger, illiteracy, ignorance and exploitation. We have however, yet to go a long way. What is most significant is an honest commitment and political will to act in that direction by spreading awareness and creating conditions where girls could live in dignity and be treated as an asset rather than a burden.

20

The Girl Child

Leila Seth

Where have all the young girls gone?
Some were aborted before they were born:
A few were buried or choked with coarse paddy:
Others were smothered, starved or drowned in a well;
Poisoned with berries of oleander till dead,
So that dowry need not be paid or in-laws fed,
Or daughters raped, beaten or burnt -
This is the sad story of the girl child's hell.

Father, why do you discriminate against me
When I can be as good as my brother?
Mother, nurture, nourish and educate me and you will see
That I will not be a burden but will control my own destiny,
And you will have nothing to fear (if brother is not there),
I will look after both of you in your old age;
I ask only to be treated equally - will you not dare -
So that I have the freedom to choose and the right to care;
And am no longer the prisoner of my gender
Unable to retaliate against injustice.
Oh Father, give me chance,
Just give a chance.
Oh Mother, break the bonds of tradition
And let me into the sunlight to dance...to dance...to dance.

Appendix - I

Universal Declaration of Human Rights

Adopted and Proclaimed by General Assembly Resolution 217 A(111) of 10 December 1948

Preamble

Whereas recognition of the inherent dignity and of the equal and inalienable rights of all members of the human family is the foundation of freedom, justice and peace in the world,

Whereas disregard and contempt for human rights have resulted in barbarous acts which have outraged the conscience of mankind, and the advent of a world in which human beings shall enjoy freedom of speech and belief and freedom from fear and want has been proclaimed as the highest aspiration of the common people,

Whereas it is essential, if man is not to be compelled to have recourse, as a last resort, to rebellion against tyranny and oppression, that human rights should be protected by the rule of law,

Whereas it is essential to promote the development of friendly relations between nations,

Whereas the peoples of the United Nations have in the Charter reaffirmed their faith in fundamental human rights, in the dignity and worth of the human person and in the equal rights of men and women and have determined to promote social progress and better standards of life in larger freedom,

Whereas Member States have pledged themselves to achieve, in cooperation with the United Nations, the promotion of universal respect for and observance of human rights and fundamental freedoms,

Whereas a common understanding of these rights and freedoms is of the greatest importance for the full realization of this pledge,

Now, therefore,

The General Assembly,

Proclaims this Universal Declaration of Human Rights as a common standard of achievement for all peoples and all nations, to the end that every individual and every organ of society, keeping this Declaration constantly in mind, shall strive by teaching and education to promote respect for these rights and freedoms and by progressive measures, national and international, to secure their universal and effective recognition and observance, both among the peoples of Member States themselves and among the peoples of territories under their jurisdiction.

Article 1

All human beings are born free and equal in dignity and rights. They are endowed with reason and conscience and should act towards one another in a spirit of brotherhood.

Article 2

Everyone is entitled to all the rights and freedoms set forth in this Declaration, without distinction of any kind, such as race, colour, sex, language, religion, political or other opinion, national or social origin, property, birth or other status.

Furthermore, no distinction shall be made on the basis of the political, jurisdictional or international status of the country or territory to which a person belongs, whether it be independent, trust, non-self-governing or under any other limitation of sovereignty.

Article 3

Everyone has the right to life, liberty and security of person.

Article 4

No one shall be held in slavery or servitude; slavery and the slave trade shall be prohibited in all their forms.

Article 5

No one shall be subjected to torture or to cruel, inhuman or degrading treatment or punishment.

Article 6

Everyone has the right to recognition everywhere as a person before the law.

Article 7

All are equal before the law and are entitled without any discrimination to equal protection of the law. All are entitled to equal protection against any discrimination in violation of this Declaration and against any incitement to such discrimination.

Article 8

Everyone has the right to an effective remedy by the competent national tribunals for acts violating the fundamental rights granted him by the constitution or by law.

Article 9

No one shall be subjected to arbitrary arrest, detention or exile.

Article 10

Everyone is entitled in full equality to a fair and public hearing by an independent and impartial tribunal, in the determination of his rights and obligations and of any criminal charge against him.

Article 11

1. Everyone charged with a penal offence has the right to be presumed innocent until proved guilty according to law in a public trial at which he has had all the guarantees necessary for his defence.

2. No one shall be held guilty of any penal offence on account of any act or omission which did not constitute a penal offence, under national or international law, at the time when it was committed. Nor shall a heavier penalty be imposed than the one that was applicable at the time the penal offence was committed.

Article 12

No one shall be subjected to arbitrary interference with his privacy, family, home or correspondence, nor to attacks upon his honour and reputation. Everyone has the right to the protection of the law against such interference or attacks.

Article 13

1. Everyone has the right to freedom of movement and residence within the borders of each State.
2. Everyone has the right to leave any country, including his own, and to return to his country.

Article 14

1. Everyone has the right to seek and to enjoy in other countries asylum from persecution.
2. This right may not be invoked in the case of prosecutions genuinely arising from non-political crimes or from acts contrary to the purposes and principles of the United Nations.

Article 15

1. Everyone has the right to a nationality.
2. No one shall be arbitrarily deprived of his nationality nor denied the right to change his nationality.

Article 16

1. Men and women of full age, without any limitation due to race, nationality or religion, have the right to marry and to found a family. They are entitled to equal rights as to marriage, during marriage and at its dissolution.
2. Marriage shall be entered into only with the free and full consent of the intending spouses.
3. The family is the natural and fundamental group unit of society and is entitled to protection by society and the State.

Article 17

1. Everyone has the right to own property alone as well as in association with others.
2. No one shall be arbitrarily deprived of his property.

Article 18

Everyone has the right to freedom of thought, conscience and religion; this right includes freedom to change his religion or belief, and freedom, either alone or in community with others and in public or private, to manifest his religion or belief in teaching, practice, worship and observance.

Article 19

Everyone has the right to freedom of opinion and expression; this right includes freedom to hold opinions without interference and to seek, receive and impart information and ideas through any media and regardless of frontiers.

Article 20

1. Everyone has the right to freedom of peaceful assembly and association.
2. No one may be compelled to belong to an association.

Article 21

1. Everyone has the right to take part in the government of his country, directly or through freely chosen representatives.
2. Everyone has the right to equal access to public service in his country.
3. The will of the people shall be the basis of the authority of government; this will shall be expressed in periodic and genuine elections which shall be by universal and equal suffrage and shall be held by secret vote or by equivalent free voting procedures.

Article 22

Everyone, as a member of society, has the right to social security and is entitled to realization, through national effort and international co-operation and in accordance with the organization and resources of each State, of the economic, social and cultural rights indispensable for his dignity and the free development of his personality.

Article 23

1. Everyone has the right to work, to free choice of employment, to just and favourable conditions of work and to protection against unemployment.
2. Everyone, without any discrimination, has the right to equal pay for equal work.
3. Everyone who works has the right to just and favourable remuneration ensuring for himself and his family an existence worthy of human dignity, and supplemented, if necessary, by other means of social protection.
4. Everyone has the right to form and to join trade unions for the protection of his interests.

Article 24

Everyone has the right to rest and leisure, including reasonable limitation of working hours and periodic holidays with pay.

Article 25

1. Everyone has the right to a standard of living adequate for the health and well-being of himself and of his family, including food, clothing, housing and medical care and necessary social services, and the right to security in the event of unemployment, sickness, disability, widowhood, old age or other lack of livelihood in circumstances beyond his control.
2. Motherhood and childhood are entitled to special care and assistance. All children, whether born in or out of wedlock, shall enjoy the same social protection.

Article 26

1. Everyone has the right to education. Education shall be free, at least in the elementary and fundamental stages. Elementary education shall be compulsory. Technical and professional education shall be made generally available and higher education shall be equally accessible to all on the basis of merit.
2. Education shall be directed to the full development of the human personality and to the strengthening of respect for human rights and fundamental freedoms. It shall promote understanding, tolerance and friendship among all nations, racial or religious groups, and shall further the activities of the United Nations for the maintenance of peace.
3. Parents have a prior right to choose the kind of education that shall be given to their children.

Article 27

1. Everyone has the right freely to participate in the cultural life of the community, to enjoy the arts and to share in scientific advancement and its benefits.
2. Everyone has the right to the protection of the moral and material interests resulting from any scientific, literary or artistic production of which he is the author.

Article 28

Everyone is entitled to a social and international order in which the rights and freedoms set forth in this Declaration can be fully realized.

Article 29

1. Everyone has duties to the community in which alone the free and full development of his personality is possible.
2. In the exercise of his rights and freedoms, everyone shall be subject only to such limitations as are determined by law solely for the purpose of securing due recognition and respect for the rights and freedoms of others and of meeting the just requirements of morality, public order and the general welfare in a democratic society.
3. These rights and freedoms may in no case be exercised contrary to the purposes and principles of the United Nations.

Article 30

Nothing in this Declaration may be interpreted as implying for any State, group or person any right to engage in any activity or to perform any act aimed at the destruction of any of the rights and freedoms set forth herein.

Appendix - II
Convention on the Political Rights of Women

Opened for signature and ratification by General Assembly resolution 640 (VII) of 20 December 1952

ENTRY INTO FORCE: 7 July 1954, in accordance with article VI

The Contracting Parties,

Desiring to implement the principle of equality of rights for men and women contained in the Charter of the United Nations,

Recognizing that everyone has the right to take part in the government of his country directly or indirectly through freely chosen representatives, and has the right to equal access to public service in his country, and desiring to equalize the status of men and women in the enjoyment and exercise of political rights, in accordance with the provisions of the Charter of the United Nations and of the Universal Declaration of Human Rights,

Having resolved to conclude a Convention for this purpose,

Hereby agree as hereinafter provided:

Article I

Women shall be entitled to vote in all elections on equal terms with men, without any discrimination.

Article II

Women shall be eligible for election to all publicly elected bodies, established by national law, on equal terms with men, without any discrimination.

Article III

Women shall be entitled to hold public office and to exercise all public functions, established by national law, on equal terms with men, without any discrimination.

Article IV

1. This Convention shall be open for signature on behalf of any Member of the United Nations and also on behalf of any other State to which an invitation has been addressed by the General Assembly.

2. This Convention shall be ratified and the instruments of ratification shall be deposited with the Secretary-General of the United Nations.

Article V

1. This Convention shall be open for accession to all States referred to in paragraph 1 of article IV.

2. Accession shall be effected by the deposit of an instrument of accession with the Secretary-General of the United Nations.

Article VI

1. This Convention shall come into force on the ninetieth day following the date of deposit of the sixth instrument of ratification or accession.

2. For each State ratifying or acceding to the Convention after the deposit of the sixth instrument of ratification or accession the Convention shall enter into force on the ninetieth day after deposit by such State of its instrument of ratification or accession.

Article VII

In the event that any State submits a reservation to any of the articles of this Convention at the time of signature, ratification or accession, the Secretary-General shall communicate the text of the reservation to all States which are or may become Parties to this Convention. Any State which objects to the reservation may, within a period of ninety days from the date of the said communication (or upon the date of its becoming a Party to the Convention), notify the Secretary-General that it does not accept it. In such case, the Convention shall not enter into force as between such State and the State making the reservation.

Article VIII

1. Any State may denounce this Convention by written notification to the Secretary-General of the United Nations. Denunciation shall take effect one year after the date of receipt of the notification by the Secretary-General.

2. This Convention shall cease to be in force as from the date when the denunciation which reduces the number of Parties to less than six becomes effective.

Article IX

Any dispute which may arise between any two or more Contracting States concerning the interpretation or application of this Convention, which is not settled by negotiation, shall at the request of any one of the parties to the dispute be referred to the International Court of Justice for decision, unless they agree to another mode of settlement.

Article X

The Secretary-General of the United Nations shall notify all Members of the United Nations and the non-member States contemplated in paragraph I of article IV of this Convention of the following:

(a) Signatures and instruments of ratification received in accordance with article IV;

(b) Instruments of accession received in accordance with article V;

(c) The date upon which this Convention enters into force in accordance with article VI;

(d) Communications and notifications received in accordance with article VII;

(e) Notifications of denunciation received in accordance with paragraph I to article VIII;

(f) Abrogation in accordance with paragraph 2 of article VIII.

Article XI

1. This Convention, of which the Chinese, English, French, Russian and Spanish texts shall be equally authentic, shall be deposited in the archives of the United Nations.

2. The Secretary-General of the United Nations shall transmit a certified copy to all Members of the United Nations and to the non-member States contemplated in paragraph I of article IV.

Appendix - III

Convention on the Elimination of All Forms of Discrimination Against Women

Adopted and opened for signature, ratification and accession by General Assembly Resolution 34/180 of 18 December 1979

ENTRY INTO FORCE 3 September 1981, in accordance with article 27(1)

The States Parties to the present Convention,

Noting that the Charter of the United Nations reaffirms faith in fundamental human rights, in the dignity and worth of the human person and in the equal rights of men and women,

Noting that the Universal Declaration of Human Rights affirms the principle of the inadmissibility of discrimination and proclaims that all human beings are born free and equal in dignity and rights and that everyone is entitled to all the rights and freedoms set forth therein, without distinction of any kind, including distinction based on sex,

Noting that the States Parties to the International Covenants on Human Rights have the obligation to ensure the equal rights of men and women to enjoy all economic, social, cultural, civil and political rights,

Considering the international conventions concluded under the auspices of the United Nations and the specialized agencies promoting equality of rights of men and women,

Noting also the resolutions, declarations and recommendations adopted by the United Nations and the specialized agencies promoting equality of rights of men and women,

Concerned, however, that despite these various instruments extensive discrimination against women continues to exist,

Recalling that discrimination against women violates the principles of equality of rights and respect for human dignity, is an obstacle to the participation of women, on equal terms with men, in the political, social, economic and cultural life of their countries, hampers the growth of the prosperity of society and the family and makes more difficult the full development of the potentialities of women in the service of their countries and of humanity,

Concerned that in situations of poverty women have the least access to food, health, education, training and opportunities for employment and other needs,

Convinced that the establishment of the new international economic order based on equity and justice will contribute significantly towards the promotion of equality between men and women,

Emphasizing that the eradication of *apartheid* all forms of racism, racial discrimination, colonialism, neo-colonialism, aggression, foreign occupation and domination and interference in the internal affairs of States is essential to the full enjoyment of the rights of men and women,

Affirming that the strengthening of international peace and security, the relaxation of international tension, mutual co-operation among all States irrespective of their social and economic systems, general and complete disarmament, in particular nuclear disarmament under strict and effective international control, the affirmation of the principles of justice, equality and mutual benefit in relations among countries and the realization of the right of peoples under alien and colonial domination and foreign occupation to self-determination and independence, as well as respect for national sovereignty and territorial integrity, will promote social progress and development and as a consequence will contribute to the attainment of full equality between men and women,

Convinced that the full and complete development of a country, the welfare of the world and the cause of peace require the maximum participation of women on equal terms with men in all fields,

Bearing in mind the great contribution of women to the welfare of the family and to the development of society, so far not fully recognized, the social significance of maternity and the role of both parents in the family and in the upbringing of children, and aware that the role of women in procreation should not be a basis for discrimination but that the upbringing of children requires a sharing of responsibility between men and women and society as a whole,

Aware that a change in the traditional role of men as well as the role of women in society and in the family is needed to achieve full equality between men and women,

Determined to implement the principles set forth in the Declaration on the Elimination of Discrimination against Women and, for that purpose, to adopt the measures required for the elimination of such discrimination in all its forms and manifestations,

Have agreed on the following:

PART I

Article 1

For the purposes of the present Convention, the term "discrimination against women" shall mean any distinction, exclusion or restriction made on the basis of sex which has the effect or purpose of impairing or nullifying the recognition, enjoyment or exercise by women, irrespective of their marital status, on a basis of equality of men and women, of human rights and fundamental freedoms in the political, economic, social, cultural, civil or any other field.

Article 2

States Parties condemn discrimination against women in all its forms, agree to pursue by all appropriate means and without delay a policy of eliminating discrimination against women and, to this end, undertake:

(a) To embody the principle of the equality of men and women in their national constitutions or other appropriate legislation if not yet incorporated therein and to ensure, through law and other appropriate means, the practical realization of this principle;

(b) To adopt appropriate legislative and other measures, including sanctions where appropriate, prohibiting all discrimination against women;

(c) To establish legal protection of the rights of women on an equal basis with men and to ensure through competent national tribunals and other public institutions the effective protection of women against any act of discrimination;

(d) To refrain from engaging in any act or practice of discrimination against women and to ensure that public authorities and institutions shall act in conformity with this obligation;

(e) To take all appropriate measures to eliminate discrimination against women by any person, organization or enterprise;

(f) To take all appropriate measures, including legislation, to modify or abolish existing laws, regulations, customs and practices which constitute discrimination against women;

(g) To repeal all national penal provisions which constitute discrimination against women,

Article 3

States Parties shall take in all fields, in particular in the political, social, economic and cultural fields, all appropriate measures, including legislation, to ensure the full development and advancement of women, for the purpose of guaranteeing them the exercise and enjoyment of human rights and fundamental freedoms on a basis of equality with men,

Article 4

1. Adoption by States Parties of temporary special measures aimed at accelerating *de facto* equality between men and women shall not be considered discrimination as defined in the present Convention, but shall in no way entail as a consequence the maintenance of unequal or separate standards; these measures shall be discontinued when the objectives of equality of opportunity and treatment have been achieved.

2. Adoption by States Parties of special measures, including those measures contained in the present Convention, aimed at protecting maternity shall not be considered discriminatory.

Article 5

States Parties shall take all appropriate measures:

(a) To modify the social and cultural patterns of conduct of men and women, with a view to achieving the elimination of prejudices and customary and all other practices which are based on the idea of the inferiority or the superiority of either of the sexes or on stereotyped roles for men and women;

(b) To ensure that family education includes a proper understanding of maternity as a social function and the recognition of the common responsibility of men and women in the upbringing and development of their children, it being understood that the interest of the children is the primordial consideration in all cases.

Article 6

States Parties shall take all appropriate measures, including legislation, to suppress all forms of traffic in women and exploitation of prostitution of women.

PART - II

Article 7

States Parties shall take all appropriate measures to eliminate discrimination against women in the political and public life of the country and, in particular, shall ensure to women, on equal terms with men, the right:

(a) To vote in all elections and public referenda and to be eligible for election to all publicly elected bodies;

(b) To participate in the formulation of government policy and the implementation thereof and to hold public office and perform all public functions at all levels of government;

(c) To participate in non-governmental organizations and associations concerned with the public and political life of the country.

Article 8

States Parties shall take all appropriate measures to ensure to women, on equal terms with men and without any discrimination, the opportunity to represent their Governments at the international level and to participate in the work of international organizations.

Article 9

1. States Parties shall grant women equal rights with men to acquire, change or retain their nationality. They shall ensure in particular that neither marriage to an alien nor change of nationality by the husband during marriage shall automatically change the nationality of the wife, render her stateless or force upon her the nationality of the husband.

2. States Parties shall grant women equal rights with men with respect to the nationality of their children.

PART - III

Article 10

States Parties shall take all appropriate measures to eliminate discrimination against women in order to ensure to them equal rights with men in the field of education and in particular to ensure, on a basis of equality of men and women:

(a) The same conditions for career and vocational guidance, for access to studies and for the achievement of diplomas in educational establishments of all categories in rural as well as in urban areas; this equality shall be ensured in pre-school, general, technical, professional and higher technical educations, as well as in all types of vocational training;

(b) Access to the same curricula, the same examinations, teaching staff with qualifications of the same standard and school premises and equipment of the same quality;

(c) The elimination of any stereotyped concept of the roles of men and women at all levels and in all forms of education by encouraging co-education and other types of education which will help to achieve this aim and, in particular, by the revision of textbooks and school programmes and the adaptation of teaching methods;

(d) The same opportunities to benefit from scholarships and other study grants;

(e) The same opportunities for access to programmes of continuing education, including adult and functional literacy programmes, particularly those aimed at reducing, at the earliest possible time, any gap in education existing between men and women;

(f) The reduction of female student drop-out rates and the organization of programmes for girls and women who have left school prematurely;

(g) The same opportunities to participate actively in sports and physical education;

(d) Access to specific educational information to help to ensure the health and well-being of families, including information and advice on family planning.

Article 11

1. States Parties shall take all appropriate measures to eliminate discrimination against women in the field of employment in order to ensure, on a basis of equality of men and women, the same rights, in particular;

(a) The right to work as an inalienable right of all human beings;

(b) The right to the same employment opportunities, including the application of the same criteria for selection in matters of employment;

(c) The right to free choice of profession and employment, the right to promotion, job security and all benefits and conditions of service and the right to receive vocational training and retraining, including apprenticeships, advanced vocational training and recurrent training;

(d) The right to equal remuneration, including benefits, and to equal treatment in respect of work of equal value, as well as equality of treatment in the evaluation of the quality of work;

(e) The right to social security, particularly in cases of retirement, unemployment, sickness, invalidity and old age and other incapacity to work, as well as the right to paid leave.

(f) The right to protection of health and to safety in working conditions, including the safeguarding of the function of reproduction.

2. In order to prevent discrimination against women on the grounds of marriage or maternity and to ensure their effective right to work, States Parties shall take appropriate measures:

(a) To prohibit, subject to the imposition of sanctions, dismissal on the grounds of pregnancy or of maternity leave and discrimination in dismissals on the basis of marital status;

(b) To introduce maternity leave with pay or with comparable social benefits without loss of former employment, seniority or social allowances;

(c) To encourage the provision of the necessary supporting social services to enable parents to combine family obligations with work responsibilities and participation in public life, in particular through promoting the establishment and development of a network of child-care facilities;

(d) To provide special protection to women during pregnancy in types of work proved to be harmful to them.

3. Protective legislation relating to matters covered in this article shall be reviewed periodically in the light of scientific and technological knowledge and shall be revised, repealed or extended as necessary.

Article 12

1. States Parties shall take all appropriate measures to eliminate discrimination against women in the field of health care in order to ensure, on a basis of equality of men and women, access to health care services, including those related to family planning.

2. Notwithstanding the provisions of paragraph 1 of this article, States Parties shall ensure to women appropriate services in connection with pregnancy, confinement and the post-natal period, granting free services where necessary, as well as adequate nutrition during pregnancy and lactation.

Article 13

States Parties shall take all appropriate measures to eliminate discrimination against women in other areas of economic and social life in order to ensure, on a basis of equality of men and women, the same rights, in particular;

(a) The right to family benefits;

(b) The right to bank loans, mortgages and other forms of financial credit;

(c) The right to participate in recreational activities, sports and all aspects of cultural life.

Article 14

1. States Parties shall take into account the particular problems faced by rural women and the significant roles which rural women play in the economic survival of their families, including their work in the non-monetized sectors of the economy, and shall take all appropriate measures to ensure the application of the provisions of the present Convention to women in rural areas.

2. State Parties shall take all appropriate measures to eliminate discrimination against women in rural areas in order to ensure, on a basis of equality of men and women, that they participate in and benefit from rural development and, in particular, shall ensure to such women the right:

(a) To participate in the elaboration and implementation of development planning at all levels;

(b) To have access to adequate health care facilities, including information, counselling and services in family planning;

(c) To benefit directly from social security programmes;

(d) To obtain all types of training and education, formal and non-formal, including that relating to functional literacy, as well as, *inter alia,* the benefit of all community and extension services, in order to increase their technical proficiency;

(e) To organize self-help groups and co-operatives in order to obtain equal access to economic opportunities through employment or self-employment;

(f) To participate in all community activities;

(g) To have access to agricultural credit and loans, marketing facilities, appropriate technology and equal treatment in land and agrarian reform as well as in land resettlement schemes;

(h) To enjoy adequate living conditions, particularly in relation to housing, sanitation, electricity and water supply, transport and communications.

PART - IV

Article 15

1. States Parties shall accord to women equality with men before the law.

2. States Parties shall accord to women, in civil matters, a legal capacity identical to that of men and the same opportunities to exercise that capacity. In particular, they shall give women equal rights to conclude contracts and to administer property and shall treat them equally in all stages of procedure in courts and tribunals.

3. States Parties agree that all contracts and all other private instruments of any kind with a legal effect which is directed at restricting the legal capacity of women shall be deemed null and void.

4. States Parties shall accord to men and women the same rights with regard to the law relating to the movement of persons and the freedom to choose their residence and domicile.

Article 16

1. States Parties shall take all appropriate measures to eliminate discrimination against women in all matters relating to marriage and family relations and in particular shall ensure, on a basis of equality of men and women:

(a) The same right to enter into marriage;

(b) The same right freely to choose a spouse and to enter into marriage only with their free and full consent;

(c) The same rights and responsibilities during marriage and at its dissolution;

(d) The same rights and responsibilities as parents, irrespective of their marital status, in matters relating to their children; in all cases the interests of the children shall be paramount;

(e) The same rights to decide freely and responsibly on the number and spacing of their children and to have access to the information, education and means to enable them to exercise these rights;

(f) The same rights and responsibilities with regard to guardianship, wardship, trusteeship and adoption of children, or similar institutions where these concepts exist in national legislation; in all cases the interests of the children shall be paramount;

(g) The same personal rights as husband and wife, including the right to choose a family name, a profession and an occupation;

(h) The same rights for both spouses in respect of the ownership, acquisition, management, administration, enjoyment and disposition of property, whether free of charge or for a valuable consideration.

2. The betrothal and the marriage of a child shall have no legal effect, and all necessary action, including legislation, shall be taken to specify a minimum age for marriage and to make the registration of marriages in an official registry compulsory.

PART - V

Article 17

1. For the purpose of considering the progress made in the implementation of the present Convention, there shall be established a Committee on the Elimination of Discrimination against Women (hereinafter referred to as the Committee) consisting, at the time of entry into force of the Convention, of eighteen and, after ratification of or accession to the Convention by the thirty-fifth State party, of twenty-three experts of high moral standing and competence in the field covered by the Convention. The experts shall be elected by States Parties from among their nationals and shall serve in their personal capacity, consideration being given to equitable geographical distribution and to the representation of the different forms of civilization as well as the principal legal systems.

2. The members of the Committee shall be elected by secret ballot from a list of persons nominated by States Parties. Each State Party may nominate one person from among its own nationals.

3. The initial election shall be held six months after the date of the entry into force of the present Convention. At least three months before the date of each election the Secretary-General of the United Nations shall address a letter to the States Parties inviting them to submit their nominations within two months. The Secretary-General shall prepare a list in alphabetical order of all persons thus nominated, indicating the States Parties which have nominated them, and shall submit it to the States Parties.

4. Elections of the members of the Committee shall be held at a meeting of States Parties convened by the Secretary-General at United Nations Headquarters. At the meeting, for which two thirds of the States Parties shall constitute a quorum, the persons elected to the Committee shall be those nominees who obtain the largest number of votes and an absolute majority of the votes of the representatives of States Parties present and voting.

5. The members of the Committee shall be elected for a term of four years. However, the terms of nine of the members elected at the first election shall expire at the end of two years; immediately after the first election the names of these nine members shall be chosen by lot by the Chairman of the Committee.

6. The election of the five additional members of the Committee shall be held in accordance with the provisions of paragraphs 2, 3 and 4 of this article, following the thirty-fifth ratification or accession. The terms of two of the additional members elected on this occasion shall expire at the end of two years, the names of these two members having been chosen by lot by the Chairman of the Committee.

7. For the filling of casual vacancies, the State Party whose expert has ceased to function as a member of the Committee shall appoint another expert from among its nationals, subject to the approval of the Committee.

8. The members of the Committee shall, with the approval of the General Assembly, receive emoluments from United Nations resources on such terms and conditions as the Assembly may decide, having regard to the importance of the Committee's responsibilities.

9. The Secretary-General of the United Nations shall provide the necessary staff and facilities for the effective performance of the functions of the Committee under the present Convention.

Article 18

1. States Parties undertake to submit to the Secretary-General of the United Nations, for consideration by the Committee, a report on the legislative, judicial, administrative or other measures which they have adopted to give effect to the provisions of the present Convention and on the progress made in this respect;

(a) Within one year after the entry into force for the State concerned;

(b) Thereafter at least every four years and further whenever the Committee so requests.

2. Reports may indicate factors and difficulties affecting the degree of fulfilment of obligations under the present Convention.

Article 19

1. The Committee shall adopt its own rules of procedure.

2. The Committee shall elect its officers for a term of two years.

Article 20

1. The Committee shall normally meet for a period of not more than two weeks annually in order to consider the reports submitted in accordance with article 18 of the present Convention.

2. The meetings of the Committee shall normally be held at United Nations Headquarters or at any other convenient place as determined by the Committee.

Article 21

1. The Committee shall, through the Economic and Social Council, report annually to the General Assembly of the United Nations on its activities and may make suggestions and general recommendations based on the examination of reports and information received from the States Parties. Such suggestions and general recommendations shall be included in the report of the Committee together with comments, if any, from States Parties.

2. The Secretary-General of the United Nations shall transmit the reports of the Committee of the Commission on the Status of Women for its information.

Article 22

The specialized agencies shall be entitled to be represented at the consideration of the implementation of such provisions of the present Convention as fall within the scope of their activities. The Committee may invite the specialized agencies to submit reports on the implementation of the Convention in areas falling within the scope of their activities.

PART - VI

Article 23

Nothing in the present Convention shall affect any provisions that are more conducive to the achievement of equality between men and women which may be contained:

(a) In the legislation of a State Party; or

(b) In any other international convention, treaty or agreement in force for that State.

Article 24

States Parties undertake to adopt all necessary measures at the national level aimed at achieving the full realization of the rights recognized in the present Convention.

Article 25

1. The present Convention shall be open for signature by all States.
2. The Secretary-General of the United Nations is designated as the depositary of the present Convention.
3. The present Convention is subject to ratification. Instruments of ratification shall be deposited with the Secretary-General of the United Nations.
4. The present Convention shall be open to accession by all States. Accession shall be effected by the deposit of an instrument of accession with the Secretary-General of the United Nations.

Article 26

1. A request for the revision of the present Convention may be made at any time by any State Party by means of a notification in writing addressed to the Secretary-General of the United Nations.
2. The General Assembly of the United Nations shall decide upon the steps, if any, to be taken in respect of such a request.

Article 27

1. The present Convention shall enter into force on the thirtieth day after the date of deposit with the Secretary-General of the United Nations of the twentieth instrument of ratification or accession.
2. For each State ratifying the present Convention or acceding to it after the deposit of the twentieth instrument of ratification or accession, the Convention shall enter into force on the thirtieth day after the date of the deposit of its own instrument of ratification or accession.

Article 28

1. The Secretary-General of the United Nations shall receive and circulate to all States the text of reservations made by States at the time of ratification or accession.
2. A reservation incompatible with the object and purpose of the present Convention shall not be permitted.
3. Reservations may be withdrawn at any time by notification to this effect addressed to the Secretary-General of the United Nations, who shall then inform all States thereof. Such notification shall take effect on the date on which it is received.

Article 29

1. Any dispute between two or more States Parties concerning the interpretation or application of the present Convention which is not settled by negotiation shall,

at the request of one of them, be submitted to arbitration. If within six months from the date of the request for arbitration the parties are unable to agree on the organization of the arbitration, any one of those parties may refer the dispute to the International Court of Justice by request in conformity with the Statute of the Court.

2. Each State Party may at the time of signature or ratification of the present Convention or accession thereto declare that it does not consider itself bound by paragraph 1 of this article. The other States Parties shall not be bound by that paragraph with respect to any State party which has made such a reservation.

3. Any State Party which has made a reservation in accordance with paragraph 2 of this article may at any time withdraw that reservation by notification to the Secretary-General of the United Nations.

Article 30

The present Convention, the Arabic, Chinese, English, French, Russian and Spanish texts of which are equally authentic, shall be deposited with the Secretary-General of the United Nations.

IN WITNESS WHEREOF the undersigned, duly authorized, have signed the present Convention.

Appendix - IV

The Vienna Declaration and Programme of Action

Adopted 25 June 1993 by the World Conference on Human Rights

3. The equal status and human rights of women:

36. The World Conference on Human Rights urges the full and equal enjoyment by women of all human rights and that this be a priority for Governments and for the United Nations. The World Conference on Human Rights also underlines the importance of the integration and full participation of women as both agents and beneficiaries in the development process, and reiterates the objectives established on global action for women towards sustainable and equitable development set forth in the Rio Declaration on Environment and Development and chapter 24 of Agenda 21, adopted by the United Nations Conference on Environment and Development (Rio de Janeiro, Brazil, 3.14 June, 1992).

37. The equal status of women and the human rights of women should be integrated into the mainstream of United Nations system-wide activity. These issues should be regularly and systematically addressed throughout relevant United Nations bodies and mechanisms. In particular, steps should be taken to increase cooperation and promote further integration of objectives and goals between the Commission on the Status of Women, the Commission on Human Rights, the Committee for the Elimination of Discrimination against Women, the United Nations Development Fund for Women, the United Nations Development Programme and other United Nations agencies. In this context, co-operation and co-ordination should be strengthened between the Centre for Human Rights and the Division for the Advancement of Women.

38. In particular, the World Conference on Human Rights stresses the importance of working towards the elimination of violence against women in public and private life, the elimination of all forms of sexual harassment, exploitation and trafficking in women, the elimination of gender bias in the administration of justice and the eradication of any conflicts which may arise between the rights of women and the harmful effects of certain traditional or customary practices, cultural prejudices and religious extremism. The World Conference on Human Rights calls upon the General Assembly to adopt the draft declaration on violence against women and urges States to combat violence against women in accordance with its provisions. Violations of the human rights of women in situations of armed conflict are violations of the fundamental principles of international human rights and humanitarian law. All violations of this kind, including in particular murder, systematic rape, sexual slavery, and forced pregnancy, require a particularly effective response.

39. The World Conference on Human Rights urges the eradication of all forms of discrimination against women, both hidden and overt. The United Nations should encourage the goal of universal ratification by all States of the Convention on the Elimination of All Forms of Discrimination against Women by the year 2000. Ways and means of addressing the particularly large number of reservations to the Convention should be encouraged. Inter alia, the Committee on the Elimination of Discrimination against Women should continue its review of reservations to the Convention. States are urged to withdraw reservations that are contrary to the object and purpose of the Convention or which are otherwise incompatible with international treaty law.

40. Treaty monitoring bodies should disseminate necessary information to enable women to make more effective use of existing implementation procedures in their pursuits of full and equal enjoyment of human rights and non-discrimination. New procedures should also be adopted to strengthen implementation of the commitment to women's equality and the human rights of women. The Commission on the Status of Women and the Committee on the Elimination of Discrimination against Women should quickly examine the possibility of introducing the right of petition through the preparation of an optional protocol to the Convention on the Elimination of All Forms of Discrimination against Women. The World Conference on Human Rights welcomes the decision of the Commission on Human Rights to consider the appointment of a special rapporteur on violence against women at its fiftieth session.

41. The World Conference on Human Rights recognizes the importance of the enjoyment by women of the highest standard of physical and mental health throughout their life-span. In the context of the World Conference on Women and the Convention on the Elimination of All Forms of Discrimination against Women, as well as the Proclamation of Tehran of 1968, the World Conference on Human Rights reaffirms, on the basis of equality between women and men, a woman's right to accessible and adequate health care and the widest range of family planning services, as well as equal access to education at all levels.

42. Treaty monitoring bodies should include the status of women and the human rights of women in their deliberations and findings, making use of gender-specific data. States should be encouraged to supply information on the situation of women *de jure* and *de facto* in their reports to treaty monitoring bodies. The World Conference on Human Rights notes with satisfaction that the Commission on Human Rights notes with satisfaction that the Commission on Human Rights adopted at its forty-ninth session resolution 1993/46 of 8 March 1993 stating that rapporteurs and working groups in the field of human rights should also be encouraged to do so. Steps should also be taken by the Division for the Advancement of Women in cooperation with other United Nations bodies, specifically the Centre for Human Rights, to ensure that the human rights activities of the United nations regularly address violations of women's human rights, including gender-specific abuses. Training for United Nations human rights and humanitarian relief personnel to assist them to recognize and deal with human rights abuses particular to women and to carry out their work without gender bias should be encouraged.

43. The World Conference on Human Rights urges Governments and regional and international organizations to facilitate the access of women to decision-making posts and their greater participation in the decision-making process. It encourages further steps within the United Nations Secretariat to appoint and promote women staff members in accordance with the Charter of the United Nations, and encourages other principal and subsidiary organs of the United Nations to guarantee the participation of women under conditions of equality.

44. The World Conference on Human Rights welcomes the World Conference on Women to be held in Beijing in 1995 and urges that human rights of women should play an important role in its deliberations, in accordance with the priority themes of the World Conference on Women of equality, development and peace.

Appendix - V
Document 107

General Assembly Resolution adopting the Declaration on the Elimination of Violence against Women
A/RES/48/104, 20 December 1993

The General Assembly,

Recognizing the urgent need for the universal application to women of the rights and principles with regard to equality, security, liberty, integrity and dignity of all human beings,

Noting that those rights and principles are enshrined in international instruments, including the Universal Declaration of Human Rights,[1] the International Covenant on Civil and Political Rights,[2] the International Covenant on Economic, Social and Cultural Rights,[2] the Convention on the Elimination of All Forms of Discrimination against Women[3] and the Convention against Torture and Other Cruel, Inhuman or Degrading Treatment or Punishment[4],

Concerned that violence against women is an obstacle to the achievement of equality, development and peace, as recognized in the Nairobi Forward - Looking Strategies for the Advancement of Women[5], in which a set of measures to combat violence against women was recommended, and to the full implementation of the Convention on the Elimination of All Forms of Discrimination against Women,

Affirming that violence against women constitutes a violation of the rights and fundamental freedoms of women and impairs or nullifies their enjoyment of those rights and freedoms, and concerned about the longstanding failure to protect and promote those rights and freedoms in the case of violence against women,

Recognizing that violence against women is a manifestation of historically unequal power relations between men and women, which have led to domination over and discrimination against women by men and to the prevention of the full advancement of women, and that violence against women is one of the crucial social mechanisms by which women are forced into a subordinate position compared with men,

Concerned that some groups of women, such as women belonging to minority groups, indigenous women, refugee women, migrant women, women living in rural or remote communities, destitute women, women in institutions or in detention, female

---

[1]*Resolution* 217 A (III)

[2]See resolution 2200 A (XXI), annex.

[3]Resolution 34/180, annex.

[4]Resolution 39/46, annex.

[5]Report of the World Conference to Review and Appraise the Achievements of the United Nations Decade for Women: Equality, Development and Peace, Nairobi, 15-26 July 1985 (United Nations Publication, Sales No. E 85.IV.10), chap, 1, Sec. A.

children, women with disabilities, elderly women in situations of armed conflict, are especially vulnerable to violence,

Recalling the conclusion in paragraph 23 of the annex to Economic and Social Council resolution 1990/15 of 24 May 1990 that the recognition that violence against women in the family and society was pervasive and cut across lines of income, class and culture had to be matched by urgent and effective steps to eliminate its incidence,

Recalling also Economic and Social Council resolution 1991/18 of 30 May 1991, in which the Council recommended the development of a framework for an international instrument that would address explicitly the issue of violence against women,

Welcoming the role that women's movements are playing in drawing increasing attention to the nature, severity and magnitude of the problem of violence against women,

Alarmed that opportunities for women to achieve legal, social, political and economic equality in society are limited, *inter alia*, by continuing and endemic violence,

Convinced that in the light of the above there is a need for a clear and comprehensive definition of violence against women, a clear statement of the rights to be applied to ensure the elimination of violence against women in all its forms, a commitment by States in respect of their responsibilities, and a commitment by the international community at large to the elimination of violence against women,

Solemnly proclaims the following Declaration on the Elimination of Violence against Women and urges that every effort be made so that it becomes generally known and respected:

Article 1

For the purposes of this Declaration, the term "violence against women" means any act of gender-based violence that results in, or is likely to result in, physical, sexual or psychological harm or suffering to women, including threats of such acts, coercion or arbitrary deprivation of liberty, whether occurring in public or in private life.

Article 2

Violence against women shall be understood to encompass, but not be limited to, the following:

(a) Physical, sexual and psychological violence occurring in the family including battering, sexual abuse of female children in the household, dowry-related violence, marital rape, female genital mutilation and other traditional practices harmful to women, non-spousal violence and violence related to exploitation;

(b) Physical, sexual and psychological violence occurring within the general community, including rape, sexual abuse, sexual harassment and intimidation at work, in educational institutions and elsewhere, trafficking in women and forced prostitution;

(c) Physical, sexual and psychological violence perpetrated or condoned by the State, wherever it occurs.

Article 3

Women are entitled to the equal enjoyment and protection of all human rights and fundamental freedoms in the political, economic, social, cultural, civil or any other field. These rights include, *inter alia* :

(a) The right to life;[6]
(b) The right to equality;[7]
(c) The right to liberty and security of person;[8]
(d) The right to equal protection under the law;[7]
(e) The right to be free from all forms of discrimination;[7]
(f) The right to the highest standard attainable of physical and mental health;[9]
(g) The right to just and favourable conditions of work;[10]
(h) The right not to be subjected to torture, or other cruel, inhuman or degrading treatment or punishment,[11]

Article 4

States should condemn violence against women and should not invoke any custom, tradition or religious consideration to avoid their obligations with respect to its elimination. States should pursue by all appropriate means and without delay a policy of eliminating violence against women and, to this end, should :

(a) Consider, where they have not yet done so, ratifying or acceding to the Convention on the Elimination of All Forms of Discrimination against Women or withdrawing reservations to that Convention;

(b) Refrain from engaging in violence against women;

(c) Exercise due diligence to prevent, investigate and, in accordance with national legislation, punish acts of violence against women, whether those acts are perpetrated by the State or by private persons;

(d) Develop penal, civil, labour and administrative sanctions in domestic legislation to punish and redress the wrongs caused to women who are subjected to violence; women who are subjected to violence should be provided with access to the mechanisms of justice and, as provided for by national legislation, to just and effective remedies for the harm that they have suffered; States should also inform women of their rights in seeking redress through such mechanisms;

(e) Consider the possibility of developing national plans of action to promote the protection of women against any form of violence, or to include provisions for that purpose in plans already existing, taking into account, as appropriate, such cooperation as can be provided by non-governmental organizations, particularly those concerned with the issue of violence against women;

(f) Develop, in a comprehensive way, preventive approaches and all those measures of a legal, political, administrative and cultural nature that promote the protection of

---

[6]Universal Declaration of Human Rights, article 3; and International Covenant on Civil and Political Rights, article 6.

[7]International Covenant on Civil and Political Rights, article 26.

[8]Universal Declaration of Human Rights, article 3; and International Covenant on Civil and Political Rights, article 9.

[9]International Covenant on Economic, Social and Cultural Rights, article 12.

[10]Universal Declaration of Human Rights, article 23; and International Covenant on Economic, Social and Cultural Rights, articles 6 and 7.

[11]Universal Declaration of Human Rights, article 5; International Covenant on Civil and Political Rights, article 7; and Convention against Torture and Other Cruel, Inhuman or Degrading Treatment or Publishment.

women against any form of violence, and ensure that the re-victimization of women does not occur because of laws insensitive to gender considerations, enforcement practices or other interventions;

(g) Work to ensure, to the maximum extent feasible in the light of their available resources and, where needed, within the framework of international cooperation, that women subjected to violence and, where appropriate, their children have specialized assistance, such as rehabilitation, assistance in child care and maintenance, treatment, counselling, and health and social services, facilities and programmes, as well as support structures, and should take all other appropriate measures to promote their safety and physical and psychological rehabilitation;

(h) Include in government budgets adequate resources for their activities related to the elimination of violence against women;

(i) Take measures to ensure that law enforcement officers and public officials responsible for implementing policies to prevent, investigate and punish violence against women receive training to sensitize them to the needs of women;

(j) Adopt all appropriate measures, especially in the field of education, to modify the social and cultural patterns of conduct of men and women and to eliminate prejudices, customary practices and all other practices based on the idea of the inferiority or superiority of either of the sexes and on stereotyped roles for men and women;

(k) Promote research, collect data and compile statistics, especially concerning domestic violence, relating to the prevalence of different forms of violence against women and encourage research on the causes, nature, seriousness and consequences of violence against women and on the effectiveness of measures implemented to prevent and redress violence against women; those statistics and findings of the research will be made public;

(l) Adopt measures directed towards the elimination of violence against women who are especially vulnerable to violence;

(m) Include, in submitting reports as required under relevant human rights instruments of the United Nations, information pertaining to violence against women and measures taken to implement the present Declaration;

(n) Encourage the development of appropriate guidelines to assist in the implementation of the principles set forth in the present Declaration;

(o) Recognize the important role of the women's movement and non-governmental organizations world-wide in raising awareness and alleviating the problem of violence against women;

(p) Facilitate and enhance the work of the women's movement and non-governmental organizations and cooperate with them at local, national and regional levels;

(q) Encourage inter-governmental regional organizations of which they are members to include the elimination of violence against women in their programmes, as appropriate.

Article 5

The organs and specialized agencies of the United Nations system should, within their respective fields of competence, contribute to the recognition and realization of the rights and the principles set forth in the present Declaration and, to this end, should, *inter alia*:

(a) Foster international and regional cooperation with a view to defining regional strategies for combating violence, exchanging experiences and financing programmes relating to the elimination of violence against women;

(b) Promote meetings and seminars with the aim of creating and raising awareness among all persons of the issue of the elimination of violence against women;

(c) Foster coordination and exchange within the United Nations system between human rights treaty bodies to address the issue of violence against women effectively;

(d) Include in analyses prepared by organizations and bodies of the United Nations system of social trends and problems, such as the periodic reports on the world social situation, examination of trends in violence against women;

(e) Encourage coordination between organizations and bodies of the United Nations system to incorporate the issue of violence against women into ongoing programmes, especially with reference to groups of women particularly vulnerable to violence;

(f) Promote the formulation of guidelines or manuals relating to violence against women, taking into account the measures referred to in the present Declaration;

(g) Consider the issue of the elimination of violence against women, as appropriate, in fulfilling their mandates with respect to the implementation of human rights instruments;

(h) Cooperate with non-governmental organizations in addressing the issue of violence against women.

Article 6

Nothing in the present Declaration shall affect any provision that is more conducive to the elimination of violence against women that may be contained in the legislation of a State or in any international convention, treaty or other instrument in force in a State.

Appendix - VI

UNESCO's Statement on Women's Contribution to a Culture of Peace*

United Nations Educational, Scientific and Cultural Organization

Statement

On the eve of the twenty-first century, a dynamic movement towards a culture of peace derives inspiration and hope from women's visions and actions.

It is important to draw strength from cultural diversity and redefine the concept of security so that it encompasses ecological, economic, social, cultural and personal security. To replace unequal gender relations with authentic and practical equality between women and men is imperative in order to allow for true participatory democracies.

Ours is still an armed and warring planet. In the first half of this decade alone, more than 90 conflagrations of various kinds have taken a vast toll of human life, impeded social and economic development and depleted the world's resources. Women continue to experience systematic violations of their human rights and to be largely excluded from decision-making. In situations of war and military occupation, women are to an alarming degree the victims and targets of atrocities and aggression.

To combat war as the ultimate expression of the culture of violence, we must address issues such as violence against women in the home, acts and reflexes of aggression and intolerance in everyday life, the banalization of violence in the media, the implicit glorification of war in the teaching of history, trafficking in arms and in drugs, recourse to terrorism and the denial of fundamental human rights and democratic freedoms.

A culture of peace requires that we confront the violence of economic and social deprivation. Poverty and social injustices such as exclusion and discrimination weigh particularly heavily on women. Redressing the flagrant asymmetries of wealth and opportunity within and between countries is indispensable to addressing the root causes of violence in the world.

Equality, development and peace are inextricably linked. There can be no lasting peace without development, and no sustainable development without full equality between men and women.

---

*The Statement on Women's Contribution to a Culture of Peace was prepared by UNESCO for the 'Fourth World Conference on Women: Action for Equality, Development and Peace', held in Beijing in September 1995. The original signatories were women Presidents and Prime Ministers in office, Nobel Prize laureates and heads of United Nations organizations.

The new millennium must mark a new beginning. We must dedicate ourselves to averting violence at all levels, to exploring alternatives to violent conflict and to forging attitudes of tolerance and active concern towards others. Human society has the capacity to manage conflict so that it becomes part of a dynamic of positive change. Always provided it involves the full participation of women, action to remedy a pervasive culture of violence is not beyond the capacity of the people and governments of the world.

Efforts to move towards a culture of peace must be founded in education; as stated in UNESCO's Constitution: *since wars begin in the minds of men, it is in the minds of men that the defences of peace must be constructed.*

Girls and women constitute a large majority of the world's educationally excluded and unreached. Ensuring equality of educational access and opportunity between the sexes is a pre-requisite for achieving the changes of attitudes and mind-sets on which a culture of peace depends.

Equality in education is the key to meeting other requirements for a culture of peace. These include: full respect for the human rights of women; the release and utilization of women's creative potential in all aspects of life; power sharing and equal participation in decision-making by women and men; the reorientation of social and economic policies to equalize opportunities and new and more equitable patterns of gender relations - presupposing a radical reform of social structures and processes.

Women's capacity for leadership must be utilized to the full and to the benefit of all in order to progress towards a culture of peace. Their historically limited participation in governance has led to a distortion of concepts and a narrowing of processes. In such areas as conflict prevention, the promotion of cross-cultural dialogue and the redressing of socio-economic injustice, women can be the source of innovative and much needed approaches to peace building.

Women bring to the cause of peace among people and nations distinctive experiences, competence, and perspectives. Women's role in giving and sustaining life has provided them with skills and insights essential to peaceful human relations and social development. Women subscribe less readily than men to the myth of the efficacy of violence, and they can bring a new breadth, quality and balance of vision to a joint effort of moving from a culture of war towards a culture of peace.

To this end, we the undersigned, commit ourselves to:

• support national and international efforts to ensure equal access to all forms of learning opportunities, with a view to women's empowerment and access to decision-making;

• promote relevant quality education that imparts knowledge of the human rights of men and women, skills of non-violent conflict resolution, respect for the natural environment, inter-cultural understanding and awareness of global inter-dependence, which are essential constituents of a culture of peace;

• encourage new approaches to development that take account of women's priorities and perspectives;

• oppose the misuse of religion, cultural and traditional practices for discriminatory purposes;

• seek to reduce the direct and indirect impact of the culture of war on women - in the form of physical and sexual violence or the neglect of social services for excessive military expenditure;

• increase women's freedom of expression and involvement in the media as well as the use of gender-sensitive language and images;

• promote knowledge and respect for international normative instruments concerning the human rights of girls and women and ensure widespread dissemination in order to further the well-being of all, men and women, including the most vulnerable groups of societies;

• support governmental and intergovernmental structures as well as women's associations and NGOs committed to the development of a culture of peace based on equality between women and men.

• We, the signatories, appeal to women and men of goodwill and of diverse cultural backgrounds, religious beliefs, ethnic and social origins to join us in a global endeavour to build, in solidarity and compassion, a culture of peace in the domestic realm and in the public sphere.

• Only together, women and men in parity and partnership, can we overcome obstacles and inertia, silence and frustration and ensure the insight, political will, creative thinking and concrete actions needed for a global transition from the culture of violence to a culture of peace.

Appendix - VII

Beijing Declaration

We, the Governments participating in the Fourth World Conference on Women.

Gathered here in Beijing in September 1995, the year of the fiftieth anniversary of the founding of the United Nations.

Determined to advance the goals of equality, development and peace for all women everywhere in the interest of all humanity.

Acknowledging the voices of all women everywhere and taking note of the diversity of women and their roles and circumstances, honouring the women who paved the way and inspired by the hope present in the world's youth.

Recognize that the status of women has advanced in some important respects in the past decade but that progress has been uneven, inequalities between women and men have persisted and major obstacles remain, with serious consequences for the well-being of all people.

Also recognize that this situation is exacerbated by the increasing poverty that is affecting the lives of the majority of the world's people, in particular women and children, with origins in both the national and international domains.

Dedicate ourselves unreservedly to addressing these constraints and obstacles and thus enhancing further the advancement and empowerment of women all over the world, and agree that this requires urgent action in the spirit of determination, hope, co-operation and solidarity, now and to carry us forward into next century.

We reaffirm our commitment to:

The equal rights and inherent human dignity of women and men and other purposes and principles enshrined in the Charter of the United Nations, to the Universal Declaration of Human Rights and other international human rights instruments, in particular the Convention on the Elimination of All Forms of Discrimination against Women and the Convention on the Rights of the Child, as well as the Declaration on the Elimination of Violence against Women and the Declaration on the Right to Development;

Ensure the full implementation of the human rights of women and of the girl child as an inalienable, integral and indivisible part of all human rights and fundamental freedoms.

Build on consensus and progress made at previous United Nations conferences and summits - on women in Nairobi in 1985, on children in New York in 1990, on environment and development in Rio de Janeiro in 1992, on human rights in Vienna in 1993, on population and development in Cairo in 1994 and on social development in Copenhagen in 1995 with the objective of achieving equality, development and peace;

Achieve the full and effective implementation of the Nairobi Forward-Looking Strategies for the Advancement of Women;

The empowerment and advancement of women, including the right to freedom of thought, conscience, religion and belief, thus contributing to the moral, ethical, spiritual and intellectual needs of women and men, individually or in community with others and thereby guaranteeing them the possibility of realizing their full potential in society and shaping their lives in accordance with their own aspirations.

We are convinced that:

Women's empowerment and their full participation on the basis of equality in all spheres of society, including participation in the decision-making process and access to power, are fundamental for the achievement of equality, development and peace;

Women's rights are human rights;

Equal rights, opportunities and access to resources, equal sharing of responsibilities for the family by men and women, and a harmonious partnership between them are critical to their well-being and that of their families as well as to the consolidation of democracy;

Eradication of poverty based on sustained economic growth, social development, environmental protection and social justice requires the involvement of women in economic and social development, equal opportunities and the full and equal participation of women and men as agents and beneficiaries of people-centred sustainable development;

The explicit recognition and reaffirmation of the right of all women to control all aspects of their health, in particular their own fertility, is basic to their empowerment;

Local, national, regional and global peace is attainable and is inextricably linked with the advancement of women, who are a fundamental force for leadership, conflict resolution and the promotion of lasting peace at all levels;

It is essential to design, implement and monitor, with the full participation of women, effective, efficient and mutually reinforcing gender-sensitive policies and programmes, including development policies and programmes, at all levels that will foster the empowerment and advancement of women;

The participation and contribution of all actors of civil society, particularly women's groups and networks and other non-governmental organisations and community-based organisations, with full respect for their autonomy, in co-operation with Governments, are important to the effective implementation and follow-up of the Platform for Action;

The implementation of the Platform for Action requires commitment from Governments and the international community. By making national and international commitments for action, including those made at the Conference, Governments and the international community recognize the need to take priority action for the empowerment and advancement of women.

We are determined to:

Intensify efforts and actions to achieve the goals of the Nairobi Forward-Looking Strategies for the Advancement of Women by the end of this century;

Ensure the full enjoyment by women and the girl child of all human rights and fundamental freedoms and take effective action against violations of these rights and freedoms;

Take all necessary measures to eliminate all forms of discrimination against women and the girl child and remove all obstacles to gender equality and the advancement and empowerment of women;

Encourage men to participate fully in all actions towards equality;

Promote women's economic independence, including employment, and eradicate the persistent and increasing burden of poverty on women by addressing the structural causes of poverty through changes in economic structures, ensuring equal access for all women, including those in rural areas, as vital development agents, to productive resources, opportunities and public services;

Promote people-centred sustainable development, including sustained economic growth, through the provision of basic education, life-long education, literacy and training, and primary health care for girls and women;

Take positive steps to ensure peace for the advancement of women and, recognizing the leading role that women have played in the peace movement, work actively towards general and complete disarmament under strict and effective international control, and support negotiations on the conclusion, without delay, of a universal and multilaterally and effectively verifiable comprehensive nuclear-test-ban treaty which contributes to nuclear disarmament and the prevention of the proliferation of nuclear weapons in all its aspects;

Prevent and eliminate all forms of violence against women and girls;

Ensure equal access to and equal treatment of women and men in education and health care and enhance women's sexual and reproductive health as well as education;

Promote and protect all human rights of women and girls;

Intensify efforts to ensure equal enjoyment of all human rights and fundamental freedoms for all women and girls who face multiple barriers to their empowerment and advancement because of such factors as their race, age, language, ethnicity, culture, religion, or disability, or because they are indigenous people;

Ensure respect for international law, including humanitarian law, in order to protect women and girls in particular;

Develop the fullest potential of girls and women of all ages, ensure their full and equal participation in building a better world for all and enhance their role in the development process.

We are determined to:

Ensure women's equal access to economic resources, including land, credit, science and technology, vocational training, information, communication and markets, as a means to further the advancement and empowerment of women and girls, including through the enhancement of their capacities to enjoy the benefits of equal access to these resources, inter alia, by means of international co-operation;

Ensure the success of the Platform for Action, which will require a strong commitment on the part of Governments, international organisations and institutions at all levels. We are deeply convinced that economic development, social development and environmental protection are inter-dependent and mutually reinforcing components of sustainable development, which is the framework for our efforts to achieve a higher quality of life for all people. Equitable social development that recognizes empowering the poor, particularly women living in poverty, to utilize environmental resources sustainably is a necessary foundation for sustainable development. We also recognize that broad-based and sustained economic growth in the context of sustainable development is necessary to sustain social development and social justice. The success of the Platform for Action will also require adequate mobilization of resources at the national and international levels as well as new and additional resources to the developing countries from all available funding mechanisms, including multilateral, bilateral and private sources for the advancement of women; financial resources to strengthen the capacity of national, sub-regional, regional and international institutions; a commitment to equal rights, equal responsibilities and equal opportunities and to the equal participation of women and men in all national, regional and international bodies and policy-making processes; and the establishment or strengthening of mechanisms at all levels for accountability to the world's women;

Ensure also the success of the Platform for Action in countries with economies in transition, which will require continued international co-operation and assistance;

We hereby adopt and commit ourselves as Governments to implement the following Platform for Action, ensuring that a gender perspective is reflected in all our policies and programmes. We urge the United Nations system, regional and international financial institutions, other relevant regional and international institutions and all women and men, as well as non-governmental organisations, with full respect for their autonomy, and all sectors of civil society, in co-operation with Governments, to fully commit themselves and contribute to the implementation of this Platform for Action.

Appendix - VIII

Empowerment of Women Under the Indian Constitution in the Self-Government Institutions

PART IX

THE PANCHAYATS

243(d) "Panchayat" means an institution (by whatever name called) of self-government constituted under Article 243B, for the rural areas.

243B Constitution of Panchayats:

(1) There shall be constituted in every State, Panchayats at the village, intermediate and district levels in accordance with the provisions of this Part.

243C: Compostion of Panchayats:

(2) All the seats in a Panchayat shall be filled by persons chosen by direct election from territorial constituencies in the Panchayat area and, for this purpose, each Panchayat area shall be divided into territorial constituencies in such manner that the ratio between the population of each constituency and the number of seats allotted to it shall, so far as practicable, be the same throughout the Panchayat area.

243D: Reservation of Seats:

(3) Not less than one-third (including the number of seats reserved for women belonging to the Scheduled Castes and the Scheduled Tribes) of the total number of seats to be filled by direct election in every Panchayat shall be reserved for women and such seats may be allotted by rotation to different constituencies in a Panchayat.

(4) The offices of the Chairpersons in the Panchayat or any other level shall be reserved for the Scheduled Castes, the Scheduled Tribes and women in such manner as the Legislature of a State may, by law, provide.

Provided further that not less than one-third of the total number of offices of Chairpersons in the Panchayats at each level shall be reserved for women.

PART - IXA

THE MUNICIPALITIES

243P. Definitions:

(e) "Municipality" means an institution of self-government constituted under Art. 243Q.

243Q. Constitution of Municipalities:

(1) There shall be constituted in every State -

(a) A Nagar Panchayat (by whatever named called) for a transitional area, that is to say, an area in transition from a rural area to an urban area;

(b) a Municipal Council for a smaller urban area; and

(c) a Municipal Corporation for a larger urban area.

in accordance with the provisions of this Part;

243T. Reservation of seats:

(2) Not less than one-third of the total number of seats reserved under Clause (1) shall be reserved for women belonging to the Scheduled Castes or as the case may be, the Scheduled Tribes.

(3) Not less than one-third (including the number of seats reserved for women belonging to the Scheduled Castes and the Scheduled Tribes) of the total number of seats to be filled by direct election in every Municipality shall be reserved for women and such seats may be allotted by rotation to different constituencies in a Municipality.

(4) The officers of Chairpersons in the Municipalities shall be reserved for the Scheduled Castes, the Scheduled Tribes and women in such manners as the Legislature of a State may, by law, provide.

Appendix - IX

Chronology of Women's Right to Vote*

1893	New Zealand
1901	Australia
1906	Finland
1913	Norway
1915	Denmark, Greenland, Iceland
1917	Canada
1918	Austria, Ireland, Poland, Sweden, United Kingdom, USSR
1919	Belgium, Germany, Luxembourg, Netherlands
1920	Czechoslovakia, USA
1923	Mongolia
1928	Equador
1931	Portugal, Spain, Sri Lanka
1932	Maldives, Thailand, Uruguay
1934	Brazil, Cuba, Turkey
1935	Burma
1936	Puerto Rico
1937	Philippines
1941	Panama
1942	Dominican Republic
1944	Bermuda, Bulgaria, France, Guadeloupe, Jamaica, Martinique
1945	Albania, Guatemala, Indonesia, Italy, Japan, Senegal, Solomon Islands
1946	Cameroon, Djibouti, Liberia, Romania, Trinidad and Tobago, Vietnam, Yugoslavia
1947	Bolivia, Malta, Pakistan, Venezuela
1948	Israel, Korea, Singapore, Surinam
1949	Chile, China, Costa Rica, Syria
1950	El Salvador, Haiti, India, Peru
1951	Antigua and Barbuda, Barbados, Dominica, Nepal
1952	Argentina, Bolivia, Cote d'lvoire, Greece
1953	Bhutan, Mexico, Sudan
1954	Belize, Nigeria
1955	Ethiopia, Ghana, Honduras, Nicaragua
1956	Benin, Burkina Faso, Cambodia, Central African Republic, Chad, Comoros, Egypt, Gabon, Guinea, Laos, Mali, Mauritania, Mauritius, Niger, Somalia, Togo, Tunisia
1957	Colombia, Lebanon, Malaysia
1959	Madagascar, Tanzania
1960	Cyprus
1961	Burundi, Gambia, Rwanda, Sierra Leone
1962	Algeria, Bahamas, Monaco, Paraguay, Uganda
1963	Congo, Equatorial Guinea, Iran, Kenya, Libya, Morocco
1964	Afghanistan, Malawi, Zambia
1965	Botswana
1966	Guyana, Lesotho
1967	Grenada, St. Christopher-Nevis, St. Lucia, St. Vincent and Grenadines, Yemen, Zaire
1968	Nauru, Swaziland
1971	Switzerland
1972	Bangladesh
1973	Jordan, San Marino
1975	Angola, Cape Verde, Papua New Guinea
1977	Guinea Bissau, Mozambique
1978	Zimbabwe
1980	Iraq, Vanuatu
1984	Liechtenstein
1989	Namibia

Note: This table includes those countries for which information could be gathered and verified from the variety of existing sources, but does not encompass all countries.

*Extract from: Women and Human Rights by Katarina Tomasevski (with a few corrections).

Index